PHANTOM SOLDIERS

PHANTOM SOLDIERS

Raymond Lamont Brown

Drake Publishers Inc
New York · London

Published in 1975 by
Drake Publishers, Inc.
381 Park Avenue South
New York, New York 10016

ISBN: 0-87749-777-X
LC: 74-22585

Printed in the United States of America.

Foreword

Raymond Lamont Brown believes in a spirit universe just as real as the world of the living, for ghosts do not all rattle chains and haunt draughty old gothic mansions, or appear headless and wearing old-fashioned clothes; they are just as likely to use the telephone, drive a car, play a musical instrument or enjoy a game of chess. Science and reason have still not explained what really happens beyond the grave, but there is more testimony today of ghosts as realities than the derogatory theories of the sceptical would have us believe. As a sequel to the popular *Phantoms, Legends, Customs & Superstitions of the Sea,* this intriguing and often spine-chilling book traces military occultism from the days when men first went to war. Every type of ghost is dealt with and illustrated with authenticated testimony, mostly from eye-witnesses. Ghosts of Cromwellian cavalrymen, Lancastrian pikemen and Roman legionaries jostle for attention with World War II spectral bombardiers, ghostly Korean mercenaries and phantom GIs in this book, which records many of the world's most famous superstitions, customs, taboos and omens concerning soldiers and war.

Contents

Illustrations

Plates

Illustrations within text

Acknowledgements

The copyright for all illustrations belongs to the author except in the following cases: pages 20, 23, 36, 45 & 54 *Ian Heath;* pages 25, 47, 88 & 105 (top) *Aerofilms Limited;* pages 26 (top) & 48 (top) *Yorkshire Post;* page 27 *Tate Gallery;* page 28 (top) *City of Peterborough Libraries;* page 46 (bottom) *National Maritime Museum, London;* page 65 (top), 87 (bottom) & 167 *Department of the Environment;* page 66 *Leabharlaan Náisíunta Nah Eireann;* page 67 (top) *Colonel Francis Claridge;* page 68 (top) *Somerset County Library;* page 68 (bottom) *Mrs Cynthia Muhl;* page 85 (both) *National Portrait Gallery;* page 86 (top) *Press and Journal, Aberdeen;* page 86 (bottom) *Cambridge City Libraries;* page 87 (top) *British Railway Archives;* page 105 (bottom) *County of Leicester Record Office;* page 107 (top) *Barnet and Finchley Photographic Society;* page 107 (centre) *Canon S. J. Burling;* page 107 (bottom) *Borough of Colchester Libraries;* page 108 (top) *Revd Geoffrey C. Smith;* page 108 (bottom) *Bord Fáilte Eireann;* page 125 (both) *Watney Mann;* page 127 (top left) *Regimental HQ Records, Argyll & Sutherland Highlanders;* page 127 (top right) *Liaison Office, HQ Welsh Guards;* page 127 (bottom) *US Department of the Army;* page 128 (both) *Psychic News;* page 148 (both) *Messrs Wilkinson Swords Ltd;* page 166 (top) *Cairo Museum;* page 166 (bottom) *Australian War Memorials Commission.*

PHANTOM SOLDIERS

Introduction

I believe in ghosts! Why not? Today a belief in atomic energy, television, and laser beams is commonplace when once they would have been considered black magic. Some people are born colour-blind, tone-deaf, or without the use of one or other of their senses. So why can't one be born to see things that others cannot? Why can't some eyes and ears register vibrations and rays invisible to the 'normal senses' of others?

Certainly animals, in some conditions, have a greater capacity for psychic cognizance than humans; similarly, some humans exhibit distinct physical advantages over others. So why cannot a human have some genetic pattern which throws out hypersensitivity to psychic matter? A quick glance at the factor known as 'genius' gives some indication of how man can be controlled by 'powers' outside himself, or deep from within that part of the mind which makes him a brilliant brain surgeon, a physicist, or whatever. See how Peter Ilich Tchaikovsky (1840-93) explains his genius: 'Generally speaking, the germ of a composition comes suddenly and unexpectedly. It would be vain to try to put into words that immeasurable sense of bliss which comes over me directly a new idea awakens in me and begins to assume a definite form. I forget everything and behave like a madman. Everything within me starts pulsing and quivering; hardly have I begun the sketch ere one thought follows another . . . In the midst of this magic process it frequently happens that some external interruption awakes me from my somnambulistic state; . . . dreadful indeed are such interruptions. Sometimes they break the thread of inspiration for a considerable time so that I have to seek it again—often in vain'.

In their prose and verse writings men such as Keats (*Hyperion*), Blake (*Milton*), Shelley (*Prefaces*) and Kipling (*Autobiography*), admit to supernatural influences on their lives. It is almost as if, while they write, they become 'mediums' possessed by a ghost (the popular description of an inhabiting spirit, which to the initiated is either 'soul', or 'spirit being'). In 1917 Count Maurice Maeterlinck (1862-1949) averred: 'But here and there we have around us wandering intelligences, already enfranchised from the narrow and burdensome laws of space and matter, that sometimes know things that we do not know. Do they emanate from ourselves, are they manifestations of faculties as yet unknown, or are they external, objective and independent of ourselves? Are they merely alive in the sense in which we speak of our bodies, or do they belong to bodies which have ceased to exist? That is what we cannot yet decide; but it must be acknowledged that, once we admit their existence, which at this date is hardly contestable, it becomes less difficult to argue that they belong to the dead. This at least may be said: if experiences such as these do not demonstrate positively that the dead are able directly, demonstrably and almost personally, to mingle with our existence and to remain in touch with us, they prove that they continue to live in us much more ardently, profoundly, vividly and passionately than has hitherto been believed: and that, in itself, is more than we dared hope'. As Larmartine said: '*Ce n'est pas moi qui pense; ce sont mes idées qui pensent pour moi*' (It is not I who thinks; my ideas think for me). In this field lies the rationality in believing in ghosts.

'I no more doubt that these queer things do happen than I doubt the fact that I am writing these words . . . People do not reflect that if one ghost tale out of a thousand is true the circumstance is of much stronger scientific interest than radium or wireless telegraphy. I merely want the occult to be explained on scientific grounds'. This is how Andrew Lang commented in the *Independent* in 1906. Since his day science has played a big part in psychic research, but academic superstition and arrogance still remain.

On the surface it would appear that science, in its broadest sense, is the enemy of psychic studies. This attitude could not be more wrong. Fundamentally it has been proved that scientists, out of all the professions, are likely to have, or to have had psychic experiences. This statement is based on data received from research just completed by students from Duke University, North Carolina. It echoes what the Boston Society for Psychical Research suggested in official blurb in the late 1920s: '. . . A scientific man is exactly as likely to have a psychical experience as a man whose profession is the inculcation of religion, and the preoccupation with purported spiritual realities no more tends to induce such experiences than preoccupation with minerals, chemicals, bugs, beasts, or the physiological or mental characteristics of human beings. Then, so far as chance has led us to discover their stories, the appalling fact seems to loom up, that scientists are more likely to have psychical experiences than are clergymen and theologians'. Of course, this must be so: there are more scientists than clergy, and ghosts choose their own time to materialise, for they are self-contained, self-governing beings!

We have now gone beyond the delusion that ghosts cannot exist; too many scientists of standing have established that there is room for them in the universe and that there are more positive physical and chemical reasons for the existence of ghosts than not. 'One thing the Society for Psychical Research has proved beyond cavil', Dr James H. Hyslop wrote, 'is the fact that apparitions do occur. We need not care what explanation offers itself. The multiplication of the phenomena puts them on the same footing with meteors and comets and all other sporadic or residual facts. Their regular occurrence after a definite type suggests some other law than hallucination, extensive as that is'.

Basically the work of such as Marconi, Rutherford, Brown and Einstein has proved the probability of conditions under which developed civilizations can use telepathy, ESP and allied phenomena to transcend time and space. Today, with all the scientific material available, it might be said that a disbelief in ghosts is more irrational than a belief.

Disbelief in spectres of the dead is a comparatively recent attitude of mind, for as late as the 17th century ghosts still had a respectable standing. Shakespeare, for instance, wrote for a public which accepted ghosts as stock characters on the stage, thus he could count on their being taken seriously: Caesar in the tent of Brutus before the battle of Philippi; Banquo sitting in Macbeth's chair at the feast; the elder Hamlet on the battlements of Elsinore; and the ghosts of such as Earl Rivers, Lord Grey, Prince Edward, King Henry VI, the Duke of Clarence and Sir Thomas Vaughan which all played an important part in *The Tragedy of King Richard III*.

In the 18th century Dr Samuel Johnson declared in *Rasselas* that he believed in ghosts because of the fact that all races of men everywhere in all ages had reported apparitions of their dead, but were greatly puzzled by them. In this he was predating the late Professor Gustav Stomberg's (of the Mount Wilson Observatory) comments on apparitions of the dead in his *Soul of the Universe:* 'All races on earth seem to have recorded them and many are so well authenticated that we have no right to doubt them. The reason why they are usually ignored by investigators who have not themselves had any such experiences is that it seems entirely impossible to explain them scientifically'.

Immanuel Kant was not as sure as Dr Johnson however: 'I do not care wholly to deny all truth to the various ghost stories,' he wrote in *Traüme Eines Geistersehers*, 'but with the curious reservation that I doubt each one of them singly yet have some belief in them all taken together'. An attitude quite typical of the 18th century intellectuals was expressed by Madam du Deffard who, when asked if she believed in ghosts, replied: 'No, but I'm afraid of them!'

In the main, ghosts vanished from the stage in the 19th century when the penchant for more bloody horror developed. But the so-called 'Age of Science' led to a greater investigation of ghost phenomena, and among the investigators were top rank scientists like Alfred Russell Wallace, Sir William Crookes, Sir William Barrett, Professor Rayleigh, Sir Oliver Lodge and William James, who all demanded that psychic phenomena should be investigated like any other mysterious occurrences in nature.

Subsequently, the questions most asked by those interested in the occult were undoubtedly: What are ghosts? How real are they? Why do ghosts so frequently follow the course of long-vanished tracks? By what criteria do places become haunted? Do ghosts exist wholly in the mind of the percipient, or have they a separate existence? Why do some people see ghosts and others never at all? How is it that psychic or paranormal phenomena occur at different times, in the same place, to quite different people, having no contact with one another? How is it that ghosts appear almost invariably clothed and why in period dress? From what source do ghosts receive their power of materialisation? Hypotheses on these and many other questions relating to military ghosts are offered in this book, but initially must come conclusions based on modern psychic research.

Modern dictionaries only offer prosaic and restricted definitions of ghosts, such as this: 'An apparition, wraith, disembodied spirit of the dead manifesting itself to the senses of the living'. In truth a ghost is a law unto itself. Consequently, down the centuries, researchers have offered a multitude of definitions of ghosts to suit their own academic briefs.

The theory that a ghost might be some type of psychiatric puppet was first put forward by psychic researcher G. N. M. Tyrrell. He believed that a ghost could be an image projected by the subconscious mind, in time of crisis, on the receptive conscious mind of the viewer. As he pointed out, this example of a ghost picture involves that type of mental function we know to be vital for the framing of an idea, inspiration, or a train of thought.

Consequently, Tyrrell put forward the idea that the ghost itself was an unfinished entity until it found expression in the mind of the recipient. A ghost, therefore, proceeded from within the viewer and not from a psychic agency outside the thought processes of the witness. Because of man's willingness to 'see' ghosts, thought Tyrrell, this was enough for the psychic entity to exist.

Dr Nandor Fodor, the internationally famous psycho-analyst, saw ghosts in a different academic light. He averred that ghosts were the merging of two self-propitiating energies; one from a past age and one from the future. He theorised that a genuinely haunted house was affected by some sort of absorbed emotional unpleasantness from former owners. Thus, for instance, if a murder had taken place in a house, its psychic aura of horror was absorbed by the fabric of the house. Years, or even centuries later this horror could be drawn out of the house's substance by a similar, but not necessarily so awful emotional disturbance. Fodor saw houses in which people had radiated happiness as being immune from haunting.

Another psychic investigator, Edmund Gurney, gave his opinion on collective sightings of ghosts, saying that they were some kind of telepathic infectious mental state. One person seeing a ghost passes on what he sees telepathically to another or others; so all see the same ghost.

H. H. Price, Wykeham Professor of Logic in the University of Oxford won fame for his theory on ghosts which stated that certain powerful thoughts could be trapped in the atmosphere much as radio waves are absorbed and perpetuated by the upper atmosphere of the earth. Price too said that these mental images could become a part of the atmosphere of a particular location—a house, a castle, an abbey, for instance—and that this atmosphere could be disturbed at a later date by powerful emotions of hatred, sorrow or fear. Thus reagitated, these thoughts could be replayed on the mind of that person present who was suffering the emotion.

What makes Price's theory interesting is that the person imparting the original emotion plays no direct part in the subsequent replay; only his thoughts are re-enacted. This put an entirely new slant on the possibilities of haunting. Professor Price put forward this theory, which is now known to psychic researchers as the Charged Psychic Ether Theory, in his presidential address to the Society for Psychical Research in 1939. In this he was extending the researches set out by Dr C. A. Mace in his fifth Myers Memorial Lecture (1938).

Among the many things established by these eminent psychic scientists was that a ghost must be classified as a supernatural being. Its movements are more than an illusion, for they can be scientifically traced to a pinpointed cause.

Even though scientists still argue among themselves as to the detailed causes of ghostly phenomena, they seem to be generally agreed on classification. In the jargon of parapsychology (that branch of behavioral science which undertakes to examine such phenomena), a *ghost* is a stranger to the one who perceives it; an *apparition* is well-known to the percipient (parent, relative or friend) and a *vision* is the appearance of a religious figure (saints, angels, etc). A *poltergeist*, however, is a projection of psychic energy that finds its potential through the frustrated creativity of adolescence, and emanates from the living rather than from the dead.

These basic categories are subdivided again into a further six classifications: *harbingers of death,* who appear with pale minatory fingers and sightless eyes and beckon the percipient to doom, or bring their gloomy presage of death to others; *local, or resident ghosts; phantasms of the living; telepathic apparitions; ghosts that were never human* (animals and objects); and *ghostly music, lights and allied phenomena.*

The question of evidence which can be adduced pointing to the reality of the existence of ghosts, is one of vast significance, because its implications for the nature of human personality are immense, but only if it can be shown in simple terms that there is such a thing as 'a real ghost', that is, something objective, existing by itself and not a figment of the imagination. This book then, sets out to provide two types of possible evidence, physical and mental.

The reason why ghosts so frequently follow the course of long vanished tracks, incidentally, is that the ghosts are materialising in the time sequence of their own mortal life, which is superimposed on a later time sequence. Thus there are innumerable accounts of ghosts walking above or below the existing level of the ground, disappearing through solid walls and doors, climbing staircases that no longer exist: all structural changes which were made after their mortal death. For the same reason ghosts invariably materialise in the dress of their period (ie, shrouds). No place, of course, is likely to be haunted more than others; aircraft factories, council flats, pubs and theatres have all attracted ghosts.

A ghost of course can be an illusion, for we cannot wholly trust our senses. But there are some people who are more able to see ghosts than others. This doesn't mean that they are prone to hallucination; only that some people are born with the ability as a trick of the mind, as with geniuses. For instance, people like John Stuart Mill (1806-73) who had a Stanford University rating of IQ 200, and who began to learn Greek at the age of three, was using a talent with which he had been born; a talent which might just as easily have taken the form of an ability to see ghosts.

One of the most perplexing questions of all is where ghosts get their power. Thomas Alva Edison, however, may have left us a clue to this enigma. Edison theorised that energy, like matter, is indestructible. He further hypothesised that the vibrations of every word ever uttered still echo in the ether: thus a ghost may be able to replay such scenes as if running an old film, using this 'power' from the ether.

The selection of material herein collected is first of all taken from the narration of people of unimpeachable integrity, and could be quadrupled. Enough has been set out however, to show the variety of these mysterious psychic occurrences. Many readers will scan some of the stories with a critical eye, but they must honestly assess the stories as being from people who are arch-sceptics. Unwilling testimony is the most conclusive in psychic matters. Shorter anecdotes are the experiences of friends, but for the classic tales I have gone to printed sources, which the reader may consult if he wishes to study the material in detail.

This book does not set out to prove anything, for the immense majority of the greatest minds of all ages have firmly believed that the personality survives after death; this book is concerned only with presenting facts and occurrences, with an added exercise in hypothesis. 'At some future day it will be proven—I cannot say when and where—', wrote Immanuel Kant, 'that the human soul is, while in earthlife, already in an uninterrupted communication with the living in another world; that the human soul can act upon these beings and receive, in return, impressions of them without being conscious of it in the ordinary personality'. If this book can help in creating the right state of mind for further personal investigation by the reader of psychic phenomena, then this will be an added bonus. As Thackeray said: 'It is all very well for you who have never seen a ghost to talk as you do, but had you seen what I have witnessed, you would hold a different opinion!!'

Chapter 1

Phantoms at war

The Ancient Greeks, who gave battlefield heroes the stature of gods, also invented the ghost tale as a storytelling form; soldiers and ghosts have been inseparable ever since. It was Greek scribes, for instance, who first wrote that battlefields were heavily populated with ghosts, and by way of example they often quoted the case of Marathon, a plain near Athens where the Greeks defeated the Persians in 490 BC. From that time this battlefield was deemed to ring on many a night with the sounds of war, and men engaged in bloody conflict. These ghostly combatants were seen by anyone brave enough to visit the battlefields after dark.

Such sights were not really intended for mortal eyes, the Greek chroniclers wrote, and those who beheld the spectacle were inviting personal misfortune. British soldier phantoms locked in perpetual occult battle, however, are not so selective in their audience, and have appeared on many occasions to a variety of people.

Classic cases from the records of English battlefield hauntings seem to stem mainly from the period 1642-45, which corresponds with the early part of the English Civil War. Records of military psychic phenomena usually highlight the ghostly occurrences at Edgehill and Marston Moor. From the basic research work done by Christina Hole and Alasdair Alpin MacGregor, linked with that of Lt-Col A. H. Burne, the investigator in military psychic phenomena can assess the occult aspects of these two great battles.

Combatants at Edgehill

The Battle of Edgehill, October 23 1642, was the first pitched battle of the English Civil War. The last battle to be fought in England between two English armies had been at Bosworth Field (August 22 1485) and, in the intervening 157 years, much change had taken place in the muniments of war. Apart from helmets and breast-plates, armour had been abandoned, and infantrymen were armed with pikes and muskets. Indeed, some of the muskets were so heavy that they had to be fired from crutch-supports. Furthermore, by 1642 heavy cannon had been introduced to the field of battle, as were small grape-shot sakers and a variety of other field guns. But most important of all was the introduction of cavalrymen, armed with pistols and swords.

The two opposing armies at Edgehill were under the respective commands of King Charles I, who had raised his standard at Nottingham in August 1642, and the Parliamentarian (Roundhead) Robert Devereux, 3rd Earl of Essex (whose ghostly predecessor still walks the Tower of London, see page 114), who had left London on September 9. Charles had proceeded to Shrewsbury, collecting his troops on the way, and on October 23 1642, after various tactical manoeuvres, the two armies confronted each other at Edgehill, near Kineton, Warwickshire. Today the hill is still a commanding spot and rises some 600 feet for three miles in a boomerang shape, the long arm overlooking Kineton plain, with the rear above the Warwick-Stratford road and Essex's route to London.

Although the Royalist Army outnumbered that of Essex and commanded an elevated position at Edgehill, both sides had secured generals with war experience. A particularly outstanding soldier was King Charles' brilliant nephew Prince Rupert of the Palatinate in Germany. The old idea of battle was the *caracole;* this involved a brisk cavalry trot to about 50 yards from the enemy line, a barrage of pistols and then a swift retreat to make way for a barrage from the second line of horse—there was little close conflict or actual swordplay. But Rupert introduced the Swedish methods of Gustavus Adolphus. Not all of Rupert's men, therefore, were armed with pistols, and he instructed them to bunch together and gallop through the enemy using their swords at close range.

At the beginning of the battle Rupert was on the right wing facing Parliamentarian Ramsay's horse, with the Royalist Wilmot's cavalry fronting Fielding on the left. Parliamentarian Essex, however, had placed a cavalry reserve under Balfour, the capable Scottish soldier, and Stapleton, in a wood behind his infantry.

On the advice of Rupert, King Charles marched his army downhill at 1400 hours

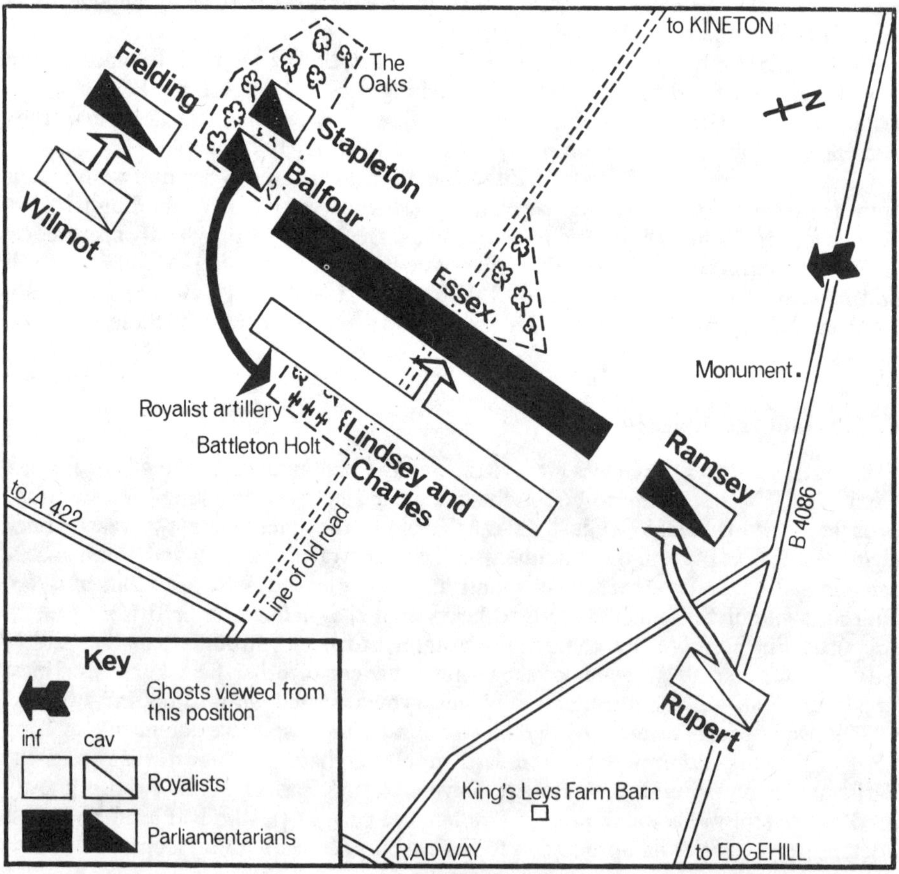

and immediately engaged the enemy on the plain. When Rupert charged, therefore, it meant that the impetus of his horsemen (and his superiority in numbers) carried all before him. Rupert, however, rashly pursued his fleeing enemy more than two miles from the field, until held up by the arrival of John Hampden's regiment with the artillery. Wilmot met with similar success. But Balfour swept the Royalists back through Battleton Holt and captured the Royalist guns.

While Rupert raced forward the Royalist infantry had been broken, for the Parliamentarians had thus wheeled to the right and a great hand-to-hand fight took place round the Royalist Standard, which was captured (later to be regained by Captain John Smith). Rupert's horsemen returned in disorder and were incapable of retrieving the king's fortunes. Throughout the night the two armies remained facing each other and in the morning marched away, the Royalists to Oxfordshire and the Parliamentarians to Warwick.

Thus the first campaign of the Civil War in the end took the form of a race between the armies of Charles and Essex to London; but Essex, by permitting Charles to take Banbury unmolested, yielded the fruits of victory to the Royalists. While Charles had in fact the edge over the Parliamentarians and Rupert's advance guard captured Brentford, the king delayed his march to London and was forced to withdraw to winter quarters at Oxford. The basic details thus recounted of the battle of Edgehill are indeed relevant, for the whole, in great detail, was to be re-enacted in phantom form two months later; not just for a fleeting moment, but for many hours and on different occasions.

For details of the phantom battle replayed at Edgehill, the researcher has to turn to a curious tract which was first reprinted in 1860 as an appendix to Lord Nugent's *Memorials of John Hampden, his Party, & his Times*. The tract, with the lengthy title *A Great Wonder in Heaven, shewing the late Apparitions and Prodigious Noyses of War and Battels, seen on Edge-Hill, neere Keinton, in Northamptonshire.—Certified under the Hands of WILLIAM WOOD, Esquire, and Justice of the Peace in the said Countie, SAMUEL MARSHALL, Preacher of God's Word in Keinton, and other Persons of Qualitie,* was based on the findings of the commission set up by the king, who was anxious to have a 'report upon these prodigies, and to tranquillise and disabuse the alarms of a country town . . .' (first published by Thomas Jackson, London, January 23 1643).

According to this account, several shepherds, farm workers and travellers, who were out between midnight and one o'clock on the Saturday morning before Christmas heard the sound of distant drums gradually drawing towards them and 'the noise of soldiers, as it were, giving out their last groans'.

Alarmed by all this unexpected clamour, the shepherds and the other witnesses were about to run away, when '. . . on a sudden, whilst they were in their cogitations, appeared in the air the same incorporeal soldiers that made these clamours, and immediately, with ensigns displayed, horses neighing, which also to these men were visible, the alarum or entrance of this game of death was one army which gave the first charge, having the King's colours, and the other the Parliament's at their head, to the front of the battle, and so pell-mell, to it they went. The battle appeared to the King's forces having at first the best, but afterwards to be put to apparent rout. But till two or three in the morning in equal scale continued this dreadful fight, the clattering of arms, noises of cannon, cries of soldiers, so amazing and terrifying the poor men than they could not believe they were mortal or give credit to their eyes and ears; run away they durst not, for fear of being made a prey of these infernal soldiers, and so they, with much fear and affright, stayed to behold the success of the business, which at last suited to this effect. After some three hours' fight, that army which carried the King's colours withdrew, or rather, appeared to fly; the other remaining, as it were, masters of the field stayed a good space triumphing and expressing all the signs of joy and conquest, and then, with all their drums, trumpets, ordnance and soldiers, vanished'.

Thereupon the terrified witnesses hastened to Kineton and told what they had seen to William Wood and Samuel Marshall. The next night a party, including Wood and Marshall, went to the place where the ghosts had been seen and saw the battle fought again, exactly as the first group had seen it the night before. A week later the whole thing was re-enacted on two succeeding nights. This was too much for William Wood and several of his friends, who 'forsook their habitations thereabout and retired themselves to other more secure dwellings; but Mr Marshall stayed and some others; and so successively the next Saturday and Sunday the same tumults and prodigious sights and actions were put in the state and conditions they were formerly'.

Col Lewis Kirke, Capt Dudley, Capt Wainman and three other officers were sent by King Charles (then at Oxford) to enquire more fully into the matter. They too saw and heard the ghosts and 'recognised on the Royalist side several of their personal friends who had been killed'. The curious tract of Wood and Marshall ends in the rather religio-moral literary tone of the time: 'What this doth portend, God only knoweth and time perhaps will discover; but doubtlessly it was a signe of His wrath against this Land, for these civil warres, which He in His good time [*will*] finish and send a sudden peace between his Majestie and Parliament . . .'

Lord Nugent's comments on this historic document, to be found in the 1860 edition, are worth a mention. Nugent suggested that 'a well supported imposture', or some 'wild and stormy night among the Warwickshire hills, might possibly have influenced the minds of a peasantry in whose memory lingered terrors of battle; but this hardly explained how the minds of certain officers, sent there expressly to correct the illusion, could have been affected in this way'. 'It will also be observed', continued Nugent, 'that no inference is attempted by the witnesses to assist any notion of a judgement or warning favourable to the interests or passions of their own party. It is a pure, inexplicable working of fancy upon the minds of shrewd and well-educated men, in support of the superstitions of timid and vulgar ones, who had, for several nights, been brought to consent to the same belief'.

Those who wish to view the battlefield as it is today, with the hope of seeing the ghosts of Edgehill themselves, can proceed to Edgehill from Banbury by the A41 to Warwick, and then turn left after about six and a half miles along the B4086. The battlefield itself (O/S 145-357-492) is War Department property, but permission may be obtained to view the site if a written application is made to the Officer Commanding, CAD Kineton, Warwickshire.

It should be remembered, however, that in 1642 there were no trees on the heights where Charles spent the night before the battle. But the view from the top of Edgehill Tower Inn gives the visitor the best impression of the King's view on the morning of the battle. The phantoms at Edgehill incidentally, are the only ones which the Public Records Office at London accept as authentic.

The ghost of Sir Edmund Verney—Charles I's standard-bearer at Edgehill—is said to appear at Claydon House, Middle Claydon, Bucks, whenever trouble threatens either his country or his family. Sir Edmund was killed at Edgehill, and died clutching the standard so tightly that his hand had to be hacked off: it was eventually returned to his family for burial. He was one of those recognised amongst the spectral combatants.

After the battle, a Cromwellian dragoon corporal named Jeremiah Stone came to the Anchor Inn, Warwick, with a bag of spoil he had looted from the dead. Being wounded himself, the dragoon gave the bag to the landlord for safe keeping. When he recovered, however, the innkeeper denied all knowledge of the bag and threw the soldier out. The Roundhead promptly drew his sword and tried to break down the door, whereupon the landlord had him arrested.

While he lay in prison—vouches a broadsheet of 1642 in which John Finch a shoemaker 'being an eyewitness doth testify to the same'—the soldier was visited by the Devil who offered to act as attorney at his coming trial. Gratefully accepting, the next day the soldier came to trial and was defended by the Devil, who suggested to the court that the inn might be searched to discover if the bag of loot was there or not. The landlord denied stealing the bag, and wished that the Devil might take him if he told a lie. At that very moment the Devil promptly obliged, 'seized upone his bodie and carried him over the Market-place, nothing left behind but ane terrible stinke'.

Bloodshed on Marston Moor

On the evening before the Parliamentarians succeeded at Marston Moor, near York (O/S 97-491-525), on July 2 1644, a troop of phantom horsemen was seen galloping over the heights of Helvellyn, a mountain in the lake district of Cumberland, between Thirlmere and Ullswater, where no ordinary horse could pass with safety. But the most curious rumours of the ghosts of Marston Moor were not well attested until some 300 years after the battle. The best authenticated account is given in the papers of the late Sir Ernest Bennett.

Thomas Horner, a commercial traveller from Ripon, and his friend Arthur Wright, were driving from Filey to Harrogate via Wetherby on Saturday November 5 1932. The evening was not very pleasant, but the slight mist did not necessitate the use of

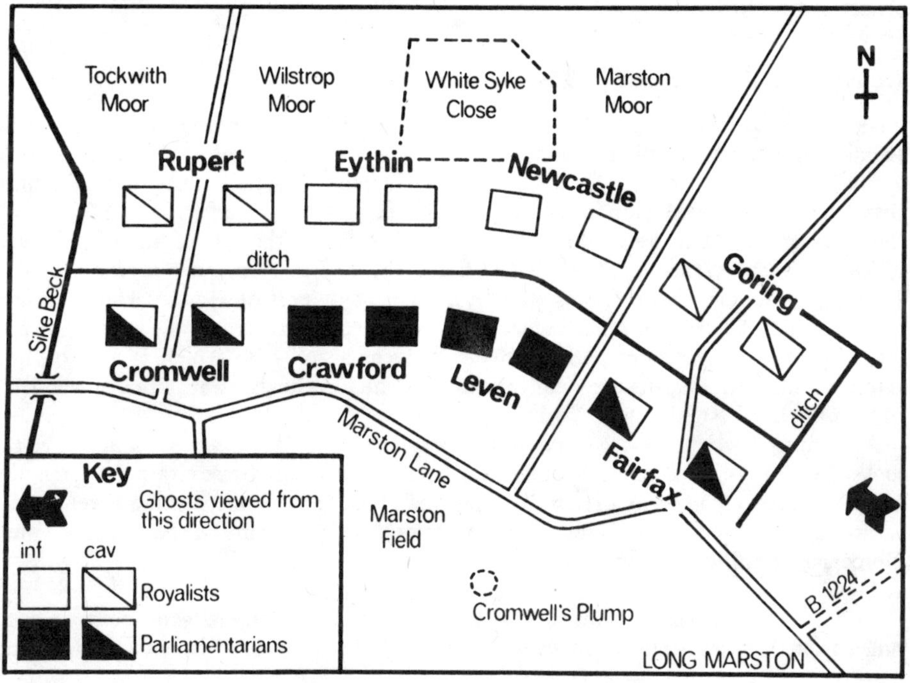

headlights. As they were crossing Marston Moor a bus approached, and at the same moment Arthur Wright called out that there were some pedestrians in front of the car. Tom Horner braked and the two watched the walkers carefully as they straggled across the road. The pedestrians were dressed in long dark cloaks, with dark top-boots, or leggings, and large hats turned up at the side with cockades. The overall colour of their dress was white. Their hair was unusually long for the fashions of 1932, and their general appearance was strange enough to impress both Horner and Wright.

Starting up again Tom Horner dipped his now searching headlights to pass the approaching bus, for the mist had thickened. Once the two vehicles had passed, Horner and Wright looked again to see where the strangely dressed men had gone, but to their surprise could see them nowhere. Horner and his friend were so intrigued by the strangers' quick disappearance, that they got out of the car to search for them in case they had been knocked down while passing the bus. The road was completely empty.

Thomas Horner later told Sir Ernest that it was impossible for anyone to have hidden; there was a grass verge by the roadside, and the hedge was too high to jump. Furthermore Horner and Wright had only been a few feet away from the strangers as they passed the bus. Horner seems to have seen three men, whereas Wright saw only two; even so, this discrepancy may have been caused by their different positions in the car. They were both sincerely convinced that the pedestrians they had seen were not labourers, gypsies or poachers. Where these phantoms were seen is in fact the general direction of the main escape route taken by the Royalist stragglers who were ultimately taken to Chester by Prince Rupert. The costume of the figures Horner and Wright saw corresponded with the contemporary accounts of the undyed serge jackets of the 'Whitecoats' commanded by Lord Eythin (second in command to William Cavendish, Marquis of Newcastle).

Today the best view of Marston Moor, which may be reached along the B1224 from York to Wetherby, is from the footpath leading to Cromwell's Plump, near the southern aspect of the battlefield.

Ghost soldiers haunt the golf course

The various battles and seiges of the English Civil War have greatly contributed to Britain's military ghost phenomena, but none seems to have given such *lasting* occult aura as the siege of Howley Hall, the ruins of which are situated on the slope of a hill between Batley and Morley in Yorkshire. This siege took place in June 1643, when the Royalist Newcastle assailed the fortified house, then in the care of Sir John Savile of Lupset, near Wakefield. Newcastle blasted the hall to ruins and imprisoned Sir John in Pontefract Castle. Long afterwards the major part of Howley Hall was let to various families as a summer lodge. Today the swards in front of the ruin, and the farmhouse which once belonged to the hall, form a golf club which is a favourite retreat of mill-owners, business and professional men from the nearby heavy woollen district of the West Riding of Yorkshire.

According to verified local rumour, Howley Hall Golf Club is not as peaceful as it looks, for it is reputed to be haunted not by one ghost but by several; the strange, aimless spectres from that dreadful siege which wander over the putting greens and fairways. Both Mr Gordon Bunney, a mathematics teacher from Leeds, and Mr Tom Gomersall, a mill-worker from nearby Batley Carr, are on record as having seen ghosts at Howley.

Very recently however, a director of a Dewsbury mill, situated some four or five miles from Howley, told an investigator of the 'uneasy feeling' he and many club

Edgehill in Warwickshire was the scene in 1642 of one of the hardest fought battles in the English Civil War. Ghosts of the combatants have frequently been sighted here.

The Monument to the Battle of Marston Moor (1644). Phantom steeds are heard galloping along this road bearing their riders to the battle scene.

Howley golf course, near Batley, Yorkshire, where Roundhead phantoms play golf.

'The Morning of Sedgemoor' by Edgar Bundy. The spectral re-enactment of this bloody battle, first fought on July 6 1685, has been attested by many witnesses.

A vivid portrayal of the attack on Woodcroft Castle in 1648. The hapless Dr Michael Hudson can be seen hanging from the battlements which he now haunts.

A map of the site of the Battle of St Albans. Phantom men-at-arms mingle with the shoppers in the streets of this ancient Hertfordshire town.

members still have when out on Howley Links: 'One evening I was going round the course on my own. I think there was one other couple, well ahead of me, and I was feeling very relaxed and looking forward to a couple of drinks in the clubhouse, when I had the most peculiar feeling. Dusk was drawing in, and I was just about to make a short putt when I felt certain that I was being watched. I paused and looked around, but there was no one in my vicinity at all. It was as if a whole crowd of invisible watchers were standing around the green, surrounding me. The experience was stifling and most unpleasant. I felt terribly depressed all of a sudden and couldn't get away quickly enough.'

One other British battlefield has retained its forbidding aura right up to modern times. No one who visits Culloden, where the Jacobite hopes were destroyed by the Duke of Cumberland* in 1746, fails to experience the awful sense of despair which seems to cling to every tree and rock hereabouts. Because of this few hikers picnic here, and no camper is advised to pitch his tent on Culloden's field, for there have been too many others who have experienced 'a disturbed night' in the past.

Spectres over Sedgemoor

The same rebellious century which spawned the English Civil War also witnessed the Battle of Sedgemoor, July 6 1685, where the troops of James II fought those of his nephew the Duke of Monmouth (the natural son of Charles II). One case in particular of phantoms at Sedgemoor is satisfactorily accounted by Alasdair Alpin MacGregor in *Phantom Footsteps*. Apparently a Mr and Mrs Harold Robinson were motoring across Sedgemoor, Somerset, one day, when they suddenly saw in front of them a large number of troopers armed with scythes and billhooks and attired in 17th-century costume. Unfortunately the Robinsons did not leave a written account of what they saw but, in a letter to Alpin MacGregor, their son Philip assured that: 'As far as I remember, my mother cried out to my father to stop the car for fear of running into a number of people carrying staves and pikes'.

James Wentworth Day notes that a Sedgemoor revenant (Monmouth himself) was also seen by his childhood tutor Charles Hugh Rose, MA, of Keble College, Oxford, while driving in a gig with his friend the squire of Hutton Court (near Weston-super-Mare) on July 3 1912. Rose was so sure of what he had seen that he compared his ghost with Sir Godfrey Kneller's (1646-1723) portrait of Monmouth and found an exact likeness.

Woodcroft and Woodmanton

Woodcroft Manor, Peterborough, is another house associated with Civil War sieges. Dr Michael Hudson, one of the royal chaplains, was the hero of this affair of 1648. With a view to containing the many bands of Parliamentary marauders who were pillaging Huntingdonshire, this militant cleric collected a band of yeomen and urged rebellion in the name of the king. After some initial success Dr Hudson was obliged to fall back on Woodcroft Manor. Here he was presently besieged by Parliamentarians. At last, driven to the roof of the manor's round Edwardian tower, Dr Hudson engaged several Roundheads in hand to hand swordsmanship. The soldiers beat him back to the tower's parapet and, refusing to accept his offer of surrender, forced him off the

* The ghost of William Augustus (1721-65), Duke of Cumberland, soldier son of George II, is said to haunt the Cumberland Head Hotel, Beighton, Derbyshire.

walkway. Dr Hudson clung desperately to the battlements until a Roundhead officer in charge hacked off the cleric's fingers; Dr Hudson fell into the moat. Still alive the plucky parson crawled from the muddy moat only to be despatched by Roundhead pikemen.

Again and again Dr Hudson's ghost has been seen battling on the roof of Woodcroft Manor, while on the ground his companions are seen fighting off Roundhead pikemen. With the apparitions come the ghostly sounds of the clash of steel and cries of: 'Quarter, I pray give me quarter!' and 'Mercy! Have mercy on me!'

At Woodmanton, Wiltshire, a small valley known as Patty's Bottom is said to be haunted on certain nights by the sound of tramping soldiers and the occasional appearance of headless horses rushing wildly to and fro. This might represent the earliest known haunted battlefield in Britain for, according to local tradition, a great battle was once fought near here between invading Romans and the British defenders. So terrible was the carnage, said local chroniclers, that Patty's Bottom was awash with blood.

St Albans' gory field

As far as psychic researchers can tell, however, the earliest well recorded haunted battlefield in Britain is that of St Albans. This battle of May 22 1455 was the first of the War of the Roses, that series of disjointed wars between the Yorkists and Lancastrians, the rival families in power at the English court.

One of the oldest towns in England, St Albans has not changed its main streets in shape or direction since 1455. With the exception of London Road, Holywell Hill, George Street, St Peter's Street and Shropshire Lane knew the fiercest of the battle in which the Yorkists under Warwick captured King Henry VI.

An old house called Battlefield once stood in the heart of St Albans and was haunted periodically by the noise of galloping horses and the clash of steel on steel. This house was supposed to stand near the line of the Lancastrian defences during the battle. Although nothing supernatural was ever seen, the haunting was persistent. Even when the house was demolished and a row of modern shops built on the site, the phantom noises were still heard in their due season.

Phantom French Dragoons

In his many researches into ghostly phenomena, the veteran occultist-writer James Wentworth Day records how he saw spectral *cavalerie* outside a shell-shattered wood on the crest of the Ravelsberg Hills above Neuve Eglise. It was late November 1918 and Wentworth Day was accompanied by Corporal James Barr of the 298 POW Company on a foraging trip along this part of the French-Belgian frontier. While searching among the ruins of an old *auberge* the two soldiers suddenly caught sight of a party of German Uhlans in 1914 uniforms. With lances couched, the soldiers were charging down out of a small wood headlong at a patrol of French Dragoons, clad in breastplates and plumed helmets.

They watched lances splinter and sabres gleam as the cavalry clashed and clamoured. The whole vision lasted but a few moments, then the entire company of men disappeared. Wentworth Day subsequently checked the records and found that such a skirmish had taken place in August 1914 within a few days of the outbreak of war. The graves of the German and French cavalrymen who appeared in ghost form can still be seen in the local churchyard.

Angels of Mons

The most famous of all World War I ghostly tales (besides the ghostly white cavalry seen by German troops in the Bethune sector of the Western Front, which caused them to retreat) is undoubtedly that called the 'Angels of Mons'. The phenomenon is said to have occurred at the beginning of World War I, during the retreat from Mons, when the British Expeditionary Force, which was outnumbered by more than two to one, narrowly escaped annihilation by the German First Army.

On day three of the retreat (August 26 1914), the position of the 2nd Corps of the British Expeditionary Force was particularly critical. Fighting through the previous night the enemy had encircled them. At 1530 hours the 2nd Corps began to retire under increasingly heavy fire. As dusk fell the British soldiers waited for the final *coup d'assommoir*, but here and there as the soldiers peered towards the German lines they saw a mirage shimmering over the enemy. Slowly, one by one, figures began to materialise in the haze; figures tall and winged like angels. The German troops waited poised on the brink of final attack, but in the unearthly lull the British gained precious time and marched through the night to safety.

For some time no reports of the retreat from Mons mentioned any vision but, on September 29 1914, a journalist called Arthur Machen had published a story in the *Evening News* (London) called 'The Bowmen'. In it he recounted how a British soldier in the retreat murmured the Latin motto *adsit anglis Sanctus Georgius* (may St George be a present help to the English) as he waited to make a last ditch stand. As he did so, he felt something like an electric shock and instead of the noise of battle he heard voices shouting 'St George! St George!', and before him, hanging over the enemy, was a 'sort of shining thing' which resolved itself into the glittering figure of St George in armour, flanked by an army of bowmen such as had fought at Crécy (1346) and Agincourt (1415). As this phantom army rained a torrent of arrows on the German lines, the British soldiers made their way to safety, marvelling at what they had seen.

Machen's story triggered off wild speculation, and the journalist was besieged by correspondents from all over Britain. Was the story fact or fiction? Machen publicly announced that the story was pure fantasy and that the idea for the feature had come to him while he sat in church one Sunday listening to the sermon. Even so, Machen's explanation did not scotch the story. People started to inform him that letters had been received from soldiers at the time telling of the same phantom bowmen before the feature had been published. Harold Begbie, the editor of *The Occult Review* even published a 'verbatim statement' to the effect from a lance-corporal, given to a Red Cross Superintendent in France by the nurse to whom the soldier had dictated the story.

The soldier's tale recounted how, on the hot clear evening of August 26 1914 while the British were waiting, the lance-corporal saw in the sky '. . . a strange light which seemed to be quite distinctly outlined and was not a reflection of the moon, nor were there any clouds in the neighbourhood. The light became brighter and I could see quite distinctly three shapes, one in the centre having what looked like out-spread wings; the other two were not so large, but were quite plainly distinct from the centre one. They appeared to have a long loose-hanging garment of a golden tint, and they were above the German line facing us'.

Begbie theorised that Machen must have 'received a telepathic vision of the battlefield at Mons from the brain of a dying . . . British soldier'. Machen however, remained adamant that the story was fiction. The story nevertheless became a legend. Copies of the picture 'The Bowmen of Mons' by A. Forester sold widely, and the legend inspired popular songs like Paul-Paree's 'The Angel of Mons Valse', which was published by the Lawrence Wright Music Co of London.

Certainly there is no reasonable explanation of what really did happen at the retreat from Mons. The facts, however, are these: 160,000 German soldiers with 600 heavy guns bore down on 70,000 exhausted British soldiers with only 300 guns. Yet, at the end of the day, 56,000 of the British soldiers escaped to safety. Why so many were allowed to survive is a complete mystery. The official military theory is that the Germans were too exhausted to pursue the retreating British relentlessly enough to destroy them utterly. But the occult, and popularly held belief was that a miracle had occurred. Thus a large proportion of the British population was prepared to believe in the intervention of St George and his host of 'angel bowmen'.

Colonel Sien's vanishing army

While some lost soldiers materialise as battling ghosts, others work the reverse. Consider this incident in China just before World War II. By December 1937 the Japanese Imperial Army had advanced so far that the Chinese city of Nanking (Kiangning) was threatened with destruction (it fell to General Iware Matsui on December 18 1937). The terrain to the south of the city was such that the supreme Chinese commander Chiang Kai-shek decided to stage a last ditch stand there among the rolling hills. To this end he signalled for more troops to be sent from lines in the north.

As night fell the Chinese troops, reinforced by some 3,000 extras, were well entrenched on the south with heavy artillery backing up a two-mile front. The Commander, Col Li Fu Sien, retired for the night, fully confident that the new lines would repel any surprise attack by the Japanese. A few hours before dawn, Col Sien was awakened by his aide-de-camp who reported that he was unable to contact the right wing of the new defence line. Repeated signals brought no response and the aide suggested that close inspection was needed.

On arrival at the place where he had seen the lines erected, the colonel stopped in amazement. Along the two-mile front not a man was to be seen. There was no sign anywhere of a breach by the Japanese. The heavy artillery remained loaded but unattended and many of the cooking fires were still lit. The whole company of some 3,000 Chinese soldiers had disappeared entirely, never to be seen or heard of again. There was no record in the Japanese documents of Chinese prisoners being captured. No one knows to this day where the soldiers went, but some believe that it was a ghostly materialisation in reverse.

A phosphorescent GI

Even during the reality of World War II, incidents occurred that had ghostly appurtenances. In one case the lack of spirituality did nothing to lessen the fright of some American 4.2-inch mortar crewmen in the Alsatian forests.

Peeking through the sombre, fir-covered hills, they suddenly stared wild- and wide-eyed as a helmeted shadow walked slowly towards them, its bodily edges emanating a glowing, silvery mist. Two or three of the GIs pressed against the clay of their dugouts, and one hid behind a tree. The apparition stopped in the stillness of the forest a few feet away from one of the guns. It spoke out—'Hey fellas, it's me!'—and only after a few frightening seconds in which the adrenalin lessened its overtime coursing, did the soldiers realize that one of their platoon, while handling white phosphorous shells, had come afoul of a leaking casing. It had been enough to cover him with the eerie halo, yet not burn him. An almost ghostly end indeed!

Boullan and Dubus' occult battle

The world's most curious battle, however, occurred under very different circumstances and far away from the conventional battlefield. It comprised the prolonged conflict of 'spells' conducted through space over a distance of 300 miles.

The major protagonist in this was a defrocked French priest called Joseph-Antoine Boullan who lived at Lyons. Boullan, when he was 51 in 1875, had become a disciple of the occultist and 'miracle-worker' Pierre Vintras, and on Vintras' death Boullan declared publicly that he had been chosen to succeed his mentor as High Priest of the Church of the Carmel.

Vintras had founded the Church of the Carmel some years before. Although it had nothing to do with the Carmelite Order of the Roman Catholic Church (commonly known in medieval England as 'white friars' from the white mantle forming part of their habit), Vintras' group was apparently named after the mountains in Israel, some 18 miles long, running in a north-westerly direction between the Plains of Esdraelon (Jezreel) and Sharon, to the Bay of Acre. Here where the Carmelite Order was founded in 1156, was the site of Elijah's triumph over the prophets of Baal. But Vintras' scriptural theories were very different from the accepted gospel.

Most of the pontiffs consecrated by Vintras refused to accept Boullan as their spiritual leader; nevertheless Boullan continued the work of Vintras in Lyons helped and supported by his middle-aged housekeeper Julie Thibault, known as Priestess of the Carmel and the Apostolic Woman. Together they celebrated such curious rituals as the 'Sacrifice of the Glory of Melchizedek', or the 'Provictimal Sacrifice of Mary'. Only a few close associates, however, were allowed to participate in the prime acts of Abbé Boullan's mystic-erotic liturgy 'Les Unions de la Vie' (The Unions of Life).

Joseph-Antoine Boullan taught that 'since the Fall of our first parents, was the result of an act of culpable love, it was through acts of love accomplished in a religious spirit that the Redemption of Humanity could and should be achieved'. Boullan maintained that life was a ladder which one could successfully climb by having sexual intercourse with celestial beings, and which one could help inferior beings to climb by copulating with them. Such a doctrine may be described as the advocation of the satanic witchcraft of incubism and succubism (belief in sexual intercourse with male and female spirits). Boullan and his followers, as the existing documents show, deluded themselves into believing that such copulation with imaginary spirits of the dead would lead them to their own salvation. They believed that the most powerful way to reach salvation was to copulate with the dead spirits of such military figures as Attila the Hun, Charlemagne and so on.

In Paris, some 300 miles away from Boullan at Lyons, were ranged in opposition Edouard Dubus, a young poet addicted to magic and morphine, the Marquis Stanislaus de Guaita, another morphinomaniac, who had just revived the ancient Rosicrucian Order, a young occultist called Oswald Wirth, and the self-styled talented novelist, Sâr Joséphin Péladan. Guaita and Wirth had infiltrated the Carmel at Lyons and in 1887 publicly proclaimed that Boullan was 'a pontiff of infamy', 'a base idol of the mystical Sodom, a magician of the worst type, a wretched criminal, and evil sorcerer, and the founder of an infamous sect' (*Le Temple du Satan*, Guaita et al: Paris, 1891), and that they were out to get him.

Boullan remembered Guaita and Wirth as his 'guests in Lyons' and, as he had shown them his 'most lethal spells and incantations', he was afraid that they would kill him by magic. The Carmel house in Lyons was therefore set on a war footing and Boullan and Julie Thibault conducted an occult battle against their opponents in Paris. At about the same time the novelist and naturalistic writer Joris-Karl Huysmans became interested in Boullan and wrote a book about him (*Là-Bas:* Paris, 1891).

Huysmans, however, became involved in Boullan's occult battle with the Paris occultists and experienced 'fluidic fisticuffs—blasts of cold air—which struck at his face at night, and which affected his cat at the same time'. To repel these occult bombardments from 'Stanislaus de Guaita's occult war machine' in Paris, Huysmans shut himself up with Boullan's occult weapons and tried some personal incantations. Robert Baldick (*The Life of J-K Huysmans*, Oxford, 1955) writes: 'A tablet of exorcising paste would be burnt in the fireplace, a defensive circle drawn on the floor. And then . . . "brandishing the miraculous host in his right hand, and with his left hand pressing the blessed scapular cloak of the Elijan Carmel to his body, he would recite conjurations which dissolved the astral fluids, and paralysed the powers of the sorcerers" '.

Throughout 1891 Boullan performed many elaborate rites to 'protect' himself and Huysmans. By some sort of mediumistic divination, Julie Thibault was able to warn Boullan of the more deadly 'occult military manifestations of evil' from the Paris group. The occult battle raged on until, on January 3 1893, Boullan died suddenly. In a Paris paper Jules Bois, a friend of Huysmans, published an article accusing Guaita and his associates of murdering Boullan with an occult army. The authorities, of course, took no action, but after a duel between Jules Bois and Guaita, the quarrels seem to have been peacefully resolved. Edouard Dubus was later committed to an asylum and Guaita died of an overdose in 1898, at the age of 27.

Mysteries at Flodden

The mists lie heavy over Crookham Ford, Northumberland, shrouding that scene of pity and grief. In the wind sometimes, the old folk say, you can hear the clank of armour, the frenzied screams of horses and the crash of sword on shield. An old man of my youth* remembered clearly the ghostly men-at-arms he had seen careering across the main road, along which the buses run nightly between Edinburgh and London. 'To the brave of both Nations' (actually there were three nations involved Scotland, France and England) and the date September 9 1513 (September 20 by modern reckoning) set on stone near the deserted site, is all that remains of that terrible day 460 odd years ago, when Scotland lost her king and more of her kinsmen than she cares remember.

As the ghosts at Flodden are not recounted at length elsewhere, they are set down here in some detail with a brief background of events.

Actual losses at Flodden have never been really assessed, but John Riddell, the genealogical antiquary in his *Peerage and Consistorial Law* (Edinburgh, 1842) said: 'The more I look into any Scottish charter-chest, the more I am sensibly struck; almost every distinguished Scottish family having then been prematurely deprived of an ancestor or member'. Of the 80 or so men who rode from the border town of Selkirk, for instance, one returned.

Why, historians have argued, did the Scots fare so badly at Flodden, when they had so many advantages? They were amply provisioned, had superior artillery, the

* James Thompson (1872-1957), woodcutter, of Crookham and Swinton.

ground was to their advantage and their lines of communication were open and secure. Perhaps the 'secret' of the Scottish defeat lies in the character of the chief actor in the tragedy: James IV (1472-1513), King of Scots. He was at once a scholar of no mean attributes, a linguist, and a man devout to his religion; a sensualist, a lover of sport, but abstemious with food and drink. He stands at one of the watersheds in history, a foot in both the Middle Ages and the Renaissance, having the attributes of both. Although he was well equipped for a kingly role, the shadow of doubt was eternally cast across his life.

James was haunted by an oppressive guilt concerning his father's murder by intriguers. Falsely conceiving himself guilty of the crime, he undertook a lifelong penance: round his body he daily wore an iron chain, to which as the years went by, another link was added. The early petty intrigues of the Scottish court, the dangers of one faction feuding against another, took its toll on the boy who was king in suspicion and an unduly harsh cancer of hesitation.

Although the years leading up to 1513 had been peaceful in Scotland, with the throne secure, the fact that King Henry VIII of England was James' brother-in-law meant little diplomatically. Tempers were frayed by the attacking of Scottish ships by Lord High Admiral Howard off the Downs, and by the non-payment of the dowry due to Scotland in the marriage settlement between Margaret Tudor, Henry VIII's sister, and James IV. Anxious not to have a conflict with Scotland while his troops were committed in France, Henry sent Nicholas West as ambassador to soothe the Scots. He could not have sent a bigger, or more pompous dolt, and West's arrogance angered the Scots further. While the Anglo-Scottish marriage had forged some links between the two countries, Scotland was more strongly tied by tradition and treaty to France, a country now being invaded by Henry.

The deciding factor came from the Queen of France, Anne of Brittany, while Henry's troops were fighting in France. She begged James to stab the English in the back. James agreed and on August 12 1513, the largest army ever to leave Scotland crossed the Tweed at Coldstream, taking all before it to encamp on a high plateau sheltered by Flodden Edge; a wide natural battlement, well wooded around its base with a good series of communications.

Estimates of the size of the Scottish army at Flodden are very varied, from 10,000 suggested by Robert Lindesay of Pitscottie, to the 100,000 noted in Hall's chronicles. In spite of wastage from desertion and the usual medieval toll from camp sickness, the Scottish army was probably only slightly superior to the 20,000 men under the command of the English leader, the Earl of Surrey. Surrey was at Pontefract, Yorkshire, when he heard on August 25 1513 that the Scots had crossed the Tweed. By the time he had reached Newcastle, five days later, he was joined by Lord Thomas Dacre and his men from the northern estates: Surrey's army was now complete. At Wooler Haugh, Surrey encamped and reviewed his strength.

On the march Surrey had kept the command of the rearguard for himself and entrusted the vanguard to Admiral Lord Edward Howard. Both the vanguard and rearguard were divided into a centre and two wings. The right wing of the vanguard was commanded by the Admiral's younger brother Edmund and included some 1,500 men from Lancashire and Cheshire, many of whom were dependents of the powerful Stanley family. The 1,000 or so men on the left wing were led by the elderly Sir Marmaduke Constable. In the centre was the Admiral himself with the men of Durham marching under the banner of St Cuthbert, borrowed from the Prior of Durham Cathedral.

The right wing of the rearguard, with the main stream of 1,500 border prickers under Dacre, was reinforced by the men of Bamburgh and Tynemouth. On the left wing of the rearguard were the remaining levies from Durham and Lancashire under Sir Edward Stanley. The centre of this group was led by Surrey himself and consisted of the citizens of York, soldiers from the estates of the Bishop of Ely, and Surrey's own retinue of 500 with kinsmen of the Stanleys and the Abbot of Whitby.

Once they had arrived at Flodden Surrey's cohorts were quickly running out of provisions; so it would have been good tactics for James IV to withdraw until the English army was forced to move deeper into England to re-store. Then at least he would have had a chance to get the English army on the run. Surrey forsaw this and sent Rougecroix Pursuivant (a junior herald) to goad James into immediate battle. Rougecroix infuriated James well and the Scottish Islay Herald was despatched to Surrey with the news that the agreed date for battle was Friday September 9 1513.

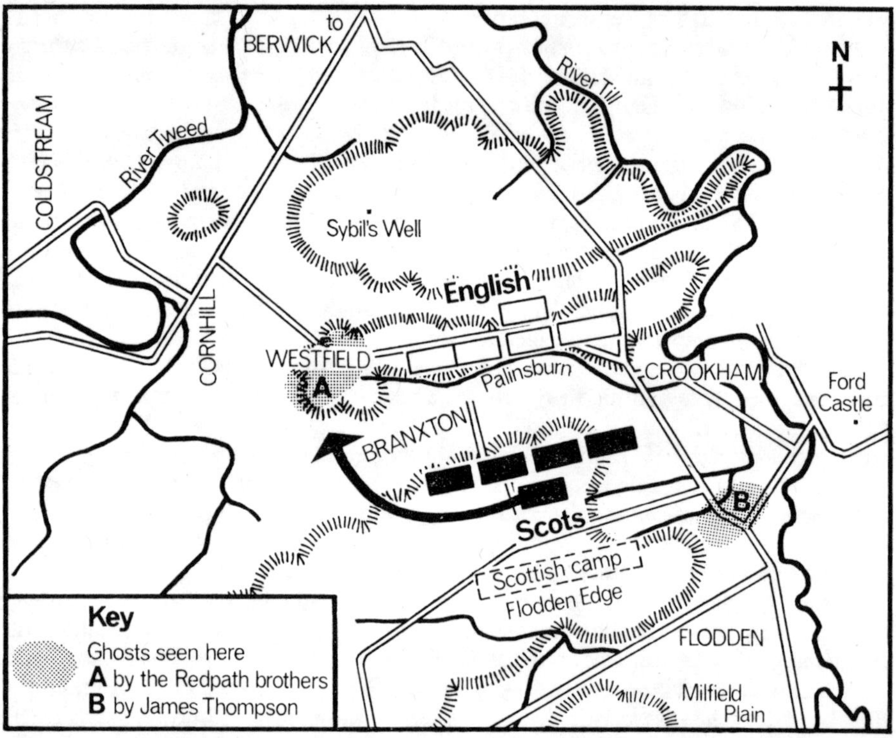

Today at Flodden Edge it is very difficult to determine the position of the Scottish camp as described by historians like Hall, George Ridpath (*The Border History of England and Scotland*, T. Cadell, London 1776) and Polydore Vergil (*Anglicae Historiae*, Guarimum Basileae 1570) as *verticem montis quem Floddonem incolae vocant, occupat* (he occupies the top of a hill which the locals call Flodden). Research by myself at the National Library of Scotland and the Scottish Record Office shows that the Scots were most probably not encamped on the southern side of Flodden Hill, but were more likely on the eastern or north-eastern side where the ghosts were seen.

Hearing of Surrey's approach James set fire to Ford Castle, where he had been stationed. Then he moved his army across the River Till to a position described by Hall in *Trewe Encountre* as being, 'enclosed in three parties with three great mountaynes* soe that ther was noe passage nor entre unto hym† but oon way, wher was laied marvelous and great ordenance of gunnes'.

Because of these guns Surrey knew a frontal attack on the Scots was out of the question. Thus Surrey decided on a dangerous move and placed himself between the Scots and their native land. At first there were some bluff moves on the part of the English who found the marshy terrain around Flodden a difficulty. Guns roared and men on both sides fell. At last the English right wing was engaged and Edmund Howard narrowly escaped death as the Scots under Huntley and Hume beat him back. Regrouping, the English retaliated and the Scots were forced to fall back to their original position. At this point the losses on both sides were heavy, and James' own divisions were hacked by Admiral Howard's halberdiers.

Now the Scottish burghers under the Earls of Crawford and Montrose descended on the Admiral with Swiss pikes lowered. Invaluable in their day this cavalry pike was useless at Flodden. The fighting raged on and James became more and more dithering in his tactics. Slowly the seasoned English soldiers began to rout and slaughter the Scottish amateurs. As the crimson and gold banner of James IV with the support banners of St Andrew and St Matthew fell in the mud beside their dead bearers, the courage seemed to leave the Scottish army. Crawford, Errol and Montrose fell in quick succession and at the end of three hours amongst the bodies of his son, two bishops, two abbots, 11 earls and 15 lords, James IV was unhorsed and hacked to death.

Some little time ago, while researching the life of Major-General Henry Darling, Burgess of Berwick-upon-Tweed, I came across a curious note. Henry Darling had been having some renovations done to his lodgings (1781) and had employed some builders from Tweedmouth. One of their number came from Cornhill-on-Tweed and 'swore most honestly, that he and his brothers had seen the King of Scots killed at Flodden'. This man, John Redpath, had been snaring rabbits with his brothers to the west of Branxton. Within a matter of minutes a heavy mist from Flodden Edge engulfed them where they stood. As they stood together, snare-nets in hand, through the mist they had seen men-at-arms fighting each other. In the midst of these ghostly soldiers was a sandy-haired man who sat helmetless, bolt upright in his saddle. For a minute or two they watched this man wheel and duck the persistent billmen on foot. At last the man was unseated, and in the midst of footsoldiers he was piked to death.

The mist cleared as quickly as it had descended and the Redpath brothers were left with a mystery. Had they seen a revenant picture of 1513? The men searched the ground for hoofprints but none could be found. Henry Darling noted 'it is well-known that James IV of Scots had red hair, and the men described his banners and shield in great heraldic detail. A remarkable fact as these men had little education and knew nothing about the muniments of war'.

* Impossible to identify today, certainly the use of the word mountain is exaggerated.
† Surrey.

Chapter 2

Gleanings from Gallipoli

The seaport town of Gallipoli (Turkish Gelibolu), on a peninsula at the north-eastern extremity of the European side of the Dardanelles, has been Turkish property since 1357. Although the British and the French fortified the neighbourhood in 1854, few people in northern Europe had heard of Gallipoli until the 1915-16 campaigns.

Shortly after the outbreak of World War I, the Turkish government, under German pressure, closed the Dardanelles to commerce. For this reason the Anglo-French fleets deployed here to force a passage. In retrospect the Gallipoli operation is seen by historians as a disaster in which nothing of importance was gained. Indeed, the conception of the campaign had been sound, but the initial landings were not made in sufficient strength, and subsequent landings were not exploited with enough vigour. Furthermore, the campaign was to have some dire consequences. The career of the British commander, Sir Ian Hamilton, was permanently wrecked by it, and Winston S. Churchill's political progress was also temporarily affected. Some historians even go so far as to say that the Gallipoli Campaign contributed greatly to the fall of the Asquith government. Moreover, ghostly occurrences, both during and after the campaign, added to the psychic phenomena relating to military phantoms.

Death on the 'Royal Edward'

One such story was recently discovered amongst the papers of the late Elliot O'Donnell, who for more than 60 years was one of Britain's foremost ghost-hunters. The story concerned a young man who had been a friend of the O'Donnell family. He had joined up at the beginning of World War I, and was sent out to Gallipoli on board the ill-fated *Royal Edward,* which was torpedoed in the Aegean Sea. The young man was reported missing believed dead.

Naturally the young soldier—whom O'Donnell partially identified by the Christian name of Howard—was sadly missed by his parents and friends. Even though Howard's mother lost her powers of speech through shock, she clung to the persistent hope that, in some way, her son had survived the wrecking of the *Royal Edward.* Her hopes were buoyed up by the fact that at the moment of his loss (the time factor was established later), Howard had appeared to his sister and had said: 'Tell Mums not to worry, Mabs, I'm all right'.

The next evening Howard had returned again in ghostly form to his now bewildered family. This time he appeared to have a gash on his forehead, but was still smiling as he had always done in life. Later his sister again saw his phantom materialise; on this occasion, in scenario form. He appeared to be clinging to a shattered piece of ship's woodwork in the sea; on the woodwork was the barely decipherable lettering R-YA- E--A-D. This time his mother, too, witnessed the manifestation.

O'Donnell, as a friend of the family, made very possible enquiry concerning Howard's fate amongst survivors of the *Royal Edward*. At length he met a shipmate who had trained with Howard, and this man told O'Donnell that the very last time he had seen Howard had been when the ship was struck. Howard had been sighted in the water clinging to wreckage, but he seemed at the time barely alive, with a terrible gash on his forehead. Howard was never seen alive again, yet his mother clung to the forlorn hope that he had survived.

Psychic investigators believe that his ghostly visitations, made at the time of his 'passing over', were actuated by his keen desire to comfort his sorrowing mother, and to assure her that his spirit still lived. This kind of case is not unusual in war-time and many similar cases have been recorded in the *Proceedings of the National Laboratory of Psychical Research*. Many believe such instances are caused by a form of telepathy in which a mortal *in extremis* can communicate with a loved one as he or she 'passes over into the realm that is called death'. One investigator, the late Dr James Coates, even quoted a case of Australian origin in which a missing man was declared dead for legal purposes, on the 'evidence' that his ghost had appeared at his sister's bedside!

Private Kirkpatrick and his ghostly donkey

A far more curious case from Gallipoli concerns a phantom soldier and his ghostly donkey. During the early 1950s Leon V. Weeks, an American archaeologist, was exploring the area of Turkish coast between Imroz and Bozca Ada, where the three major ruins of Abydos, Troy and Assos are to be found. Of the three, Abydos and Troy are the most popularly known. At Abydos, Xerxes, King of Persia, marching against Greece in 480 BC, built a bridge of boats to transport his army over the Hellespont. The site known as Troy has seen nine cities, constructed from the late Stone Age to Roman times; the most famous, of course, was the one celebrated in Homer's *Iliad*, as the scene of the Trojan War. Dr Weeks had gone there to research and photograph the area for a pilot television series.

While he was in the area Dr Weeks decided to take a closer look at the battlefields of the Gallipoli Peninsula, with the hope of turning up some relics of the campaign of 1915-16, so, near some foxhole-cratered slopes he set up camp. For the first few nights of his stay nothing unusual occurred. One particular evening, however, Dr Weeks was standing at his open tent smoking his last cigarette before retiring, when he saw a man clambering down the slopes nearby, leading a donkey. Over the donkey was slung a load which looked vaguely human. Intrigued by this, Dr Weeks stubbed out his cigarette and scrambled over the rough terrain to where he had seen the man and the donkey, yet to his surprise Dr Weeks found nothing. Not a soul was to be seen anywhere in the region. Even his shouts went unanswered. Vowing not to take more than two glasses of wine with his supper in future, Dr Weeks retired.

The next evening the archaeologist had just unpacked his supper dishes when the sound of falling rocks attracted his attention. On the hillside above him he saw the man with the donkey once more, but this time he distinguished quite clearly the body of another man slung over the animal's back; for the figure's leather boots eerily reflected the moonlight. Weeks called out to the man, but received no reply. Next morning no signs of the man or the donkey were to be found. Yet evening after evening the strange man, whose costume was decidedly military and not native, and his donkey appeared, and on each occasion the donkey bore a human load which looked like a wounded or dead soldier. Weeks could never find any evidence in daylight of anyone having clambered down the hillside, and at length he began to believe that he was seeing ghosts! He shrugged off the idea as ridiculous and returned to Troy to complete his work.

Dr Weeks had almost forgotten his strange encounter when fate jogged his memory. It so happened that Weeks was invited to dine at the house of a British colleague while on a visit to London in 1968. Over the brandy the conversation turned to philately and the colleague showed Weeks his extensive collection of Australian commemorative stamps. One stamp, the 'fivepenny khaki issue' celebrating the 50th anniversary of the Gallipoli Campaign in 1915, where ANZAC (Australia and New Zealand Army Corps) troops fought conspicuously, caught Weeks' eye; for on the obverse of the stamp was a prominent design of a man leading a donkey, on the back of which rode a wounded ANZAC soldier. Weeks immediately recognised the design as bearing a close symbolic resemblance to the man and donkey he had seen on the hillside at Gallipoli.

Carefully Dr Weeks recounted the story of his Gallipoli encounter to his colleague, who in turn explained the historical background and significance of the fivepenny stamp issue. It had been circulated in 1965 by the Australian Post Office in a set of three stamps to honour the brave deeds of an Englishman who had fought at Gallipoli.

The soldier was Private John Simpson Kirkpatrick who had been born at South Shields, County Durham, on July 6 1892. After emigrating to Australia, Kirkpatrick served during World War I in the 3rd Australian Field Ambulance. In 1915 on Gallipoli, Private Kirkpatrick acquired a donkey with which he used to carry wounded down Monash (Shrapnel) Valley to the beach. With his donkey 'Duffy', Kirkpatrick (he chose to enlist under the name of John Simpson) saved dozens of wounded comrades, until he was shot while coming down Monash Valley on May 19 1915.

His brave deeds became a saga often retold at campfire and military dinner alike. Today Dr Weeks still believes that he saw the ghost of Private Kirkpatrick and his donkey 'Duffy' re-enacting their last journey on earth, and that some kink in time (the possibility of this contingency was first hinted at by Albert Einstein, cf page 119) causes the unusual phantom to appear as if it were once again flesh and blood.

Bombadier Moore's promise

One of the most interesting discussions on psychic phenomena to which I have ever contributed, took place a few years ago aboard a BOAC jetliner while I was on my way to England from Japan. To while away the long hours Charles Richardson, a Birmingham cutlery sales executive, Father Ian O'Gorman, a Roman Catholic priest, and myself discussed the meaning of the word 'soul' and the possibility of its survival of death, with particular reference to the statement made by the late Sir William Barrett: 'I am absolutely convinced of the fact that those who have once lived on earth can and do communicate with us'. During the discussion Father O'Gorman recounted a story told to him by a south of England parish priest, Father Bates.

Father Bates had been an assistant priest during the 1920s in a very poor part of Glasgow. He had lodged with another priest, and being the younger had done all the night calls. One particularly wet evening Father Bates returned from his rounds drenched, and was drying himself off at the fire when a knock came at the door. Exhausted and tired Father Bates pretended not to hear it. His companion priest was very deaf and, not hearing the noise, continued to read the paper. A minute or so later the knock came again, and once more Father Bates ignored it. But it persisted, even louder and more violent. Father Bates sighed deeply, got up and opened the door.

In the blank darkness there was nothing and no one to be seen. He waited for a moment, but no one appeared, so he closed the door and returned to the blazing fire.

Just as Father Bates was dozing off in the fire's welcoming heat, the knock broke the silence once more and the door visibly shook on its hinges. Father Bates threw the door open and, in the flickering light from the gas lamp across the street, saw a rough-looking man with a handkerchief tied round his neck standing beckoning to him to follow. Instinctively Father Bates knew that he was being summoned to perform the last rites and, calling to the man to wait, he put on his overcoat and gathered the things he would need.

Once out in the street the man signed for Father Bates to follow him and started off at a pace which the tired priest found difficult to keep up. At length they reached the docks where the vile tenement houses formed a human warren of dank alleyways and mouldering apartments. For a moment Father Bates lost sight of his guide, but at a stone staircase at the far end of the block he again saw the man waiting for him.

The man preceded the priest up the echoing stone stairway and kept a few steps ahead. Up and up they went, until they reached the last room on the top floor. The door of the 'single-end' (a Scottish expression to describe a one-roomed apartment) was open, and the light from an oil lamp shone out into the passage. The rough-looking man entered, and silently moved to the head of a bed set in one corner of the room. Father Bates saw the figure stoop over someone in the bed and mutter something. The next moment the figure vanished into thin air leaving Father Bates alone with the dying man in the shabby bed.

'Oh, Father', gasped the man lying in the bed, 'you've come at last. Archie Moore told me he would fetch a priest and he has kept his word'.

'But where has Archie Moore gone?' asked the still puffing priest.

'He died at Gallipoli ten years ago. But Father, listen to me. You'll understand when you hear my story. Archie Moore and I were school pals. We were both orphaned young, and roamed and thieved together all over Glasgow in the old days, to keep alive when we ran away from the orphanage. Somehow there was a blood pact between us sealed by the dangers and the suffering we had encountered together. We even went out to Australia together and joined the 29th Division at the same time, and were both sent to Gallipoli. In the last week of April 1915 the 29th landed at Helles. On landing we all scrambled through the water and faced a murderous hail of bullets. Archie fell on the beach mortally injured in the chest. I saw him fall and rushed over to where he was lying, he had not long as the blood was oozing out of him with every breath he took.

'Archie's hand gripped mine. "Do one last thing for me mate, fetch the priest". I stumbled away and found the Roman Catholic *padre* for Archie, who had been a lifelong Papist, more pious than myself. The priest gave my pal the last rites, and Archie's last words to me were: "Thanks Jimmy, thanks. When it comes to your time to die, I'll do the same for you". So, Father, that's why Archie Moore came for you tonight . . .'

An old soldier's revenge

Psychic phenomena concerning ghosts which returned to kill have been investigated by Sir Oliver Lodge, Sir William Crookes and Professor James of Harvard University, among others. But not even spiritualistic fiction writers like Sir Arthur Conan Doyle ever produced a story as strange as the true case of the haunted train driver who had served with bravery at Gallipoli.

James Brierley, the driver in question, was a highly skilled railway engineer. In his youth Brierley had been apprenticed to a reputable firm of railway engineers at Doncaster, and worked faithfully for the famous LNER and LMS railway companies. He was a well-built, powerful man according to his workmates, with a clear-cut, intelligent face. He had a practical nature, and looked upon the occult as bunkum.

At the turn of the century James Brierley had moved from the north of England to London, and with his wife and daughter he set up house near King's Cross station. At length he renewed his acquaintance with Jim Robson, a fellow Doncaster railway worker, who had earlier moved to London. Eventually Brierley became Robson's fireman on the midnight express to the north. By one of those coincidences which make fact stranger than fiction, Brierley and Robson served together in the 42nd Division at Gallipoli. Later, while they still worked together, Robson married and Brierley acted as best man. It was at this point that the emotional trouble started.

It appeared that the two families often visited each other, and Brierley formed a deep attachment to Jim Robson's new wife Ellen, who was some 15 years younger than her husband. At length Jim Brierley became a driver and his regular route ran past Jim and Ellen Robson's railway cottage at Finsbury Park. So, whenever Jim Brierley had some spare time, he visited Ellen, but only, of course, when Robson was away. Eventually Ellen Robson had a baby, and the local gossips in Finsbury whispered that it was Jim Brierley's child. The gossip at length reached Jim Robson's notice and, in a fit of jealousy, during a chance meeting in the engine yard, he pulled Brierley out of his cab and threatened to kill him if he so much as looked at Ellen again.

The next morning Brierley was transferred from the local run, and was put on the early morning train running to Newcastle, via York. Even so the train was on the main line that passed Ellen and Jim Robson's cottage. Unknown to her husband, Ellen Robson so planned it that she was at the door of the cottage to wave to Jim Brierley as he passed; and on his return journey in the evening she waved a small oil lamp.

One rainy Saturday night Brierley leaned from his cab to catch the light of Ellen's signal lamp but, for the first time ever, she was not there. Brierley slowed down his engine to pass the treacherous set of points by the cottage, and he blew the thundering machine's piercing whistle; but no Ellen appeared. As Brierley cycled home, however, he noticed the newsbill of the evening paper: 'TRAGEDY IN RAILWAY COTTAGE—ENGINE DRIVER KILLS HIS WIFE—HIS CHILD—AND HIMSELF'.

Next day Jim Brierley confirmed that his former workmate, friend and Gallipoli comrade had murdered his family and then had committed suicide.

Months went by with their uneventful monotony, but James Brierley always looked out for the cottage where Ellen and Jim had lived, as he braked for the dangerous points. Then one night a strange thing happened. As usual Brierley pulled back the engine's acceleration lever to quarter speed to take the points safely, and as the pounding vehicle slowed down to make a clattering clearance of the mesh of points, Brierley leaned out of his cab to look at the cottage. Suddenly the fireman's voice called to him. His eyes big with fear, the fireman pointed to the lever which was being pulled slowly open to full speed, and standing at the controls was the wraith of Jim Robson holding the accelerator lever! But strangest of all Robson had materialised in the uniform of the 42nd Division—the one he had worn at Gallipoli!

In an instant Brierley grabbed the lever to pull it back, but it would not move. Instantly Jim Robson's wraith disappeared, but the train hit the points at excessive speed, derailed itself and hit the embankment wall. Brierley was killed instantly, but the fireman, in whom he had confided his love of Ellen Robson, lived to testify to the ghost which returned to kill for revenge!

Chapter 3

Spectral armies

The ghostly soldiers of Souter Fell

On Midsummer Eve 1735 a farm-hand at Blakehills, Cumberland, saw the eastern side of Souter Fell covered with ghostly soldiers who were marching in distinct, well-regulated groups from the north, and who disappeared near a cleft on the summit. As might be expected, when the farm-hand later recounted his story he was disbelieved.

Again on Midsummer Eve 1737 the farm-hand's employer, farmer William Lancaster, saw the army follow once more the steps described by his employee. Lancaster, however, recorded his story more lucidly. He first saw a few men on horse-back riding across the face of the mountain. At the time he thought they were fox-hunters returning home; but as foxes are mainly hunted on foot in the Lakeland mountains, he found the sight unusual enough to watch.

Ten minutes later he saw the identical men leading a great column of troops marching five abreast, in exactly the same direction his farm-hand had told him in 1735. Each troop was led by a mounted officer whom Lancaster distinctly saw riding up and down the lines of soldiers. The discipline of their serried ranks was perfect. William Lancaster apparently saw all this during mid-afternoon, but as darkness fell he noticed how the disciplined soldiers seemed to break step and lose formation, so that by the time they disappeared they had turned into a mob. Once again the testimony was not believed locally, but the hard-headed Lakeland farmer stuck to his story.

One evening in 1743 Daniel Stricket, a shepherd in the employ of John Wren of Wilton Hall, was sitting at his cottage door with his master, when both saw a man and a dog in pursuit of some horses. Stricket and Wren both saw the incident and were equally mystified. How could horses travel so quickly on a mountainside so dangerously precipitous?

Early the next morning John Wren and his shepherd set out for the steep side of Souter Fell. At the very least they expected to find the prints of horseshoes and both men had the unspoken dread of finding the corpse of the man who had pursued the horses. Yet, search the mountain as they might, they found no trace at all of the horse or its rider.

Around 1930 hours on the evening of June 23 1744, Daniel Stricket saw the re-enactment of the spectral army of Souter Fell again, and by mid-1745 there were several further reports of the phantom army being seen by credible witnesses. So, on June 23 1745, 26 people set out to keep watch for the army and to make a record of what they saw. Later, the famous English authoress, agnostic and philosophical radical Harriet Martineau (1802-76) set down what had been seen in her *The English Lakes*

(Windermere, 1858): 'Carriages were now interspersed with troops; and everybody knew that no carriages had been, or could be, on the summit of Souter Fell. The multitude was beyond imagination; for the troops filled a space of half a mile, and marched quickly till night hid them—still marching. There was nothing vaporous or indistinct about the appearance of these spectres. So real did they seem that some of the people went up the next morning to look for the hoofmarks of the horses; and awful it was to them to find not one footprint on the heather or grass. The witnesses attested the whole story on oath before a magistrate . . .'

In 1747 the *Gentleman's Magazine* published an account of the vast phantom army of Souter Fell based on the testimony of these witnesses. At the time of the sighting, of course, on the west coast of Scotland, the Stuart pretender to the British throne, Charles Edward, was exercising part of his army prior to his abortive invasion of England. This caused the editor of the *Lonsdale Magazine* some time later, to put forward the theory that what the 26 people had seen was a sort of mirage 'by a transparent vapour' of the Scottish army on the mountain top.

This, of course, did not explain the sightings of 1735, 1737 and 1744; nevertheless an English writer James Clarke, the land surveyor, in his *A Survey of the Lakes of Cumberland, Westmorland and Lancashire* (printed for the author, London, 1787) attributes all the sightings to the Jacobite rebellions. But, as Harriet Martineau wrote: 'This is not much in the way of explanation, but it is, as far as we know, all that can be had at present'.

Phantoms of a Danish army

A few miles to the south-east of Sedbergh, near the village of Dent, among the dales and fells of the West Riding of Yorkshire, the spectres of a great number of soldiers are periodically seen and heard. Accounts of such sightings have been recorded as recently as the late 1950s; some have been attested by the well-known dales family of Middleton, who have lived in the region for generations. On many occasions members of this family and their neighbours have seen 'scores upon scores of soldiers, "in the dress of ancient Danes . . . coming down the fells" '. A faint rumbling is also heard as the soldiers descend.

One member of the Middleton family was inclined to be sceptical about these household tales of the phantom Danes. But he too when he was out one day saw the soldiers: 'I never felt so petrified in my life', he later told reporters. 'I certainly don't want to see it again. All that the Middletons said [*is*] true'.

Spectral soldiers of Cadbury Fort

According to persistent legend Camelot was the capital from where King Arthur ruled over the Britons before the Saxon conquest: at least this is the explicit testimony given by Chrétien de Troyes in the romance *Lancelot* written between 1160 and 1180. Even though the oldest known stories of Arthur never refer to Camelot, neither is it located on an authentic early map, archaeologists and historians have continually asked: where was Camelot?

Today the place with the strongest claim to be the original Camelot is Cadbury Fort, a pre-Roman earthwork on an isolated hill in Somerset, not far from Glastonbury, which itself plays an important role in the legends of Arthur and the Holy Grail. Investigations by the Camelot Research Committee have found evidence that, in the early sixth century AD, Cadbury was, in fact, the stronghold of a powerful chieftain,

Reality or myth? Two versions of the Mons legend appear here, that of the Angels of Mons (above) and that of St George and the Bowmen (below). Did the spirits of medieval bowmen, led by St George, rain arrows on German troops at Mons, giving the hard-pressed 2nd Corps of the BEF time to retreat?

Private John Simpson Kirkpatrick (third from the left in the front row wearing a forage cap) and his ghostly donkey clamber down the hill of Monash Valley, Gallipoli.

The torpedoing of the Royal Edward *in the Aegean Sea caused one soldier ghost to appear to his family.*

Cadbury Fort in Somerset—the site of Camelot? It is said that King Arthur issues from the ruins with his phantom patrol.

Ghostly Danish marauders haunt the fells above Dent, Yorkshire.

Charles XII of Sweden (below) believed in psychic powers which he petitioned regularly. On the left is his uniform. It was said that the loss of a magic button foretold his death.

who may have been Arthur. But to the psychic, Cadbury is one of those places where the barrier between this world and the supernatural overlap.

Just before World War II a school-teacher who lives near Ashcott saw phantom soldiers in the vicinity of Cadbury. She was motoring home rather late one evening, and as she passed the earthwork she saw a number of bright lights moving steadily down the hill. As they drew nearer she, and the lady who was with her, saw that the lights came from torches strapped to the tips of lances being carried by a troop of armed warriors. At the head of the phantom army which disappeared into the night they saw a mounted man of great stature and imposing appearance. Who was this prominent warrior and where had the ghostly soldiers come from? The two women did not know, but local tradition points clearly in one direction: King Arthur and his knights were issuing from Cadbury on a phantom patrol!

Wild Edric and his ghostly warriors

Wild Edric is one of those real people around whom many a strange legend has evolved. Edric, a nephew of Edric Streona, Ealdorman of Mercia (the area of modern times between the Thames and the Trent, excluding East Anglia) who betrayed King Edmund (Ironside) at the battle of Ashingdon (Assandum), led the men of Shropshire when they rose against William the Conqueror. With them he harried Herefordshire as far as the River Lugg, and beseiged the town of Shrewsbury. Edric became a popular hero, but the date of his death and his burial place are not known.

Shropshire legend has it that Edric's spirit never died and that it still lurks with the ghosts of his warriors in the Shropshire lead mines out of which they ride whenever the people are in danger.

Just before the Crimean War (1854), a miner and his young daughter testified that they saw Edric and his ghostly warriors ride by at Minsterley. The father told the girl to hide her face, or she would go mad. This she did, but watched the riders through her fingers. She afterwards described Edric as 'a dark man, with short curly hair and black eyes. He was dressed in a green cloak and coat and a green cap with a white feather. He carried a horn and wore a sword hanging from a golden belt. By his side rode his wife, Lady Godda, her yellow hair hanging loose over her green dress, a white linen band with a gold ornament round her head, and a short dagger at her waist . . .'.

Certainly this is a very detailed description by a young girl whose class was illiterate and hardly imaginative. In time of peace (for Edric regularly appeared, the locals said, in time of war, or to forecast its coming) Edric and his warriors, runs the old lore, can be heard hammering in the Shropshire mines, this being considered by the superstitious as a good sign (cf, 'knockers' in the Cornish tin mines).

The phantom Highland army

The legends of the north of Scotland are rich in stories of phantom soldiers, like the spectre of the gigantic warrior called Red Hand who marches up and down the sandy beach of Loch Morlich, or 'Big Donald of the Ghosts' who is said to make regular trips to America to haunt his descendants! But undoubtedly one of the most remarkable accounts of a spectral army seen on the march is that on which Lady Frances Balfour commented in a lengthy letter to *The Times* in 1926. The original holograph narrative, to which Lady Balfour referred, was collected and docketed by George Douglas (1823-1900), the 8th Duke of Argyle (father of Lady Frances), as being written down for the entertainment of his aunt Lady Charlotte Bury.

Written out by Archibald Bell, Writer to the Signet, of Inveraray, to Colonel Campbell the younger of Shawfield, the original manuscript letter is dated November 8 1808 and reads in part as follows:

'Sir,—As you wish to have an account of the vision which my father and grandfather saw in the neighbourhood of this place, I will endeavour to comply with your request. I have heard of it with all its circumstances so often related by them both, when together, as well as by my father separately, since my grandfather's decease, that I am as fully convinced they saw the vision as if I had seen it myself. At the same time I must acknowledge that, however desirous I am to oblige Lady Charlotte and you, I commit the account of it to writing with some degree of reluctance, well knowing how little reliance is given by the more intelligent classes of people to a narration of that kind, and how little it corresponds with the ordinary course of causes and effects.

'This vision was seen by them both about 3 o'clock afternoon of a very clear sunny day in the month of June or July between the years 1746 and 1753. I cannot go nearer to ascertain the year.

'My grandfather was then a farmer in Glenary, which you know is within four miles of this place, and my father, who was at that time a young unmarried man, resided in family with him. On the morning of the day above mentioned, my grandfather, having occasion to transact some business in Glenshiray, took my father along with him. They went there by crossing the hill which separates it from Glenary, and, their business in Glenshiray being finished, a little after midday they came round by Inveraray in order to return home. At that time the road generally used from Glenshiray to Inveraray lay upon the west side of the river Shiray, all the way to the Garran Bridge, when it joined the high road which leads from Inveraray to the low country by that bridge.

'As soon as they came to that bridge and had turned towards Inveraray, upon the high road, being then as you know within sight of a part of the old town of Inveraray which has been since demolished . . . they were very much surprised to behold a great number of men under arms marching on foot towards them. At this time the foremost ranks were only advanced as far as Kilmalieu*; they were marching in regular order and as closely as they could move, from the point of the new town near the quay where Captain Gillie's house now stands, along the shore and high road, and crossing the river of Aray near the town, at or about the spot where the new bridge has since been built. Of the rear there appeared to be no end; the ground upon which the new town now stands was then surrounded by a park wall, and the road beyond it lay in a circular direction between that wall and the sea. From the nature of the ground my father and grandfather could see no further than the wall and as the army was advancing in front, the rear as regularly succeeded and advanced from the farthest verge of their view.

'This extraordinary sight, which was wholly unexpected, so much attracted their attention that they stood a considerable time to observe it. They then walked slowly on, but stopped now and then, with their eyes constantly fixed on the objects before them. Meantime the army continuing regularly to advance, they counted that it had 15 or 16 pairs of colours, and they observed that the men nearest to them were marching upon the road six or seven abreast, or in each line, attended by a number of women and children, both above and below the road, some of whom were carrying tin cans and other implements of cookery, which I am told is customary upon a march. They were clothed in red . . . and the sun shone so bright that the gleam of their arms,

* A burial ground.

consisting of muskets and bayonets, dazzled their sight . . .

'My father, who had never seen an army before, naturally put a number of questions to my grandfather* concerning the probable route and destination of the army which was now advancing towards them, and the number of which it seemed to consist. My grandfather replied that he supposed it had come from Ireland and had landed in Kintyre, and that . . . it was more numerous than the armies on both sides at the battle of Culloden . . .

'My father and grandfather were now come to the thorn bush† between the Garran bridge and the gate of the Deer Park, and at the same time the van of the army had advanced very near to that gate . . . The vanguard, they then observed, consisted of a party of 40 to 50 men, preceded by an officer on foot; at a little distance behind them another officer appeared riding upon a grey dragoon horse . . . He had on a gold laced hat and a blue hussar cloak, with wide open loose sleeves, all lined with red; he also wore boots and spurs . . .'

A few seconds later the army completely disappeared leaving Bell's father and grandfather in a state of amazement. In the letter Archibald Bell concludes that neither of the two men had been drinking and that neither of them suffered from hallucinations. No one then or since has been able to account for the 'vision'.

Colonel Shepheard's story

During World War I, Colonel Shepheard, a Sheffield steel executive, was travelling in a staff car from Hazebrouck to Wimereux (a French town in the Département du Nord on the Hazebrouck canal—it was held with tenacity by the British, but was nearly lost during the final German offensive in 1918), with a French captain as interpreter and aide. As the car swept through the French villages, Colonel Shepheard took very little notice of the unremarkable, flat, poplar-lined fields, the whitewashed farms and the war-scarred villages. In fact he was only too pleased to arrive at Wimereux where he dined with his aide. That night Colonel Shepheard retired early and soon fell asleep. His subconscious, however, stimulated by the wine and the superb French cheese he had had for dinner, replayed a curious dream incident in his conscious mind.

'I dreamed', Colonel Shepheard later related to his friends, 'that I was travelling the same road again in the same car through the same villages. But with a difference. As we approached one village the car slowed down and stopped. On either side of the road were flat fields. Suddenly out of the earth on each side of the road rose up the hooded cloaked figures of silent men—all cloaked and hooded like monks. They rose slowly, and every man stared fixedly at me. It was a queer, wistful, sad stare, like a dumb question or a dumb warning. Their cloaks were grey, almost luminous, with a fine, silvery bloom on them like moths' wings. I seemed to touch one and it came off on my fingers in a soft dust.

'I can't remember if I got out of the car or just sat and touched the man nearest me. But they stared and stared endlessly, pitifully, with a sadness which went right to my heart. Then, slowly, they all sank back into the ground—rank after rank of hooded men sinking into the earth, their eyes fixed on me to the last.

'Next morning at breakfast, I told my French aide of my dream. He listened and suddenly became excited.

' "You know the name of that village near where your car stopped?" he asked.

* He had served with the Argyle Highlanders during the 1745 Rebellion.
† Destroyed c 1920.

' "No" I said. "What was it?"

' "Crécy!" the aide replied.'

A great battle, a part of which or of its consequences was thus telepathically transmitted to Colonel Shepheard's subconscious by some kind of occult transfer, was fought on August 26 1346 at the village of Crécy-en-Ponthieu in the Département du Somme, 12 miles north-east of Abbeville. Here Edward III of England decisively defeated Philip VI of France.

Edward had invaded France through Normandy, crossed the Seine and then forded the Somme. The English formed in battle order on a wooded hill between Wadicourt and Crécy, all on foot, with the large company of Welsh archers at the front. The French nobles present at Crécy had been impatient for victory: their army was numerically superior to that of the English and they insisted on joining battle immediately, even though their archers' crossbows had been dampened by a recent shower. The wooded country thereabouts, of course, was unsuitable for a mounted charge.

As a result the French cavalry were cut to pieces by the English longbowmen and spearmen. Although the French fought bravely, their senseless repeated charges only increased their casualties. By sunset they were beaten into a disorganised retreat. Colonel Shepheard's staff car passed over the site of the main scene of carnage of this, the first major action of the Hundred Years War. An example of the grey cowls and habits seen in Shepheard's dream of Crécy field may be viewed in the 14th century *Chroniques de Gilles le Muisit*.

I am indebted to the family of the late Colonel Shepheard for permission to use this story.

Chapter 4

Raising soldiers from the dead

Down the centuries witchcraft has been all things to all men. Today most people who admit to practising what they call 'witchcraft' make it clear that they only formulate white (ie, good) incantations and spells, abhorring black (evil) magic. In my description of the rise and development of witchcraft in Europe and North America,* I showed how difficult it is for the neophyte historian of the occult to distinguish between white and black magic practice; for in history both have run in parallel. But the blackest of all black magic is undoubtedly necromancy. Derived from the Greek words meaning 'dead' and 'divination', necromancy is the very ancient method of trying to communicate with the dead. It is practised for a variety of reasons, sometimes to protect oneself against evil spells called down by others, or more often to reveal hidden treasures and to ask advice.

Necromancy can be separated into two distinct practices; one, divination by means of ghosts, and two, divination from corpses. Both were arcane (ie, hidden) sciences, and the second led to the disinterrment of corpses and the desecration of tombs. The classic instance of necromancy was the biblical 'Witch of Endor' case.

As any knowledgeable spiritualist will tell you, ghosts cannot be summoned at will, but there are many instances in history stating how evil spirits have been tempted out of their non-earthly existence to be petitioned, summoned and consulted by devotees.

General Batraville's experiments

For a long time now necromancy has played an important part in voodoo (a West African corruption of the tribal Yoruba word for 'god'), that folk religion brought to Haiti by slaves from Dahomey (the West African republic which achieved its independence from France in 1960). In 1920 the revolutionary guerrilla General Benoit Batraville was engaged in battle with American troops in Haiti† and attempted necromancy to aid his war tactics. To help his efforts further, he used an amalgam of voodoo and medieval witchcraft‡. 'Instead of the Creole incantations, he used such Latin phrases as *Exurgent mortui et acmo venuient* (I require of you dead that you come to me), coupled with the name of Astrotha, a figure of medieval European demonology. When the spirit was summoned, the general asked his questions, then laid it again by throwing a handful of graveyard dust "to the four corners of the earth"

* See: Brown, Raymond Lamont, *A Book of Witchcraft* (David & Charles, 1971).
† See: Seabrook, William, *The Magic Island* (London, 1929).
‡ See: Brown, Raymond Lamont, *A Book of Witchcraft*, pp 45-46 (David & Charles, 1971).

saying: "Go back from whence you came. From the dirt you were created, to the dirt you may return" '.

Ritual processes

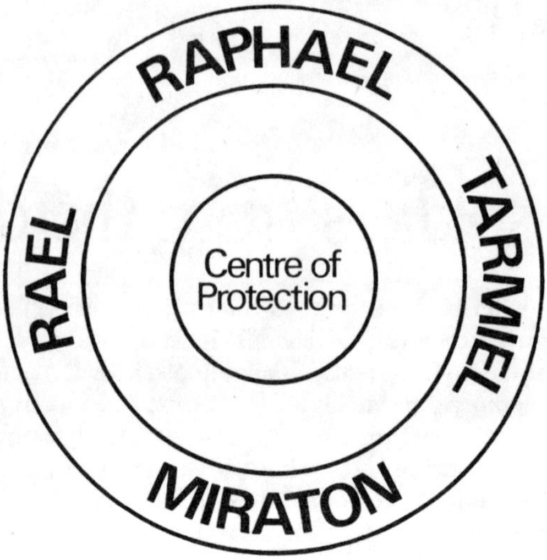

Others used a more involved ritual incorporating a circle of power, like the one pictured above, drawn on the ground (graveyard, sward, etc), set out with five 'magic points'. The necromancer stood within the circle to summon the dead spirit; usually a dead soldier for tactical questions and so on. The spirit was addressed in Latin, with the summons: '*Ego sum te peto et videre queo*' (It is I who petitions you and asks to see you), was reminded to speak only when spoken to, with: '*Ad consilium ne acces-seris, antequam voceris*', (Go not to the council chamber until I have summoned you), and was dismissed on the completion of the seance with: '*Ad regno electorum redes*', (Return to the kingdom of the chosen).

Often four black candles were burnt at the four cardinal points of the circle (here, Raphael, Tarmiel, Miraton and Rael), and the necromancer, from his position in the 'Centre of Protection', scattered red petitioning powder to the four winds as he summoned the spirit.

On the trail of treasure

In his *Memories of the Courts of Berlin, Dresden, Warsaw and Vienna in the years 1777, 1778, 1779* (London, 1799), Sir Nathaniel William Wraxall tells the story of how Prince Charles of Saxony, when in need of money, decided to raise the spirit of his dead kinsman the Chevalier de Saxe. The Chevalier de Saxe was the third son of Augustus II (1670-1733) the elector of Saxony and King of Poland. A half-brother to the libertine, drug-taking, soldier of fortune Moritz Graf von Sachsen (Maurice, Count of Saxony), the Chevalier was thought to have secreted a large sum of money somewhere in his palace at Dresden. To try to find this treasure, Prince Charles of Saxony employed the celebrated medium-operator Schrepfer of Leipzig to raise the spirit of the dead soldier.

This is how an 18th century German broadsheet describes the seance: 'Schrepfer naturally preferring darkness, as not only more private in itself, but every way better calculated for the effect of incantations; the company assembled on the appointed night. They were nineteen in number . . . persons of consideration, character and respectability. When they were met in the great gallery of Prince Charles' palace, the first object of all present was to secure the windows and doors, in order equally to prevent intrusion or deception. As far as precaution could effect it, they did so; and were satisfied that nothing except violence could procure access or entrance.

'Schrepfer commenced . . . by retiring into a corner of the gallery, where kneeling down, with many mysterious ceremonies he invoked the spirits to appear, or rather to come to his aid; for it is allowed that none were ever visible. A very considerable time elapsed before they obeyed; during which interval, he laboured apparently under great agitation of body and mind, being covered with a violent sweat, and almost in convulsions, like the Pythoness of antiquity.

'At length, a loud clatter was heard at all the windows on the outside; which was soon followed by another noise, resembling more the effect produced by a number of wet fingers drawn over the edge of glasses than anything else to which it could well be compared. This sound announced, as he said, the arrival of his good or protecting spirits and seemed to encourage him to proceed in his incantation. A short time afterwards a yelling was heard, of a frightful and unusual nature, which came, as he declared, from the malignant spirits, whose presence, as it seems, was necessary and indispensable to the completion of the catastrophe . . .

'Schrepfer continuing his invocations, the door suddenly opened with violence, and something that resembled a black ball or globe, rolled into the room. It was invested with smoke or cloud, in the midst of which appeared to be a human face like the countenance of the Chevalier de Saxe . . . From this form issued a loud and angry voice, which exclaimed '*Carl was wolte du mit mich?*' (Charles, what wouldst thou with me?).

'The prince, whose imprudent curiosity had summoned his uncle's ghost, and to whom, as the person principally responsible, the spectre addressed itself, far from manifesting self-possession, or attempting any reply, betrayed the strongest marks of horror and contrition. Throwing himself on his knees, he called on Heaven for mercy; while others of the terrified party earnestly besought the magician to give the only remaining proof of his art for which they now were anxious, by dismissing the apparition.'

With some reluctance Schrepfer dismissed the wraith of the Chevalier de Saxe. Never again did Prince Charles of Saxony attempt to consult the dead for money; or, at least, if his treasury ran dry he preferred the good old 18th century stop-gap of borrowing from the aristocracy to seances!

Chapter 5

Classic European evanescences

Death of the soldier king

Swedish folklore contains many stories of the *Liten Man i Gratt* (Little Man in Grey), the legendary spectre who for centuries had delivered grim prognostications concerning the Swedish royal house. One of the most celebrated of these psychic messages was to Charles XII (1682-1718), who had succeeded his father Charles XI as King of Sweden in 1697. From his accession Charles XII had been fraught with military and political difficulties. The commencement of his troubles was undoubtedly the Great Northern War of 1699, in which Russia, Poland and Denmark had allied in an attempt to crush what they assumed to be a weak Sweden, under a king who was little more than a boy. So Charles was forced into a military career in which he was to show himself an outstanding commander.

The cold, which slashes the limbs like a Saracen's blade, lies over the woods of Finland for most of the year. The pine trees bend in the wind, and the bare white birches bow in supplication to the gods of the tempest, as the icy blasts gain force at dusk. One such evening a handful of men gathered round a crackling fire. Somehow they feared the Finnish cold less than the terror of the harsh words which one man was delivering; for he, like the wintry cold, could bring destruction. It was Charles XII of Sweden who spoke; and although the other men round the fire had been long in his service, they feared the king's actions now. Formerly his brilliance as a soldier had enabled him to inspire his men in victory and defeat; but his lust for military conquest had grown insatiable, and rather than accept offers of peace he preferred to fight against unrealistic odds.

Charles, at this time, considered it necessary to consult once more the occult advisor, called the Little Man in Grey, as to the next move in the current military campaign. His men disagreed and were quarrelsome. 'But Your Majesty', said one, 'we will be killed. It is a long way to the dwelling of the Little Man in Grey, and your enemies in Finland are as numerous as the trees hereabouts.'

'*Tystnad*—Silence!' barked the king haughtily. 'Had I listened to my tiresome advisors I should not have defeated the Danes in 1700, and forced the reparation of Travendal. Neither would I have triumphed at Narva against 6,000 Russian cavalry. Remember! Aye, a seance is required. And I shall go alone.'

A bolder courtier ventured: 'Yes, Your Majesty, many victories, but at Poltava, when the birds froze on the wing . . .'

'Yes', interrupted a cavalry officer bitterly, 'your orders led to defeat . . .'

'Defeat! Defeat!' spat the king. 'And so? It would not have happened had I not listened to some chair-bound fool's advice. Had I not taken the advice to attack the Czar, there would not have been any surrender of my troops at Perevolochna. I would not have been forced to flee to Turkey'.

The soldiers and courtiers rose as the king stood trembling with anger. One of the assembled chiefs-of-staff approached the king, however, and whispered: '*Tusen Ursäkter Eders Majestät*—A thousand pardons Your Majesty. May I ask this only? If you have no faith in your councillors, will you take the advice of this ghostly seer?'

All saw the king's face flush in the flickering campfire's light: 'My generals, admirals and troops are all alike—they're blind, deaf and dumb. Only the dead need not see, hear or talk—the dead *know*. Thus must I consult the dead. Prepare for my trip adjuvant. The rest await my return!'

So, with this, His Majesty King Charles XII of Sweden, on a bitter day in the winter of 1714, rode alone through the dense woods of Finland until he reached a certain clearing. Hitching his horse to a nearby tree, and gathering his travelling cloak around him against the cold, Charles awaited at this fabled spot where the prophetic dead walk.

Carefully he worked out what he must do. Stooping on the frozen ground, he traced a circle with the tip of his sword. Standing within the circle, the king searched for his tinder box. At last he found it in his topcoat. Striking the jewelled lid three times the king recited:

Kom kvickt! Kom kvickt! Kom kvickt!
Fran dunge eller skog eller dal
Och för Kungen av Sverige
Hans öde och framtid berätta.
(Come quick! Come quick! Come quick!
From copse or wood or dell
And to the King of Sweden
His fate and fortune tell.)

After this the king burned a cone of specially prepared herbs, crossed himself three times and stood waiting. Longer and longer he lingered in the cold. As he began to regret his journey for the tenth time, something happened. A flurry of snow fell from the trees and he felt a hand on his shoulder. Turning he saw the figure of a small grey man.

Startled, the king stepped back a pace. From somewhere in the trees a woman's voice resounded: 'Sweden has a very impulsive and obstinate king. He has won great renown and has great capacity, but he will jeopardise everything through excessive vanity.' As the voice died away, the king asked: 'Tell me, good Spirit, what can I do to save my country and vanquish my enemies?'

'Your last mistake was a fatal one,' said another ghostly voice from deep in the pinewood. 'You should not have returned to Sweden from exile in Turkey.' Impetuously Charles was about to bark that he was no longer welcome by Sultan Ahmed III, who on January 31 1713 had launched 3,000 Janissaries against the exiled Swedes encamped at Bender; but the king held his tongue. The ghost continued: 'You should have taken up service in the Sultan's army. To remain in Sweden, even now, means that you will only perish miserably, and your ghost will haunt that country for three generations.'

A calm silence fell on the clearing as the king listened, his fear increasing. But now it was the Little Man in Grey's turn to speak. He handed the king a gold encrusted finger ring: 'Wear this ring as long as you live. It will help you. It will vanish from your finger on the day of your death. Take also this magic button and sew it onto your dress-uniform. It will protect you until your time comes. Guard it well, however, for its loss will cause your death.'

Charles took the ring and slipped it on his finger. It felt as cold as ice; the button he slipped into his pocket. Meanwhile the Little Man in Grey had disappeared, and Charles went back to his troops. Thereafter he raised an army which was strong enough to prevent his being attacked by his enemies; and in 1717 he began an assault on Norway. In November 1718 Charles was beseiging Frederikshall. He and his chiefs-of-staff had come within 300 yards of the fort, when one of the officers, to whom Charles had told the story of the gold ring and the button, noticed that the ring was missing.

'Your Majesty! Look! The ring has gone, and the button is no longer sewn to your coat!'

Looking down at his hand, the king shrugged his shoulders. 'Who knows where they are? But the Little Man in Grey was wrong for once. We are winning! Look the fort is almost ours!'

With these words the king looked over the parapet of the foremost trench, and the next moment he was shot through the skull. Today, as prophesied, the ghost of Sweden's soldier king, Charles XII, still walks, but has done so for more than the three forecast generations; sometimes at Frederikshall, sometimes in the woods of Finland, and sometimes at his palace in Stockholm. Psychic phenomena concerning the king remain very modern: very recently, for instance, the Swedish Spiritualist magazine *Utan Grans*, gave one example. In its pages Captain-Doctor John Nihlen told how, with two army comrades, he sheltered for a night in a mountain cabin. Dr Nihlen was at the time on a winter ski patrol along the Swedish-Norwegian border, operating at some distance from his regiment.

During his first watch period (midnight to 0200 hours), Dr Nihlen became aware of a strange noise 'like an echo, a cracking sound I could not identify'. As the noise came nearer, Dr Nihlen aroused his comrades: 'fear gripped me', he records. 'There was something disastrous about this sound that grew stronger, came closer and filled the silent night with a new, frightening tone. We all stood listening, holding our breath . . . We strained our eyes to see down into the valley. Far away we could discern dark shadows moving back and forth. Suddenly we heard a human voice, so loud in the still night, we could distinguish the words. A man was giving orders in old Swedish: "Attention . . . Turn about . . . March forward". The dark shadows in the valley began to move, the sound of the tramping feet became stronger. It was men marching, coming in our direction'.

For a time Dr Nihlen and his comrades stood by their cabin doorway transfixed, watching the ghostly shadows grow and take on recognisable shape. First two horsemen materialised, followed by a column of troops in 18th century uniform. 'Tightly grouped, a hundred men or more, their faces ghost-like under the northern lights, they marched in perfect time up through the valley, past our cabin towards the east'. Troop after troop of soldiers passed the cabin, and by now their uniform was recognisable as Carolean.

Fascinated by what they had seen, Dr Nihlen made a careful report and sent a copy to a friend who was a military historian. From the data the historian was able to identify definitely the soldiers as Caroleans: these troops with the king at the head had marched across the Norwegian border in 1718.

'What makes the story remarkable', says Nihlen, 'is the old Swedish commands we heard. These were the very words of command used by the Caroleans. Thus they establish the period precisely'.

Strangely enough the manner of Charles XII's death has given rise to a curious type of military occultism: after his death both the bullet which killed him and his clothes took on talismanic aspects. In particular, tradition mentions the magic button given to him by the Little Man in Grey.

The prophylactic properties of the button are mentioned time and time again: 'The old people said that while Charles wore the button no bullets could kill him. Bullets hitting him bounded off and fell into his topboots. In the evenings he took off the boots and out fell the bullets . . . when he was shot they say that the button was missing from his coat'. In some traditions the bullet that killed Charles was a silver one, and this reflects the widespread European superstition that a hero (or witch, or 'protected person') could only be killed with a silver bullet; as, for example, the Roundheads believed that they could only kill Prince Rupert's 'magic advisors' (his two dogs!) with silver bullets.

Both Nils Ahnland (*Sanning och Sägen am Carl XII's Död*, Stockholm, 1941), Albert Sandklef (*Kulknappen och Carl XII's Död*, Lund, 1941), and others have examined the legends of Charles' death and the possibility of his assassination by one of his own men, who may or may not have played on the occultism surrounding the king. Many believe that Charles was actually killed by the magic button itself. Tradition relates how the king lost the button a little before his death. Apparently it was picked up by one of his officers. The officer knew of the magic button's powers and about the superstition which said that the king could only be killed by a silver missile. The soldier is said to have fired it at the king.

In 1924 a button was found in the area of a gravel pit at Deragård, near Oxnevalla, the traditional spot where the magic button is said to have landed after it had pierced Charles' skull. Certainly the rifles issued to Swedish officers in 1716, and used in the Frederickshall campaign, could have fired such a button. The button is now on display at Varberg Museum. Today only Charles XII's ghost knows the truth, and no one has been able to pin it down long enough to ascertain it*.

From Major Van Hoek's journal

Major Van Hoek served for many years in the Danish Guards, and latterly in the Royal Netherlands Army. His hobby was folklore and his particular passion, collecting ghost stories. After 50 years he had amassed notebook after notebook of tales of spectres, ghosts and wraiths. This story, called *Het Spook Hand* (The Spectre Hand), comes from his collection and was one of his favourites:

'In the August of 1870 I found myself with three fellow soldiers, when on a northern tour, at the Hotel de Scandinavia, in the long and handsome Carl Johan Gade of Christiana, Norway. A single day, or little more, had sufficed us to "do" all the lions of the little Norwegian capital—the royal palace, a stately white building, guarded by slouching Norski riflemen in long coats, with wide-awakes and green plumes; the great brick edifice wherein the Storthing is held, and where the red lion appears on everything, from the king's throne to the hall-porter's coal-scuttle; the castle of Aggerhuis and its petty armoury, with a single suit of mail, and the long muskets of the Scots who fell at Rhomsdhal; after which there is nothing more to be seen; and when the little Tivoli gardens close at ten, all Christiana goes to sleep till dawn next morning.

'English carriages being perfectly useless in Norway, we had ordered four of the

* Swedish chronicles relate how Charles XII, accompanied by his Chamberlain and state physician, witnessed the trial of the assassin of Gustavus III, which occurred nearly a century later.

native carrioles for our departure, as we were resolved to start for the wild mountainous district named the Dovrefeld, when a delay in the arrival of certain letters compelled me to remain two days behind my companions, who promised to await me at Rodnaes, near the head of the magnificent Rans-fiord; and this partial separation with the subsequent circumstances of having to travel alone through districts that were totally strange to me, with but a slight understanding of the language, were the means of bringing to my knowledge the story I am about to relate.

'The *table d'hôte* is over by two o'clock in the fashionable hotels of Christiana, so about four in the afternoon I quitted the city, the streets and architecture of which resemble portions of den Haag, with stray bits of old Amsterdam. In my carriole, a comfortable kind of gig, were my portmanteau and gun-case; these with my whole person, and indeed the body of the vehicle itself, being covered by one of those huge tarpaulin cloaks furnished by the carriole company in the Store Stangade.

'Though the rain was beginning to fall with a force and density peculiarly Norse, when I left behind me the red-tiled city with all its green-coppered spires, I could not but be struck by the bold beauty of the scenery, as the strong little horse at a rasping pace tore the light carriole along the rough mountain road, which was bordered by natural forests of dark and solemn-looking pines, interspersed with graceful silver birches. The greenness of the foliage contrasted powerfully with the blue of the narrow fiords that opened on every hand, and with the colours in which the toy-like country houses were painted, their timber walls being always snowy white, and their shingle roofs a flaming red. Even some of the village spires wore the same sanguinary hue, presenting thus a singular feature in the landscape.

'The rain increased to an unpleasant degree; the afternoon seemed to darken into evening, and the evening into night sooner than usual. Dense masses of vapour came rolling down the steep sides of the wooded hills, over which the sombre firs spread everywhere and up every vista that opened, like a sea of cones. As the houses became fewer and further apart, and not a single wanderer was abroad, I had but the pocket-map of my *Baedeker* to guide me. I soon became convinced that instead of pursuing the route to Rodnaes I was somewhere on the banks of Tyri-fiord, at least three Norwegian miles in the opposite direction, my little horse worn out, the rain still falling in a continual torrent, night already at hand, and mountain scenery of the most tremendous character everywhere around me. I was in an almost circular valley (encompassed by a chain of hills), which opened before me, after leaving a deep chasm that the road enters, near a place which I afterwards learned bears the name of Krogkleven.

'Owing to the steepness of the road, and some decay in the harness of my hired carriole, the traces parted, and then I found myself, with the now useless horse and vehicle, far from any house, homestead, or village where I could have the damage repaired or procure shelter. The rain still pouring like a sheet of water, the thick, shaggy, and impenetrable woods of Norwegian pine towering all about me, their shadows rendered all the darker by the unusual gloom of the night.

'To remain quietly in the carriole was unsuitable to a temperament so impatient as mine. So I drew it aside from the road, spread the tarpaulin over my small stock of baggage and the gun-case, haltered the pony to it, and set forth on foot, stiff, sore, and weary, in search of succour; and though armed only with a Norwegian tolknife, having no fear of thieves or of molestation.

'Following the road on foot in the face of the blinding rain, a German shepherd's blanket and oilskin my sole protection now, I perceived ere long a side-gate and little avenue, which indicated my vicinity to some estate. After proceeding about three hundred yards or so, the wood became more open, a light appeared before me, and

I found it to proceed from a window on the ground floor of a little two-storeyed mansion, built entirely of wood. The sash, which was divided in the middle, was unbolted, and stood partially and most invitingly open; and knowing how hospitable the Norwegians are, without troubling myself to look for the entrance-door, I stepped over the low sill into the empty room and looked about for a bell-pull, forgetting that in Norway, where there are no mantelpieces, it is generally to be found behind the door.

'The floor was, of course, bare, and painted brown; a high German stove, like a black iron pillar, stood in one corner on a stone block; the door, which evidently communicated with some other apartment, was constructed to open in the middle, with one of the quaint lever handles peculiar to Norway. The furniture was all of plain Norwegian pine, highly varnished; a reindeer-skin spread on the floor, and another over an easy chair, were the only luxuries; and on the table lay the *Illustret Tidende*, the *Aftonblat*, and other papers of that morning, with a meerschaum and pouch of tobacco, all serving to show that someone had recently quitted the room.

'I had just taken in all these details by a glance, when there entered a tall thin man of gentlemanly appearance, clad in a rough tweed suit, with a scarlet shirt, open at the throat, a simple but *dégagé* style of costume, which he seemed to wear with a natural grace. Pausing, he looked at me with some surprise and inquiringly, as I began my apologies and explanation in German.

' "*Taler de Dansk-Norsk*," said he curtly.

' "I cannot speak either with fluency, but—"

' "You are welcome, however, and I shall assist you in the prosecution of your journey. Meantime, here is cognac. I am an old soldier, and know the comforts of a full canteen, and of the Indian weed, too, in a wet bivouac. There is a pipe at your service."

'I thanked him, and (while he gave directions to his servants to go after the carriole and horse) proceeded to observe him more closely, for something in his voice and eye interested me deeply.

'There was much of broken-hearted melancholy—something that indicated a hidden sorrow—in his features, which were handsome, and very slightly aquiline. His face was pale and careworn; his hair and moustache, though plentiful, were perfectly white-blanched, yet he did not seem over forty years of age. His eyes were blue, but without softness, being strangely keen and sad in expression, and times there were when a startled look, that savoured of fright, or pain, or insanity, or of all mingled, came suddenly into them. This unpleasant expression tended greatly to neutralize the symmetry of a face that otherwise was evidently a fine one. Suddenly a light seemed to spread over it, as I threw off some of my sodden mufflings, and he exclaimed—

' "You speak Danskija, and German too, I know! Have you quite forgotten me, Herr Kaptain?" he added, grasping my hand with kindly energy. "Don't you remember Carl Holberg of the Danish Guards?"

'The voice was the same as that of the once happy, lively, and jolly young Danish officer, whose gaiety of temper and exuberance of spirit made him seem a species of madcap, who was wont to give champagne suppers at the Klampenborg Gardens to great ladies of the court and to ballet-girls of the Hof Theatre with equal liberality; to whom many a fair Danish girl had lost her heart, and who, it was said, had once the effrontery to commence a flirtation with one of the royal princesses when he was on guard at the Amalienborg Palace. But how was I to reconcile this change, the appearance of many years of premature age, that had come upon him?

' "I remember you perfectly, Carl," said I, while we shook hands; "yet it is so long since we met; moreover—excuse me—but I knew not whether you were in the land of the living."

'The strange expression, which I cannot define, came over his face as he said, with a low, sad tone—

' "Times there are when I know not whether I am of the living or the dead. It is many years since our happy days—a score or more since I was wounded at the Battle of Idstedt—and it seems as if 'twere twenty ages."

' "Old friend, I am indeed glad to meet you again."

' "Yes, old you may call me with truth," said he, with a sad, weary smile, as he passed his hand tremulously over his whitened locks, which I could remember being a rich auburn.

'All reserve was at an end now, and we speedily recalled a hundred and one past scenes of merriment and pleasure, enjoyed together—prior to the campaign of Holstein—in Copenhagen, that most delightful and gay of all the northern cities; and, under the influence of memory, his now withered face seemed to brighten, and some of its former expression stole back again.

' "Is this your fishing or shooting quarters, Carl?" I asked.

' "Neither. It is my permanent abode."

' "In this place, so rural—so solitary? Ah! you have become a Benedick—taken to love in a cottage, and so forth—yet I don't see any signs of—"

' "Hush! for godsake! You know not *who* hears us," he exclaimed, as terror came over his face; and he withdrew his hand from the table on which it was resting, with a nervous suddenness of action that was unaccountable, or as if hot iron had touched it.

' "Why?—Can we not talk of such things?" asked I.

' "Scarcely here—or anywhere to me," he said, incoherently. Then, fortifying himself with a stiff glass of Cognac and foaming seltzer, he added: "You know that my engagement with my cousin Marie Louise Viborg was broken off—beautiful though she was, perhaps *is* still, for even twenty years could not destroy her loveliness of feature and brilliance of expression—but you never know *why?*"

' "I thought you behaved ill to her—were mad, in fact."

'A spasm came over his face. Again he twitched his hand away as if a wasp had stung, or something unseen had touched it, as he said—

' "She was very proud, imperious and jealous."

' "She resented, of course, your openly wearing the opal ring which was thrown from the palace window by the princess—"

' "The ring—the ring! Oh, do not speak of *that!*" said he, in a hollow tone. "Mad?—yes, I was mad—and yet I am not, though I have undergone, and even *now* am undergoing, that which would break the heart of a *Holger Danske!* But you shall hear, if I can tell it with coherence and without interruption, the reason why I fled from society and the world—and for all these twenty miserable years have buried myself in this mountain solitude, where the forest overhangs the fiord, and where no woman's face shall ever smile on mine!"

'In short, after some reflection and many involuntary sighs—and being urged, when the determination to unbosom himself wavered—Carl Holberg related to me a little narrative so singular and wild, that but for the sad gravity—or intense solemnity of his manner bore with it, I should have deemed him utterly—mad!

' "Marie Louise and I were to be married as you remember, to cure me of all my frolics and expensive habits—the very day was fixed; you were to be the groomsman, and had selected a suite of jewels for the bride in the Kongens Nytorre; but the war that broke out in Schleswig-Holstein drew my battalion of the guards to the field, whither I went without much regret so far as my *fiancée* was concerned; for, sooth to say, both of us were somewhat weary of our engagement, and were unsuited to each other: so we had not been without piques, coldness, and even quarrels, till keeping up appearances partook of boredom.

' "I was with General Krogh when that decisive battle was fought at Idstedt between our troops and the Germanising Holsteiners under General Willisen. My battalion of the guards was detached from the right wing with orders to advance from Salbro on the Holstein rear, while the centre was to be attacked, pierced, and the batteries beyond it carried at the point of the bayonet, all of which was brilliantly done. But prior to that I was sent, with directions to extend my company in skirmishing order, among some thickets that covered a knoll which is crowned by a ruined edifice, part of an old monastery with a secluded burial-ground.

' "Just prior to our opening fire the funeral of a lady of rank, apparently, passed us, and I drew my men aside to make way for the open catafalque, on which lay the coffin covered with white flowers and silver coronets, while behind it were her female attendants, clad in black cloaks in the usual fashion, and carrying wreaths of white flowers and immortelles to lay upon the grave. Desiring these mourners to make all speed lest they might find themselves under a fire of cannon and musketry, my company opened at six hundred yards on the Holsteiners, who were coming on with great spirit. We skirmished with them for more than an hour, in the long clear twilight of the July evening, and gradually, but with considerable loss were driving them through the thicket and over the knoll on which the ruins stand, when a half-spent bullet whistled through an opening in the mouldering wall and struck me on the back part of the head, just below my bearskin cap. A thousand stars seem to flash around me, then darkness succeeded. I staggered and fell, believing myself mortally wounded; a pious invocation trembled on my lips, the roar of the red and distant battle passed away, and I became completely insensible.

' "How long I lay thus I know not, but when I imagined myself coming back to life and to the world I was in a handsome, but rather old-fashioned apartment, hung, one portion of it with tapestry and the other with rich drapery. A subdued light that came, I could not discover from where, filled it. On a buffet lay my sword and my brown bearskin cap of the Danish Guards. I had been borne from the field evidently, but when and to where? I was extended on a soft *fauteuil* or couch, and my uniform coat was open. Some one was kindly supporting my head—a woman dressed in white, like a bride; young and so lovely, that to attempt any description of her seems futile!

' "She was like the fancy portraits one occasionally sees of beautiful girls, for she was divine, perfectly so, as some enthusiast's dream, or painter's happiest conception. A long respiration, induced by admiration, delight, and the pain of my wound escaped me. She was so exquisitely fair, delicate and pale, middle-sized and slight, yet charmingly round, with hands that were perfect, and marvellous golden hair that curled in rippling masses about her forehead and shoulders, and from amid which her *piquante* little face peeped forth as from a silken nest. Never have I forgotten that face, nor shall I be *permitted*, to do so, while life lasts at least," he added, with a strange contortion of feature, expressive of terror rather than ardour; "it is ever before my eyes, sleeping or waking, photographed in my heart and on my brain! I strove to rise, but she stilled, or stayed me, by caressing gesture, as a mother would her child, with more of tenderness, perhaps, than love; while in her whole air there was much of dignity and self reliance.

' " 'Where am I?' was my first question.

' " 'With me' she answered naïvely; 'is it not enough?'

' "I kissed her hand, and said—

' " 'The bullet, I remember, struck me down in a place of burial on the Salbro Road—strange!'

' " 'Why strange?'

' " 'As I am fond of rambling among graves when in my thoughtful moods.'

' " 'Among graves—why?' she asked.

' " 'They look so peaceful and quiet.'

' "Was she laughing at my unwonted gravity, that so strange a light seemed to glitter in her eyes, on her teeth, and over her lovely face? I kissed her hands again, and she left them in mine. Adoration began to fill my heart and eyes, and faintly murmured on my lips; for the great beauty of the girl bewildered and intoxicated me; and, perhaps, I was emboldened by past success in more than one love affair. She sought to withdraw her hand, saying:

' " 'Look not thus; I know how lightly you hold the love of one elsewhere.'

' " 'Of my cousin Maria Louise? Oh! what of that! I never, never loved till now! and, drawing a ring from her finger, I slipped my beautiful opal in its place.'

' " 'And you love me?' she whispered.

' " 'Yes; a thousand times, yes!'

' " 'But you are a soldier—wounded, too. Ah! if you should die before we meet again!'

' " 'Or, if you should die ere then?' said I, laughingly.

' " 'Die—I am already dead to the world—on loving you; but, living or dead our souls are as one, and—'

' " 'Neither heaven nor the power beneath shall separate us now!' I exclaimed, as something of a melodrama began to mingle with the genuineness of the sudden passion with which she had inspired me. She was so impulsive, so full of brightness and ardour, as compared to the cold, proud, and calm Marie Louise. I boldly encircled her with my arms; then her glorious eyes seemed to fill with the subtle light of love, while there was a strange magnetic thrill in her touch, and more than all, in her kiss.

' " 'Carl! Carl!' she sighed.

' " 'What! You know my name?—and yours?'

' " 'Thyra. But ask no more.'

' " 'There are but three words to express the emotion that possessed me—bewilderment, intoxication, madness. I showered kisses on her beautiful eyes, on her soft tresses, on her lips that met mine half way; but this excess of joy, together with the pain of my wound, began to overpower me; a sleep, a growing and drowsy torpor, against which I struggled in vain, stole over me. I remember clasping her firm little hand in mine, as if to save myself from sinking into oblivion, and then—no more—no more!

' "On again coming back to consciousness, I was alone. The sun was rising, but had not yet risen. The scenery, the thickets which we had skirmished, rose dark as the deepest indigo against the amber-tinted eastern sky; and the last of the waning moon yet silvered the pools and marshes around the borders of the Langsö Lake, where now eight thousand men, the slain of yesterday's battle, were lying stark and stiff. Moist with dew and blood, I propped myself on one elbow and looked around me, with such wonder that a sickness came over my heart. I was *again* in the cemetry where the bullet had struck me down; a little grey owl was whooping and blinking in a recess of the crumbling wall. Was the drapery of the chamber but the ivy that rustled thereon?—for where the lighted buffet stood there was an old square tomb, whereon lay my sword and bearskin cap!

' "The last rays of the waning moonlight stole through the ruins on a new-made grave—the fancied *fauteuil* on which I lay—strewn with the flowers of yesterday, and

Apsley House (above) near Hyde Park in London is one of the many places haunted by the English Civil War Parliamentarian leader Oliver Cromwell (right).

Mount Kennedy in Eire was the haunt of the Banshee of Rossmore.

Among the 14 ghosts at Sandford Orcas is a soldier spectre with a guilty conscience.

Napoleon Bonaparte received several psychic messages during his lifetime; his ghost was said to visit his mother.

The quaint village of Dulverton in Somerset was the site of a conversation between Captain William Dyce and the ghost of Major George Sydenham.

The recurrent apparitions of the dead soldier Owen Howison to his mediumistic cousin have been the subject of thorough investigation by psychic researchers.

at its head stood a temporary cross, hung with white garlands and wreaths of immortelles. Another ring was on my finger now; but where was she, the donor? Oh, what opium-dream, or what insanity was this?

'"For a time I remained utterly bewildered by the vividness of my recent dream, for such I believed it to be. But if a dream, how came this strange ring, with a square emerald stone, upon my finger? And *where* was mine? Perplexed by these thoughts, and filled with wonder and regret that the beauty I had seen had no reality, I picked my way over the ghostly débris of the battlefield, faint, feverish, and thirsty, till at the end of a long avenue of lindens I found shelter in a stately brick mansion, which I learned belonged to the Count of Idstert, a noble, on whose hospitality—as he favoured the Holsteiners—I meant to intrude as little as possible.

'"He received me, however, courteously and kindly. I found him in deep mourning: and on discovering, by chance, that I was the officer who had halted the line of skirmishers when the funeral *cortège* passed on the previous day, he thanked me with earnestness, adding with a deep sigh, that it was the burial of his daughter.

'" 'Half my life seems to have gone with her—my lost darling! She was so sweet, Herr Kaptain—so gentle, and so surpassingly beautiful—my poor Thyra!'

'" '*Who* did you say?' I exclaimed, in a voice that sounded strange and unnatural, while half-starting from the sofa on which I had cast myself, sick at heart and faint from loss of blood.

'" 'Thyra, my daughter, Herr Kaptain,' replied the Count, too full of sorrow to remark my excitement, for this had been the quaint old Danish name uttered in my dream. 'See, what a child I have lost!' he added, as he drew back a curtain which covered a full-length portrait, and to my growing horror, and astonishment, I beheld, arrayed in white even as I had seen her in my vision, the fair girl with the masses of golden hair, the beautiful eyes, and the *piquante* smile lighting up her features even on the canvas, and I was rooted to the spot.

'" 'This ring, Herr Count?' I gasped.

'"He let the curtain fall from his hand, and now a terrible emotion seized him, as he almost tore the jewel from my finger.

'" 'My daughter's ring!' he exclaimed. 'It was buried with her yesterday—her grave has been violated—violated by your infamous troops.'

'"As he spoke, a mist seemed to come over my sight; a giddiness made my senses reel, then a hand—the soft little hand of last night, with my opal ring on its third finger—came stealing into mine, unseen! More than that, a kiss from tremulous lips I could not see, was pressed on mine as I sank backward and fainted! The remainder of my story must be briefly told.

'"My soldiering was over; my nervous system was too much shattered for further military service. On my homeward way to join and be wedded to Marie Louise—a union with whom was repugnant to me now—I pondered deeply over the strange subversion of the laws of nature presented by my adventure; or the madness, it might be, that had come upon me.

'"On the day I presented myself to my intended bride, and approached to salute her, I felt a hand—the *same hand*—laid softly on mine. Startling and trembling, I looked around me; but saw nothing. The grasp was firm. I passed my other hand over it, and felt the slender fingers and the shapely wrist; yet still I saw nothing, and Marie Louise gazed at my motions, my pallor, doubt and terror, with calm, but cool indignation.

'"I was about to speak—to explain—to say I know not what, when a kiss from the lips I could not see sealed mine, and with a cry like a scream I broke away from my friends and fled.

'"All deemed me mad, and spoke with commiseration of my wounded head; and when I went abroad in the streets men eyed me with curiosity, as one over whom some evil destiny hung—as one to whom something terrible had happened, and gloomy thoughts were wasting me to a shadow. My narrative may seem incredible; but this attendant, unseen yet palpable, is ever by my side, and if under any impulse, such even as sudden pleasure in meeting you I for a moment forget it, the soft and gentle touch of a female hand reminds me of the past, and haunts me, for a guardian demon—if I may use such a term—rules my destiny: one lovely, perhaps, as an angel.

'"Life has no pleasure, but only terrors for me now. Sorrow, doubt, horror and perpetual dread, have sapped the roots of existence; for a wild and clamorous fear of what the next moment may bring forth is ever in my heart, and when the touch comes my soul seems to die within me.

'"You know what haunts me now—God help me! God help me! You do not understand all this, you would say. Still less do I; but in all the idle or extravagant stories I have read of ghosts—stories once my sport and ridicule, as the result of vulgar superstition or ignorance—the so-called supernatural visitor was visible to the eye, or heard by the ear; but the ghost, the fiend, the invisible Thing that is ever by the side of Carl Holberg is only sensible to the touch—it is the unseen but tangible substance of an apparition!"

'He had got thus far when he gasped, grew livid, and passing his right hand over the left, about an inch above it, with trembling fingers, he says—

'"It is here—here now—even with you present, I feel her hand on mine; the clasp is tight and tender, and she will never leave me, but with life!"

'And then this once gay, strong, and gallant fellow, now the wreck of himself in body and in spirit, sank forward with his head between his knees, sobbing and faint.

'Four months afterwards, when with my friends, I was shooting bears at Hammerfest, I read in the Norwegian *Aftenposten,* that Carl Holberg had shot himself in bed, on Christmas Eve.'

The priest and the grisly hand

Among the papers of the Vatican State at the Palazzo della Sapienza is a set of records known as *L'Archivio Segreto Vaticano*—The Secret Archives of the Vatican, perhaps the most important archives in the world. These contain about 25 miles of book-shelves laden with parchment and paper manuscripts of great historical value. The papal archives therein deal with an international range of subjects like art, science, theology, and politics, as well as with psychic studies. Because the Roman Catholic Church has exploited superstition down the centuries to maintain its power, those who guard these archives are reluctant to release anything of a psychic nature; for knowledge and understanding of psychic phenomena is a power which the Vatican does not wish to give out freely. From time to time however, the secrecy in Roman Catholic psychic studies has been breached.

Although the Secret Archives are the papal *Curia Romana's* (the collective judicial and administrative institutions by means of which the Pope carries on the general government of his church) working files, and are quite separate from the Vatican Library, accredited researchers can be allowed to study them. One such was Father Zachary Raffaello Visconti, kinsman of the famous 17th century astrologer Visconti, contemporary of Galileo, who uncovered a ghost which nearly cost him his sanity!

Early one morning in June 1926, Father Visconti excused himself from the group of young priests, who regularly gathered near Castle Sant' Angelo, and hurried to his work at the Palazzo. He was behind in his project on miracles and psychic phenomena concerning 17th century military affairs and wanted to catch up. By a stroke of good luck he had managed to secure keys to the long gloomy bays at the Palazzo, so he was able to browse at will.

Father Visconti knew what he was looking for and selected books from the shadow of shrouded shelves, and laid them on a nearby table. As he was reaching for the last volume he required, the young priest noticed a small wooden box secreted behind a top shelf. Ordinarily he would have ignored it, as he was too busy to rummage, but he noticed it bore the personal motto *Jucunditas Crucis* (The joy of the Cross), the fleur-de-lys and the dove of the arms of Innocenzo X (Pope Innocent X—Giovanni Battista Pamphilj, 1644-55), the very period he was studying. Intrigued that the box might contain material relevant to his studies he removed more books to get the box out and returned with it to his lamplit table set in an alcove.

Encrusted with dirt, the box looked very old and seemed to be locked. As Father Visconti turned the casket over to examine the coat of arms on the side, the rusty hinges gave way and the lid of the box fell open. Replacing the box on the table the priest untied the leather thongs which secured an inner lid and parted the flap pieces. A bundle was revealed which he proceeded to unwrap. He shuddered at the contents. Inside the cloth was a mummified hand which had been severed at the wrist. With a feeling of nausea, Father Visconti rewrapped the hand in its decaying bandages and put the box back where he had found it.

For two hours the priest worked on the books he had selected, taking careful notes in his spidery hand. As he read the small Latin text of one *registro*, he felt a curious sensation in his right hand. It was as if another hand had slid over it, and then clasped it: for some reason Father Visconti seemed unable to move his right hand. Without looking away from his text, he began to draw his right hand slowly away, but instantly he felt a tight clasp and his hand was pulled back.

His first thought was that one of the novices who dusted the shelves was playing a practical joke on him—grabbing him from the gloom. He waited for a giggle of mischief, but none came. Rather angry at having been interrupted by a prank—he hated pranks—Father Visconti spun round and tried to clutch the offender's arm. To his amazement he clutched thin air! Turning up the lamp with his left hand Father Visconti was horrified to see *a hand severed at the wrist clasping his own!*

It was a strong, sinewy hand, with gnarled fingers, and a slight discoloration on one side. Father Visconti tried to shake the hand off, but the more he pulled, the more the grip of the ghastly thing tightened. After another wrench he succeeded in loosening it from his own and threw it from him. The hand fell with a sickening thud onto the desk.

Father Visconti fell back in his chair. Slowly, his consciousness returned and he realised the horrible event he had experienced. He tried to convince himself that he had imagined it all; but the truth would out. The more Father Visconti thought, the more mysterious the occurrence seemed.

At length his nerves calmed and he returned to his work forgetting that the hand lay on the floor, and at noon he retired for lunch. By one o'clock, the priest was back at his desk and worked a full two hours before any further disturbance. He had sat back in his chair while tapping his lip with the tip of his pen, when he felt a grip on his shoulder. Again the hand had appeared. This time he brushed off the severed limb with ease: it fell back on the desk among the papers.

For a moment the hand lay writhing on the table and then fell still. Remonstrating mentally with himself for being so afraid, Father Visconti fell to his knees in prayer for advice and assistance in tackling the 'demon' with which he considered he was plagued. And then he remembered Father Angelo Huanarez, from the Spanish Mission. Father Angelo had lectured on psychics to the novices of Father Visconti's year. Now he remembered what Father Angelo had said about certain classes of ghost—that they returned for a purpose. Was the hand trying to attract his attention to relay a message? He must wait and see. Father Visconti carefully placed the hand back in its casket and replaced the box behind the books.

Several weeks passed with no disturbance and Father Visconti was almost at the end of his researches. Around mid-afternoon on July 16 1926, the hand appeared again: it hovered over the desk where the priest was working and beckoned. Summoning all the courage he could, Father Visconti followed as the airborne hand moved towards the door of the library annexe.

Outside the corridor was empty and the hand glided towards the entrance of the basement. Once in the cellars, Father Visconti lost sight of the hand in the gloom. Searching around for a moment or two Father Visconti saw the hand hovering over a tomb slab reared against the wall. Father Visconti read:

RELICTA SUNT CINCTA NEGLECTA APUD ILLUM
PER GRAZIA DI DIO, QUI GIACCIONO I
RESTI MORTALI DI ORDINARI NOBILE DI
NOCERA DEI PAGANI, CAPITANO DELLE
GUARDIE A PIEDI DI S S PAPA INNOCENZO
X, INCONTRO LA SUA FINE CON CORRAGGIO
PER IL VILE ORDINE DI UN VILE
ASSASSINO

SOLA NOBILITAS VIRTUS

'Everything in his house is left neglected. By the Grace of God, here lie the mortal remains of Ordinari Nobile of Nocera dei Pagani, Captain of the footguard of His Holiness Pope Innocent X. He met his end bravely at the cowardly behest of a traitorous assassin. Virtue is the only nobility.' When the priest had finished reading, he looked again for the hand, but the grisly relic had disappeared.

Father Visconti knew that he could not let the matter rest: he must find out who Captain Nobile was. Next day he went to the Vatican Library and searched through the massive *bibliographia repertorium*. At last he came upon the entry he sought, which gave him the background to the slab inscription. Apparently Captain Nobile had been slain by an assassin at the age of only 28; his corpse had been found minus a hand!

Consulting the priest of the Catacombs, Father Visconti discovered the tomb of Captain Nobile and had the hand returned with the cadaver. As an afterthought the priest had the grave slab cemented over the tomb. From that day the young priest was never further disturbed by the phantom hand.

The ghost of Napoleon

As I shall mention in the section on astrology and soldiers, Napoleon put great faith in the occult. While at St Helena, the Emperor testified that he saw and conversed with the apparition of his deceased wife Josephine (de Beauharnais, 1763-1814, whom he divorced in 1809), who warned him of his approaching death. The story was first publicly narrated by Comte Montholon, who had heard it from Napoleon himself

In her treatise *Men that wouldn't stay dead* (1936), Ida Clyde Clarke, the American psychic researcher, told another story of Napoleon being assailed by a 'red man' while engaged in the Battle of the Pyramids. This apparition foretold his disaster (at Waterloo) as it had done for the rulers of France for many hundreds of years. Emil Ludwig too, in his bestselling history of Napoleon, testified to the occult aura around Napoleon's name and life.

An account of the appearance of the ghost of Napoleon to his mother probably first appeared in the diary of M. Gaspard Létion (1793-1857) under the date *Le premier mars, 1827* and the heading *Le phantome de Napoleon;* subsequently the story appeared in *Light,* and has had many other renditions. This version, however, is taken from Létion's holograph French:

Aged, blind and half paralysed, Napoleon's mother was living in Rome. It was a spring day in 1821. For six years she had never relaxed her efforts on behalf of her son, an exile on the volcanic island of St Helena, set in the Atlantic. At last she managed to send him a Corsican doctor, two priests, a servant and a cook.

Napoleon was very close to his mother and inherited many of her qualities. Consequently the exiled Letizia had her famous son in her thoughts for most of the time.

On a narrow camp bed, draped with shabby green silk curtains—the bed he had used at Austerlitz—Napoleon lay dying. In Rome his mother was sitting in the drawing room of her lodgings at the Palazzo Bonaparte. Downstairs the hall porter was dozing comfortably, when suddenly he was confronted by a stranger who spoke in a commanding voice: '*La Signora Madre*—I must see her at once.'

The protesting porter showed the stranger, a man in a voluminous cloak and hat, into the *piana nobile* where sat Letizia. The stranger strode majestically into her presence, his cloak drawn somewhat over his face. He remained silent until the door had been closed behind the servant, and then threw back the cloak and revealed himself, for in some mysterious way she could see him quite plainly, through all else was blurred.

Letizia, petrified with wonder for a moment, could not speak or move. Then a trembling sigh escaped her—she touched his cheek with hers, and with thin, shaking hands caressed him: 'My son!'

In those moments a flood of memories swept over her—memories of that day in 1815 when he had escaped from Elba and had come to her. She thought he had escaped from St Helena—that once more he wanted temporary shelter.

Stepping back and regarding her with an air of poignant solemnity he said: 'May the fifth, eighteen hundred and twenty-one—to-day'.

His tone of tremendous significance paralysed her intelligence. She could neither think nor feel. She could only gaze toward him with uncertain eyes.

Very slowly he stepped backward and retreated through the door that seemed softly opened for him. The next instant the heavy *portières* fell and he had vanished.

Recovering her self-control instantly, Letizia made her way from the drawing-room into the apartment beyond into which he had gone. No shadow darkened the room. She could feel its emptiness. She hastened to the ante-room where the servant was sitting: 'The gentleman where is he, where did he go?' she asked.

'*Eccellentissima Signora Madre,*' replied the man, 'no one has passed through since I conducted the gentleman into your presence, and I have not left this place for a moment'.

It was three months before Letizia learned that her son Napoleon had died on the very day and hour his wraith had visited her!

The ghost of the French general

During 1705 the great soldier-statesman Comte Camille de Tallard, Duc d'Hostun (1652-1728; taken prisoner at Blenheim 1704) was 'in exile' in Newdigate House, Nottingham. He remained a prisoner there until 1712, when he was allowed to return to France after the Peace of Utrecht. Tallard left behind him a wonderful ornamental garden surrounding Newdigate House and a fine residence. It was said that when he left Nottingham he promised to return: by all accounts he only returned in ghost form.

Some 40 years ago the *Nottingham Evening News* published this comment: 'In 1705 at Newdigate House, was exiled Marshal Tallard. This house, which still stands, is supposed to be haunted by the marshal and his friends. Tenants who have lived there assert that they have heard the jesting of the French officers, the clicking of billiard balls, and music at all bewitching hours of the night'.

This comment brought the following answer from writer Stanbury Thomson (London, August 1946): 'I can testify this newspaper comment as being true, for we ourselves lived in Newdigate House between 1927-29. Often at the midnight hour, when all was quiet and still, when the atmosphere felt very mysterious and ghostly, have we heard this great man's footsteps pass down the hall, stop at the entrance to the oldest part of the house*, and then direct his course through the original oak doorway of Newdigate House. After this those slow measured footsteps were heard to die away'.

A pot-pourri of revenants

The novels, biographies, diaries and documents which make up the bulk of European literature contain countless references to, and descriptions of, factual ghostly sightings concerning soldier phantoms. Here is a sampling of what can be found; instances, often ignored in official texts, which can tell us much about the thoughts and beliefs of major characters in political and social history.

Gaspard de Coligny (1519-72) The French soldier who served with distinction in the campaigns of Francis I and Henry II, was warned three times by a ghostly premonition to quit Paris before the Feast of St Bartholemew. On August 22 1572 an unsuccessful attempt was made on his life, but he was murdered in his own house during the Massacre of St Bartholomew two days later.

Philippa Wife of the Duke of Lorraine, when a girl in a convent, saw in a vision the Battle of Pavia (1525), then in progress. She further saw the captivity of King Francis I, her cousin.

Nero Claudius Drusus (38-9 BC) This brilliant Roman general, younger brother of the future emperor Tiberius, made it a major point of his career to deal with the Germans beyond the Rhine. In the course of three campaigns (12-9 BC) he advanced as far as the Elbe. There he was deterred by a female spectre, who told him to retrace his steps and meet his approaching end. On the return journey he was thrown from his horse and died 30 predicted days later.

Marcus Junius Brutus (c 86-42 BC) Governor of Cisalpine, Praetor and one of the leading conspirators against Julius Caesar. He was supposed to be visited by the spectre of his benefactor, who announced that they would meet again disastrously at Philippi. In the second Battle of Philippi, Brutus was defeated by Octavian and Anthony, and committed suicide.

Colin Lindsay, 3rd Earl of Balcarres (1654?-1722) When confined in Edinburgh

* There is a later wing adjoined to Newdigate House, of late 18th century construction.

Castle for his part in the Montgomery conspiracy to restore James II, he was visited by the apparition of John Graham of Claverhouse, Viscount Dundee, shot at that moment at the Battle of Killiecrankie (1689).

Dio (409-354 BC) Syracusan general. He saw a female apparition sweeping furiously in his house, to denote that his family would shortly be swept out of Syracuse, which through various accidents was shortly the case.

George Villiers, 1st Duke of Buckingham (1592-1628) Courtier, politician and soldier. He was warned of approaching assassination by the apparition of his father, Sir George Villiers, who was seen by Robert Parker, an official of the King's Wardrobe. Buckingham was assassinated by John Felton, a half-mad subaltern, at Portsmouth.

John Middleton, 1st Earl of Middleton (1619-74) He was taken prisoner by the Roundheads after the Battle of Worcester (1651). While in prison he was comforted by the apparition of the Laird of Buchan, whom he had known while trying to make a party for King Charles II in Scotland and who assured him of his escape in two days, which occurred.

Xerxes (c 519-465 BC) King of Persia, victor of Thermopylae. After giving up the idea of starting an expedition to Greece, he was persuaded to do so (451 BC) by the apparition of a young soldier, who also visited Xerxes' uncle Artabanus.

Quintus Curtius Rufus (c AD 9-79) Pro-consul of Africa. Reported by Pliny the Younger (Book VI, *Letters* 26) to have been visited by a gigantic female ('The Genius of Africa') who foretold his career.

Theodosius the Great (AD346-395) Roman Emperor of the East. On the eve of a battle against the Goths was reassured of victory by the ghosts of two dead soldiers. The ghosts were independently seen by an aide.

Sir Henry Rich, 1st Earl of Holland (1590-1649) Taken prisoner at the Battle of St Neots (1648). Said to haunt Holland House, dressed in the cap and clothes in which he was executed.

James IV (1473-1513) King of Scotland. After vespers in the chapel at Linlithgow, he was warned by an apparition against his expedition into England. He persisted and was warned again by the apparition at Jedburgh. Still ignoring the warnings he was finally overthrown and killed at the Battle of Flodden.

Catherine de'Medici (1519-89) Wife of Henry II of France. She saw in a ghostly vision the Battle of Jarnac (1569) and the death of Louis I, Prince of Condé. Story told by Margaret de Valois in her *Memoirs*.

Charles d'Angennes, Marquis de Rambouillet A sceptic, he was visited in Paris by the ghost of his cousin the Marquis de Précy saying that he had been killed in a battle in Flanders. The wraith also predicted Rambouillet's death in the Battle of Faubourg St Antoine. The case was mentioned by Augustin Calmet in his *Causes Célèbres*.

Pausanias (d 397 BC) A Spartan general and leader of the Lacedaemonians. Said by Plutarch in *Simone* to have inadvertantly caused the death of a young patrician woman; her ghost haunted him day and night urging him to surrender himself to justice.

Field-Marshal Gebhard Leberecht von Blücher (1742-1819) This famous Prussian commander (who joined forces with Wellington in the final campaign against Napoleon) told the King of Prussia that he had been warned of his approaching death by the apparition of his entire family.

Henry Edward Fox (1755-1811) British general. Went to Flanders (1794) with the Duke of York shortly before the birth of his son. Two years later he had a vision of the child—dead—and correctly described its appearance and surroundings, though the death occurred in a house unknown to him.

Benvenuto Cellini (1500-71) Italian sculptor and goldsmith of the later Renaissance, when in captivity at Rome by order of the Pope, was dissuaded from suicide by the apparition of a young combatant who frequently visited and encouraged him.

Wolfgang Amadeus Mozart (1756-91) Was visited by a strange military figure who ordered him to compose a Requiem. The apparition returned to inquire after the composition's progress. The spectre disappeared on the completion of the music, which occurred just in time for the work to be played at Mozart's own funeral.

King George III's Ghost Story told by Sir Owen Morshead in his book *Windsor Castle*. The rooms in which the incapacitated King lived during the last years of his life overlooked the North Terrace of Windsor Castle. When the guard was relieved the King would sometimes hear the tramp of soldier's feet and would go to the window. As the guard passed, the ensign in command would give 'Eyes Right' and the King would raise his hand in acknowledgement. One day after the King's death the ensign saw a bearded figure standing at the window and automatically gave the word of command. The figure raised its hand in salute: at that time the King was dead!

The ensign of that guard was Sir William Knollys subsequently Comptroller of the Household of King Edward VII as Prince of Wales, who told the story to King George V.

Chapter 6

Far Eastern shades

Soldiers of the Japanese Imperial Army helped kill my father, of that I have little doubt. Their brutal treatment of him as a civilian prisoner in Shanghai during World War II cruelly maimed him and shortened his lifespan. Over the years, however, his spiritual presence has been made known to me in various forms, and I now fully understand what Alexander Pope, the famous 18th century English poet and translator of *Homer*, was suggesting in his *Iliad:*

' 'Tis true, 'tis certain, man tho' dead, retains
Part of himself, the immortal mind remains,
The form-subsists—freed from the body's chains.'

It was, however, the writings of the late Dr George Lindsay Johnson* which first brought home to me the exciting possibility that those we call 'dead' are not deceased at all but exist on a different plane. Dr Johnson noted: 'When an animal or person dies, the organism reverts to its elementary form, but the Soul, of which life is the external or visible manifestation, continues to exist independently of the body'. And in researching the story of my late father's travels in the Far East, I found time and time again ample evidence to support Dr Johnson's claims. For instance, there are many examples in the modern folklore of Northern Burma of Allied soldiers, of World War II vintage, returning in ghost form to where they were brutally done to death by the Imperial Nipponese Army. One case in particular is of singular interest.

Japanese ill-treatment of soldiers at Moulmein, Rangoon Gaol and Kalagon have gone down in military and legal history. But many cases of brutal torture and humiliation remain only as memories. During the winter-spring of 1944 Lt-Gen Renya Mutaguchi's 18th Division of the Japanese Army faced Brig-Gen Frank D. Merrill's Marauders and the 22nd and 38th Chinese Divisions under Generals Liao and Li Jen Sun. One day a patrol of Allied troops were scouting the Hukawng Valley near Maingkwan, when they were surprised by a party of Japanese from the 18th Division.

The Allied troops were disarmed and strung up to trees by the Japanese, who tortured them in time-honoured way with fire and bamboo splinters. Eventually the Japanese left their prisoners to die. When the Japanese soldiers had gone, native Burmese cut down the six mutilated men and attempted to tend their wounds. In a short time, however, all six soldiers were dead.

Long after the war was over, natives in the region reported seeing a party of six soldiers patrolling the jungle thereabouts: on the approach of the tribesmen the soldiers always disappeared into thin air. Eventually a Dutch missionary, Jan Christiansen,

* Particularly *The Great Problem and the Evidence for its Solution* (London, 1928).

saw the ghostly patrol and recorded the fact in his diary:

'*12 May 1957: Walawbum, Burma.* Yesterday while out in the jungle near Maingkwan I was accosted by six European soldiers. As I sat resting in a clearing they surrounded me; curiously none of them uttered a word. They motioned with their gun barrels that I should lie down with my hands behind my back. I did so and they tied me up. Then I must have fainted for I remember no more. When I came to, I still lay in the clearing, but my limbs were free. The soldiers were nowhere to be seen and the grass and the leaves around showed no sign of their passing. Back at the village others confirmed that a six-man patrol was regularly to be seen hereabouts. Strangely enough, although I felt my hands being tightly bound, my wrists bore no marks of the cords . . .'*

As J. von Goëthe said: 'I am fully convinced that the Soul is indestructible, and its activity will continue through eternity'.

Malaysia also has its share of World War II ghosts. Broadcasting in the BBC Home Service in 1959, D. C. Horton described how, on being posted to Kuala Selangor, he found himself in an area notorious for its 'ghostly presences'. The house, for instance, on Kuala Selangor Hill had been occupied by Japanese officers during the war, and the wife of a police officer had a terrifying experience:

'She was sitting in her bungalow one evening, waiting for her husband to return from work, when she heard steps coming up the hill path. Coming nearer and nearer, they sounded as though they were being made by heavy boots. She thought at first that it was one of the constables coming up with a message. Then the steps came to the house and on to the veranda, but when she looked up, there was nothing there. The steps came slowly past her down the veranda, across the dining-room and into the kitchen, where they stopped. For a while she dared not move, then plucking up her courage she went over to the kitchen, but there was no sign of anyone. The only explanation was that a Japanese officer had lived there in the Occupation and had been accustomed to climb that path at about that time'.

The small island fortress of Corregidor, south of the Bataan Peninsula in the Philippines, is yet a further area saturated with the terrible actions of World War II. Here a pitifully small group of US and Filipino troops under Rear-Admiral Francis W. Rockwell, Commander of the 16th Naval District and Maj-Gen Jonathan M. Wainwright, vainly endeavoured to halt the onrush of the Japanese Imperial Army on the city of Manila. At length on May 6 1942, Wainwright was forced to surrender to the Japanese commander Lt-Gen Tomayuke Yamashita.

Now Corregidor is quiet and virtually uninhabited, but from time to time the war episodes are re-enacted. Many of the fishermen and woodcutters who live hereabouts claim to have seen ghostly sentries and patrols on duty. Others also tell of the red-headed phantom nurse in Red Cross uniform who tends wounded spectre-soldiers: one of the few quoted cases of a ghost in full colour!

To round off these references to World War II phantom soldiers in the Far East, this Reuters report of July 23 1956 from Tokyo, is of interest: 'The "ghosts" of Japanese soldiers who rise nightly to man a rusted anti-aircraft gun on the New Guinea beaches have so terrified the natives that they have asked a Japanese War Graves Commission to "appease" them. The commission, touring New Guinea to collect the remains of Japanese soldiers killed there in World War II, said it was warned by the natives who claimed that every night the ghosts visit the rusting gun on the beaches of Hollandia. During heavy shelling by the United States Navy,

* Rijksinstituut voor Oorlogsdocumentatie, Amsterdam. V57 N190 J1972/220.

April 5 1945, the gun was put out of commission and most of its crew killed. The commission reported that when the war ended the natives began to whisper that "haggard soldiers in rusty helmets" arose to man the gun emplacements at midnight. Many terrified natives took off to visit relatives in distant places. When the commission visited the area it was approached by the natives, and a Buddhist priest was asked to perform a "purification ceremony" to "appease the angry ghosts". The commission said that the rite will be performed soon'.

Chapter 7

Omens & warnings

Korean dancing ghosts

Probably it is only a matter of time until we hear how the wars in Vietnam and Cambodia have produced their own psychic phenomena. Combatants no doubt will have time to write down their reminiscences of strange happenings. Ghostly memories like those of Sgt Joe Schwaller from California who put his into doggerel:

> 'There's a place to dance in your combat pants,
> And a place to forget the fight:
> There's gals galore and no sign of war,
> In Kumsong, Saturday night.
> It's down the line, don't step on a mine,
> Far from the battle's din,
> Where you can jog to the phantom music
> Of Ching—and his violin.'

Sgt Schwaller was one of those who served in the 1950s at the war theatre near the Korean village of Kumsong. By the time he and his men acclimatised themselves, this area was decimated by bombs, and only shell-shattered rubble remained. Rats appeared to be the only inhabitants of the once active village.

During certain nights, however, just before massive air-raids or ground-shelling were due, Kumsong came to life. Soldiers returning from patrols gave testimony that ghostly music, singing and laughter were heard among the ruins. Colleagues who laughed at the ghost stories were encouraged to join the patrols. Many did so and the ghostly music was attested by several soldiers.

Banshee of Rossmore

The omens of impending conflict as experienced at Kumsong are not an unusual type of paranormal phenomenon: ghostly omens of war are quite common in the history of psychic happenings. Similarly, many of the long-established European families have their private ghosts which appear as an omen of family disaster, especially if the family has a record of military involvement. One such psychic omen bedevils the family of the present and 7th Baron Rossmore of Co Monaghan, Eire. The psychic omen takes the form of a banshee wail and occurs whenever the Rossmore heir is about to die. The late 6th Baron Rossmore (William, 1892-1958) recorded how the banshee's wail was first heard when the 1st Baron Rossmore, General Robert Cunningham (d 1801) was on his deathbed.

'Robert Rossmore was on terms of great friendship with Sir Jonah and Lady Barrington, and once when they met at a Dublin drawing-room, Rossmore persuaded the Barringtons to come over the next day to Mount Kennedy, where he was then living. As the invited guests proposed to rise early they retired to bed in good time, and slept soundly until two o'clock in the morning, when Sir Jonah was awakened by a wild and plaintive cry. He lost no time in rousing his wife, and the scared couple got up and opened the window, which looked over the grass plot beneath. It was a moonlight night and the objects around the house were easily discernible, but there was nothing to be seen in the direction whence the eerie sound proceeded.

'Now thoroughly frightened, Lady Barrington called her maid, who straightway would not listen or look, and fled in terror to the servants' quarters. The uncanny noise continued for about half an hour, when it suddenly ceased. All at once a weird cry of "Rossmore, Rossmore, Rossmore", was heard, and then all was still.

'The Barringtons looked at each other in dismay, and were utterly bewildered as to what the cry could mean. They decided, however, not to mention the incident at Mount Kennedy, and returned to bed in the hope of resuming their broken slumbers. They were not left long undisturbed, for at seven o'clock they were awakened by a loud knocking at the bedroom door, and Sir Jonah's servant, Lawyer, entered the room, his face white with terror.

' "What's the matter, what's the matter?" asked Sir Jonah. "Is anyone dead?"

' "Oh sir", answered the man, "Lord Rossmore's footman has just gone by in great haste, and he told me that my lord, after coming from the Castle, had gone to bed in perfect health but that about half past two this morning, his own man hearing a noise in his master's room went to him, and found him in the agonies of death, and before he could alarm the servants his lordship was dead." ' When she recounted the story Lady Barrington always added with relish: 'Lord Rossmore was actually dying at the moment when we heard his name pronounced.'

A banshee, incidentally, is traditionally defined in Irish and West Highland folklore books as, 'a guardian female fairy who by shrieks and wailings foretells the death of a member of the family over whose fortunes she watched'. The banshee wailing 'Rossmore, Rossmore' was heard at the demise of all six of the barons, but with particular vehemence during the last minutes of the second (Warner William Westernra, 1765-1842), the third (Henry Robert, 1792-1860), the fourth (Henry Cairns, d 1874) and the fifth (Derek Warner William, 1853-1921). The current *Kelly's Handbook* records that the present baron has no heir, so the days of the Rossmore banshee seem numbered.

Other warnings take on a more picturesque form when soldier members of other families die. In Cheshire, for instance, whenever the heir of the Brereton family was about to die, logs appeared to float on the surface of the Bagmere, a lake on their property. The logs were never seen at any other time. Another fatal sign, this time to the eldest son of the Nottinghamshire Cliftons, was the catching of a sturgeon in the River Trent near Clifton. Likewise the appearance of a spectral black dog was a death-omen for the Vaughans of Shropshire. The journal *All the Year Round* (first started in 1850 by Charles Dickens under the title *Household Words*) for December 1870 records an account of the death-omen of the Cotton family of Combermere Abbey, who were warned by the ghost of a sad girl who ran round the rooms as if in great distress.

John Otway Wynyard

Apparitions of the dying have often been seen by people at a distance, either at the actual moment of death, or just before it. Such was the famous Wynyard case. John Otway Wynyard died in England on October 15 1785. The very same day as his spectre was seen by his brother George (then a lieutenant, later a general) and by Captain John Sherbrooke (he was subsequently knighted), while both were serving with the 33rd Regiment in the maritime province of Nova Scotia, Canada. The incident actually occurred at a billet in Sydney, Cape Breton, shortly before Sherbrooke's memorable achievements in covering the retreat of the Duke of York in Flanders; and Sherbrooke left a note of the incident which was first recorded for the general public by A. Patchett Martin in 1893 (although the story had been partially recounted before).

'One evening Captain Sherbrooke and Lieutenant Wynyard were seated in the latter's room, which had two doors, the one opening into an outer passage, the other into the bedroom. These were the only means of ingress or egress, so that anyone passing into the bedroom must have remained there, unless he returned through the sitting room.

'The story goes that Sherbrooke suddenly perceived standing by the passage door, a tall youth of about twenty, pale and wan, to whom he called his companion's attention. "I have heard", said Sherbrooke, "of a man becoming as pale as death, but I never saw a living face assume the appearance of a corpse except Wynyard's at that moment".

'While they were gazing, the figure, which had turned upon Wynyard a glance of sorrowful affection glided into the bedroom. Wynyard, seizing his friend's arm, said, in a whisper, "Great heaven! My brother!" "Your brother?" replied Sherbrooke, "what do you mean? There must be some deception. Let us follow."

'They darted into the adjoining room, only to find it empty. Another young officer, Ralph Gore, coming in at this moment, proceeded to join in the search. It was he who suggested that a note should be made of the day and the hour of the apparition.

'The mail brought no letters from England for Wynyard, but there was one for Sherbrooke, which he hastily opened, and then beckoned Wynyard away. When he returned, alone, to the messroom, he said in a low voice to the man next to him: "Wynyard's brother is dead!" The first line in the letter had run "Dear John, break to your friend Wynyard, the death of his favourite brother". He had died at the very moment when the apparition appeared in his brother's room.'

Major Blomberg's last wish

Among the papers of T. M. Jarvis on psychic phenomena, published in 1823, was the curious account of the 'Apparition of Major Blomberg to the Governor of Dominica':

'Early in the American war*, Major Blomberg, the father of Dr Blomberg, was expected to join his regiment, which was at the time on service in the island of Dominica. His period of absence had expired, and his brother officers eagerly anticipated his return, as vessel after vessel arrived from England . . . His presence in the island now became indispensable; and the governor, impatient of so long an absence, was on the point of writing a remonstrance on the subject to the authorities in this country, when, as he was sitting at night in his study with his secretary, and remarking on the conduct of the absentee, with no very favourable or lenient expressions, a step was heard to ascend the stairs, and walk along the passage without. "Who can it be?" exclaimed the governor, "intruding at so late an hour". "It is Blomberg's step" replied the secretary. "The very man himself", said the governor; and, as he spoke, the door opened, and Major Blomberg stood before them. The major advanced

* ie, the war of 1812.

towards the table at which the gentlemen were sitting, and flung himself into a chair opposite the governor. There was something hurried in his manner; a forgetfulness of all the ordinary forms of greetings; and abruptly saying: "I must converse with you alone", he gave a sign for the secretary to retreat. The sign was obeyed. There was an air of conscious superiority about the manner of the visitor that admitted no dispute. "On your return to England", he continued, as soon as the apartment was cleared of the objectionable witness, "you will go to a farm house, near the village of [*Jarvis left this blank*] in Dorsetshire; you will there find two children; they are mine; the offspring and the orphans of my secret marriage. Be the guardian to those parentless infants. To prove their legitimacy, and their consequent right to my property, you must demand of the woman, with whom they are placed at nurse, the red Morocco case which was committed to her charge. Open it; it contains the necessary papers. Adieu! You will see me no more." Major Blomberg instantly withdrew.

'The Governor of Dominica, surprised at the commission, at the abrupt entrance, and the abrupt departure, rang the bell to desire some of his household to follow the major and request his return. None had seen him enter; none had witnessed his exit. It was strange! It was passing strange! There soon after arrived intelligence that Major Blomberg had embarked aboard a vessel for Dominica, which had been dismasted in a storm at sea, and was supposed to have subsequently sunk, as she was never more heard of, about the time in which the figure had appeared to the governor and his secretary.

'All that Major Blomberg had communicated was carefully stamped in the memory of his friend. On his return to England, which occurred in a few months after the apparition above described had been seen by the governor, he immediately hastened to the village in Dorsetshire, and to the house in which the children were resident.

'He found them. He asked for the casket; it was immediately surrendered. The legitimacy and the claims of the orphans of Blomberg were established, and they were admitted to the enjoyment of their rights without any controversy or dispute.

'This tale was related to the late Queen Charlotte, and so deeply interested her that she immediately adopted the son as the object of her peculiar care and favour . . .'

Disturbances at Sandford Orcas

Sandford Orcas is a sleepy old hamlet quite isolated from its neighbours near Sherborne in Dorset. Its Tudor mansion is of soft-golden-hued stone and its ghosts are as many as the trim lawns and paved walks. For a long time Sandford Orcas manor has been the favourite hunting ground for pressmen and psychical researchers alike. One ghost has proved most obliging, and appears on a snapshot taken in the garden. This ghost is of a tenant-farmer who hanged himself under the main gateway in the 1700s. Dressed in a white smock and round hat, the spectre has been seen on several occasions going past the kitchen window in broad daylight.

The present tenant of the manor of Sandford Orcas, Colonel Francis Claridge, knows his ghosts well and can recount them as well as he can the treasured items in his collection of antiques. As well as the tenant-farmer, there is the white-haired old lady who appears on the main stairs in a hand-painted red dress; an unknown Elizabethan woman who walks in the courtyard; a ghost of a military bearing who once followed two visitors into a room, and a ghostly musician, who from time to time plays a phantom harpsichord in the great hall. This latter ghost is often accompanied by the smell of tobacco and incense. The ghost of Sandford Orcas which fits into the military brief is the one who haunts the nursery wing, over the servants' quarters.

A former kitchenmaid at the manor says: 'Years ago . . . during my stay there I saw a ghost . . . who appeared at the foot of my bed and swayed. He was outlined against the bedroom window . . . He was tall, in evening dress, and his face appeared evil. For quite a while he stood there, then disappeared . . . One evening I was in the great hall near the piano in the corner. It was just as if someone was there compelling me to look at them, and yet I could see no one. I felt unable to move.'

Colonel Claridge thinks that this ghost is that of a lecherous soldier revisiting the scene of a brutal seduction of a serving maid. He always seems to appear before some minor mishap or other at the manor. 'What we hear', says the Colonel, 'are these heavy footsteps in the corridor leading to the nursery wing. If he is going to materialise, he turns left and enters the small bedroom. If he's not, he just knocks at the door. Then you hear the dragging sound, as if someone were pulling a body along the landing!'

Psychic scholars believe that some ghosts return only for a brief space of time to give a message, or redeem a promise. Then, their mission fulfilled, the ghosts vanish for ever. Apparently, say the spiritualists, some preoccupation with mortal affairs detains the ghost on the earthly plane for a while, but once the spirits rid themselves of their mission, they pass on to the next stage of spirit development of which death is only the beginning.

Thus have the murdered returned in ghostly form to bring their murderers to justice; likewise have the wealthy deceased reappeared to ensure the right disposition of their property, or maybe reveal the secret of hidden treasure. Some ghosts, however, have returned for more academic purposes. Such was the mission of the ghost who accosted a soldier in the reign of Charles II.

Captain Dyke's visitor

During cold winter evenings, as the log fire crackled in his parlour, Major George Sydenham of Dulverton, Somerset, had many erudite discussions with his friend Captain William Dyke of Skilgate, on the very existence of God and the possibility of the immortality of the soul. The two soldiers never did come to any definite conclusions, but promised each other that whosoever died first, if it were possible, would materialise before the survivor on the third night of the funeral. The hour fixed on this appointed third day was between midnight and one o'clock; further, the place for the materialisation was to be the summer-house in the major's garden.

Major George Sydenham was the first to die, and on the day appointed for the materialisation Captain Dyke went to his dead friend's house with his cousin Dr Thomas Dyke, who was to attend a sick child there. At 11.30 pm on the night of their arrival, Captain Dyke called for candles and, much against the doctor's advice, went to the summer-house to meet the wraith of Major Sydenham. Nothing happened and at two o'clock the following morning the officer gave up his search, but insisted, 'I know that my major would surely have come had he been able'.

Six weeks later Captain Dyke, again accompanied by his cousin Thomas, took his son to Eton and lodged at the Christopher Inn. Early the following morning, after dawn, the ghost of Major George Sydenham appeared beside Captain Dyke's bed. Drawing back the bedclothes the ghost called: 'Cap! Cap!' (a nickname the major had called his subordinate in life). Dyke sat up in bed and answered. The apparition continued: 'I could not come at the time appointed, but I am now come to tell you that there is a God, and a very just and terrible one, and if you do not turn over a new leaf, you shall find it so!'

Charles I (right) is said to have returned in spectral form at Marple Hall Cheshire. In his own lifetime Charles was witness to the apparition of Thomas Wentworth, Earl of Strafford (below).

The Lynn of Dee, Dubrach, Braemar is the frequent haunt of Sir Walter Scott's favourite ghost, that of Sergeant Arthur Davis.

The city of Cambridge is troubled by the phantom of Captain Wheatcroft of the 6th Dragoons.

The Central Station, Newcastle, is haunted by a ghostly colour sergeant.

The ghost of a suicidal guardsman haunts the Long Walk, Windsor Castle.

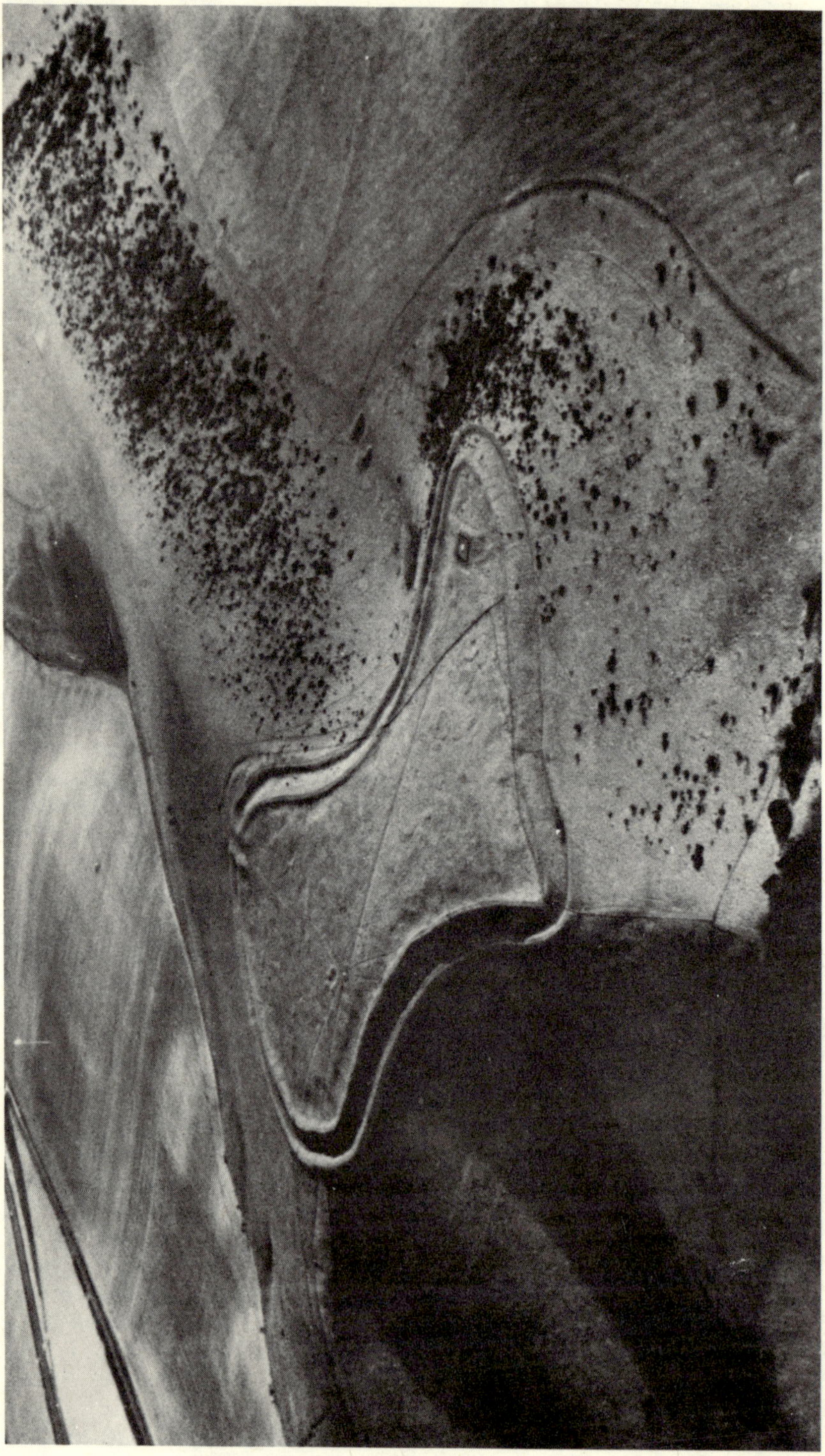

Beacon Hill, Aldershot, where the phantom of a murdered sentry is still heard running.

The ghost then walked around the bedroom for a minute or two and finally stopped by a bedside table on which lay the sword Major Sydenham had carried in life, but which was now the property of Dyke. Drawing this sword and finding it tarnished the ghost reproved: 'Captain, Captain! This sword did not used to be kept after this manner when it was mine'. With this reproach the phantom soldier disappeared. In a conversation with James Douch, recorded by T. M. Jarvis, Dr Thomas Dyke testified to the transformation in Captain Dyke's character. Before the haunting he had been a heavy drinker and wencher, now, as occultist George Sinclair expansively attested, Captain William Dyke became sober and grave.

Owen Howison's return

Until the formation of the Society for Psychical Research in 1882, there had never been a serious and scientific attempt to discover any truth in the stories of ghostly appearances, apparitions of the living and the dead, haunted houses, poltergeists, and the many claims of psychic trauma. In the main the Society set out 'to examine without prejudice or prepossession and in scientific spirit those faculties of man, real or supposed, which appear to be inexplicable on any general recognised hypothesis'

For its inception the Society attracted men and women of scientific and academic distinction. Such well known figures as Prime Minister Arthur James Balfour (1848-1930), physicist Baron Rayleigh (1842-1919) and the classical scholar Professor Gilbert Murray (1866-1957) have all been former presidents. At their headquarters in Adam and Eve Mews, London, the Society carries on its work (similar research is undertaken by the American Society for Psychical Research) and publishes its quarterly findings in the *Journal* and the *Proceedings*.

Among the many cases of apparitions and hauntings discussed and investigated by the Society, one, the case of the soldier who returned from the dead in diverse forms, is of great interest and importance. In psychic terms the phantom may be described as 'a visionary apparition', which used a piece of evidence to convince the viewer of his presence. Furthermore this phantom conveyed information to the percipient that could not have been known at the time. While the case is not in itself unusual in the annals of the psychical research societies on both sides of the Atlantic, it is something of a classic among the many tales of military ghosts and phantoms.

The central characters in this strange story are the Howison family, who had emigrated to South Africa from England in 1939. They had not been in their new home long when war was officially declared, on September 3 1939. Soon afterwards the Howison's son Owen joined the Army and served in Italy with a tank unit. When his tank received a direct hit, Owen was struck by a piece of shrapnel in his frontal skull. He was able, however, to drive his tank to the nearest medical aid centre where a severely wounded comrade could receive treatment. The next day Owen Howison died at the age of 21. Shortly afterwards on May 8 1945 the official end to World War II was declared.

A vision of the dead Owen Howison came to his cousin, Mrs Georgina Feakes, as she sat alone one day in 1949 in the lounge of her house at Bexley, Kent. With her mediumistic powers already well known to her immediate family, Mrs Feakes' first intimation that something strange was about to happen to her, was the sensation of electric shocks passing through her body. Quite aware of her psychic tendencies Mrs Feakes was not unduly disturbed. But then she saw what looked like a sphere of golden vapour coming towards her along the floor. As the vapour rapidly changed shape in front of her, Mrs Feakes saw in the golden mist the head and shoulders of her dead cousin Owen Howison.

In a letter to the boy's mother, Mrs Beatrice Howison of Main Road, Rondebosch, Capetown, South Africa, Georgina Feakes said: 'I was scared stiff as I wasn't expecting anything. My skin went cold and prickled everywhere. As I first saw him I had an impression of injury to the left of the forehead which faded until he became normal. I didn't dream it; it was not in darkness. I could see his eyes, they looked sort of amberish hazel, he looked so radiant and smiled'.

Mrs Feakes further explained that when the vision of her cousin appeared she felt a blinding flash of heat and pain all down her left side and face. It was almost as if Owen were trying to demonstrate in the only psychic transference way he knew, exactly why he died and the pain he had suffered. At the end of her vision, Georgina Feakes commented, Owen had said: 'Tell Mum'. At this point it seemed as though he were making a greater effort to speak, but failed; he then smiled and vanished.

A second vision of Owen Howison was seen by Mrs Feakes some time later. In a letter dated November 6 1949 from her home in Bexley, Mrs Feakes wrote of it to her aunt: 'Before I forget, just after I wrote to you I saw Owen, he gets much closer now, I should say he is more distinct. He had a bunch of fragile looking flowers, a violety blue. I have never seen anything like them here. He said if I told you he got them up Table Mountain, you would know I had seen him. He also said he would like to see me again in four months time.'

The story of the blue flowers of Table Mountain was to be a key factor in the case. Mrs Feakes knew nothing about the origin of the flower story so couldn't have fraudulently woven it into her own narrative.

Apparently, in 1940 Owen Howison had climbed Table Mountain (a 3,549-ft mountain of Cape Province, near Cape Town) and had brought back a sample of the Blue Afrikander (or Sandpijpie) hidden in his shirt. The boy's caution was understandable. This slender, sweet-smelling, erect plant, which flowers from June to October and grows to a height of two feet, is a protected plant in South Africa. The penalty for picking this plant was a fine of up to 40 Rand, imprisonment (with or without hard labour) of up to two months, or both. It was in fact the first time that Beatrice Howison had seen the flower, and, in her own words in a note to Professor Ian Stevenson, of the University of Virginia, who first reported the case in the *Journal* of the Society for Psychical Research in December 1964: 'The perfume of this one lovely flower lasted for nearly two weeks'.

Mrs Feakes gave Professor Stevenson other details of her vision in a letter dated January 2 1963. In this she stated: 'He said, "My tank was blown up. Tell Mum I'm not dead and remember me to Helen."' Georgina Feakes then asked of Owen: 'Give me proof please . . . so she'll believe us.' 'He whispered "watch". He opened his shirt and took out one blue flower (it has a sweet penetrating perfume) . . .[*he*] put it back in his shirt . . . "Tell Mum please, good-bye dear cousin"'.

Intrigued by the references to Helen, and not knowing anyone of that name personally, Mrs Feakes asked her aunt about the girl when Mrs Howison visited England in 1951. Her aunt, however, was evasive.

Soon afterwards Mrs Feakes had another vision of Owen Howison. This time he was more insistent about Helen: 'You did not tell Helen—poor, poor Helen', he said. It was later discovered by Professor Stevenson that Helen had been a pen friend of Owen Howison. Helen had never actually seen Owen but had been very upset over his death. Detailing this latter vision to Professor Stevenson in a letter dated April 11 1963, Mrs Feakes explained: 'when Owen has appeared it has been on bright sunny days; he has appeared solid (at least from the waist up) and his voice, far off, but real and alive. I have felt no fear of any sort, but was aware that all energy was draining from my body, perhaps that is why his visits were so brief'.

Psychical researchers can easily explain why Mrs Feakes felt tired after each visitation. One theory states that the 'ghost' draws energy from the 'medium'; so, in sapping strength the ghost tires the medium and most psychic people feel exhausted after a seance. But there seems to be no real danger to the physical body in this. In his book on spiritualism the late, controversial medium Shaw Desmond, founder of the International Institute for Psychical Research, wrote: 'It is often stated by incompletely informed people—doctors and others—that mediumship shortens the life. It does not.'

The apparition of the soldier Owen Howison may have appeared in a type of ectoplasmic vapour exuding from the body of Georgina Feakes. Again the medium Shaw Desmond explains: 'Ectoplasm is a sort of fluid which, under certain conditions, can exude through the orifices of the human body, through the ears or nostrils for instance. It is smooth and flowing, of the consistency usually of thin gum, and it can vary in colour and consistency from a cloudy whiteness to a dark oily texture. That great scientist Dr Osty has demonstrated its presence in its invisible form*.

'I myself have watched this ectoplasmic stuff exude steadily from the body of a woman medium for many minutes until it filled her lap. I have seen it literally "come out of the air" in strong light, despite the real difficulties of materialisation of any kind of light, for light tends to break up the materialisation, as every psychic scientist knows. And as Dr W. J. Crawford† and others have said, it can at times be capable of supporting heavy weights. This scientist himself watched it build up into the form of a leg and foot after coming from the body of the medium, ultimately developing a sort of ectoplasmic hand, with which it moved a table and so on. Quite recently, evidence was given in the Law Courts by a doctor who had seen it issue from the mouth of the medium and perform incredible feats of manipulation. In fact, it wrapped itself about his neck and nearly strangled him! So far as I know, this doctor was not himself a spiritualist, or in any sense credulous.'

Continuing his studies of the case of the soldier who returned, Professor Stevenson endeavoured to obtain more details of the blue flower phenomenon. He was able to ascertain without any shadow of a doubt that the incident with the flowers was only known to the Howisons.

Again Professor Stevenson testifies: 'At the time of her vision she knew that her cousin had been killed in action and probably that he had been in a tank unit. She may also have known of his head injuries'. The most likely explanation of the visions of the dead soldier is telepathic rapport between Georgiana Feakes and her aunt.

As Mrs Feakes' mediumistic powers were well known to her family circle, Mrs Howison is known to have encouraged her niece to try to have communication with Owen. 'Perhaps', says Stevenson, 'Mrs Howison's request to Mrs Feakes established a telepathic rapport between the two women which Mrs Feakes then used in elaborating her vision of her deceased cousin. I may say Mrs Feakes herself inclines to this interpretation of her experience . . .'

Nevertheless it is unlikely that the blue flower was mentioned in a letter from Mrs Feakes to Mrs Howison. Mrs Feakes now lives in Marden, Kent, and still sees the phantom of Owen Howison in the haze of golden vapour. In 1965 she wrote to Professor Stevenson to tell him that she had seen the apparition of her cousin three times in the past months. During one of these appearances he had accurately forecast a death in the family.

* See Dr Eugène Osty, *Supernormal Aspects of Energy and Matter* (London, 1933).

† Extra-mural lecturer in mechanical engineering to Belfast University.

I am indebted to Professor Ian Stevenson of the School of Medicine, Department of Neurology and Psychiatry, University of Virginia, Charlottesville, Virginia, USA, and to the Society for Physical Research, London, for supplying the basic facts of this case; also to Mrs Cynthia Muhl of Capetown—cousin of Mrs Georgina Feakes, and sister of Owen Howison—for supplying family testimony.

Charles I's restless subjects

Strange as it may seem there are few ghost stories concerning Charles I (1600-49), whose unfortunate career and continual trouble with his ministers and parliament led to some very emotional situations. Although a seemingly large number of his friends and enemies are earthbound in spirit, of this king there are no authenticated psychic accounts. Nevertheless, during his reign there were numerous omens of his impending disaster. Chronicler John Aubrey noted that, on the day when the Long Parliament first met in 1641, the sceptre fell from the hand of a carved effigy of Charles in the house of Sir Thomas Trenchard, and on the same day the picture of William Laud, Archbishop of Canterbury, fell to the ground (Laud was impeached by the Long Parliament and beheaded in 1645). Again when the bust of Charles by Bernini was transported to London by boat, a strange bird dropped blood on it, the stains of which could not be removed. Likewise, when the Royal Standard was set up at Nottingham, it was toppled by the wind. All of these were considered by the superstitious to be very bad omens.

The writer John Mastin further recorded that in 1645 Charles came to Daventry, Northamptonshire, with an army of many mounted cavaliers and some 5,000 foot-soldiers. The king intended to do battle with Cromwell's Parliamentarians then at Northampton. During the night, however, Charles was visited by the ghost of Thomas Wentworth, Earl of Strafford (1593-1641), the distinguished statesman and former Lord Deputy of Ireland. It appears that the ghost urged the king to cancel his plans and continue his march northwards, for he could never conquer by force of arms. Twice this ghost appeared to advise the king but Prince Rupert, among others, persuaded the king, who wanted to heed the ghost's advice, to remain. The disaster known as the battle of Naseby resulted.

Mastin asserted that if Charles had only heeded the spectre of Strafford, and had marched northwards, he might have met the Parliamentarians on more equal terms. The room where the ghost of Strafford appeared can still be seen at the Wheatsheaf Inn, Sheep Street, Daventry. Incidentally, the headless ghost of Marple Hall, Cheshire, which is said to be Charles I, has not been authenticated.

Chapter 8

Sir Walter Scott's favourite ghost

Ghosts, witches, and all kinds of occult phenomena interested Sir Walter Scott; so much so that he prepared for publisher John Murray (1830) a lengthy series of letters on the subject*. Thus, tales of psychic happenings were firm favourites at the meetings of the Bannatyne Club. This literary association had been founded in Edinburgh in 1823 by Sir Walter Scott and other prominent antiquaries, including David Laing of the Signet Library and printer Archibald Constable. Drawing its name from George Bannatyne (1545-1609), the famous collector of Scots poetry of the 15th and early 16th centuries, the club was formed for the publication of rare works relating to Scottish history, antiquities and literature. At its dissolution in 1861, the club had been responsible for publishing some 116 works. Among these scripts was Sir Walter Scott's favourite ghost story, for the publication of which he paid out of his own pocket in 1831.

The ghost story was entitled: 'Trial of Duncan Terig Alias Clerk, and Alexander Bane MacDonald for the Murder of Arthur Davis, Sergeant in General Guise's Regiment of Foot. June, AD MDCCLIV'. The story goes as set out below, and is built up from the depositions of Jean Ghent (Davis' wife), Donald Farquharson, Alexander Macpherson, Isobel McHardie, James MacDonald, etc, before the Curia Justiciania SDN Regis tenta in Nova Sessionis Domo Burgi de Edinburgh (1754) under Charles Erskine, Alexander Frazer, Patrick Grant and Hugh Dalrymple with John Fergusson.†

In the summer of 1749 Sergeant Arthur Davis of Lt-Gen John Guise's (c 1680-1768) regiment was posted from Aberdeen to Dubrach, Braemar, some eight miles away from the guard station at Glenshee. A man of gregarious habits, with a soldier's keen eye to accoutrements, Sergeant Davis had left his lodgings at Michael Farquharson's in Dubrach, on the morning of September 28 1749. His task that day was his twice-weekly meeting with a patrol from the Spittal of Glenshee. As he strode out to join his men Davis met a ruffian called John Growar who was wearing a tartan coat. At that time, as a consequence of the Jacobite Rebellion of 1745, clansmen were forbidden to wear the tartan; anyone doing so was liable for arrest. But being of a nationalistic nature himself, Davis only verbally warned Growar of his transgression, instructing him not to wear the plaid again, and went on his way.

On the road to Glenshee, Davis parted company with the four subordinates he had collected at Dubrach, to do a little illicit stag hunting on his own account. He told the

* See: Brown, Raymond Lamont, *Sir Walter Scott's Letters on Demonology and Witchcraft* (SR Publishers/Citadel Press Inc, 1968).
† See: Record in Edinburgh Public Library: Scottish Library Annex, XK/Scottish/2600.

men that he would meet them, and the Glenshee patrol, later. But when the two patrols met, Sergeant Davis was nowhere to be seen. A search was conducted but the popular sergeant had vanished. All that could be remembered was the distant report of Davis' gun.

Eventually Davis was posted 'missing while on duty' and his lodgings were taken over by a replacement. In June 1750 Donald Farquharson, Davis' former landlord's son, was visited by a middle-aged man called Alexander Macpherson. This man recounted the strange tale that he had been repeatedly visited at night by the ghost of the Welsh Sergeant Davis, whom Macpherson had known in life and had always admired for his seeming refinement; and more particularly for his silver watch, gold rings, purse of gold, silver buckles and dress hat.

Apparently Davis' ghost had begged Macpherson to go and seek out his mortal remains which had been buried in the peat moss on the Hill of Christie, about half a mile from the patrol road. Macpherson had been terrified of the ghost which had repeatedly begged 'Bury my bones! Bury my bones!'. And when the ghost perceived that Macpherson was afraid, it had suggested that he contact Michael and Donald Farquharson for assistance: at least that was Macpherson's garbled story.

The next morning, Donald Farquharson and Alexander Macpherson set out for the spot described by the ghost, and after some time of digging and probing among the peat, they came across the remains of a dead soldier in a shallow grave. The relics and clothes of Arthur Davis were uncovered and positively identified, but all the silk and silver trimmings, purse and valuables were gone. Obviously the sergeant had been murdered for his possessions. The two men reverently reburied the bones and both the corpse's clothes and relics were removed and sent with a report to the authorities.

A trial was arranged and Alexander Macpherson was called to give evidence, but his testimony differed greatly from the story he had told Donald Farquharson. Macpherson now said that, during late May 1750, he had been visited by a vision of a 'naked soldier', who had said, 'I am Sergeant Davis'. At first, Macpherson said, he had thought the vision to be a living man—a brother of Donald Farquharson, he added—and he was told by the vision where the murdered remains of Davis could be found.

Next day, Macpherson said, he went out and found the bones, but afterwards covered them up. On his way back to the shepherd's hut where he lived, Macpherson met John Growar (of the tartan coat). Growar threatened Macpherson that if he did not keep quiet about the bones he, Growar, would impeach him to the magistrate, Mr Shaw of Daldownie. Macpherson went on to say that he had thought it wise to visit Magistrate Shaw himself and give his testimony voluntarily. Shaw, however, had told Macpherson to remain silent and forget about the incident. Macpherson had returned home troubled and was visited the same night by Davis' ghost. This time the ghost had insisted that he go to Michael Farquharson or his son Donald.

At this point, however, the court at Edinburgh was stunned when Macpherson revealed the names of Davis' murderers—Duncan Clerk and Alexander Bane MacDonald. It should also be noted for future reference that the magistrate asked Macpherson in what language the ghost had spoken: Macpherson replied 'In the Gaelic'.

There was to come, however, an uncanny piece of testimony from Macpherson's employer Mistress Isobel MacHardie. 'One night [*in June 1750*], I had been sleeping in the sheiling, while Macpherson slept at the other end, to keep a double watch on the sheep. While I lay awake I saw something naked come in at the door, which frightened me so much that I drew the clothes over my head. When it appeared it came in in a bowing posture ...' In the morning Mistress MacHardie questioned

Macpherson about what she had seen, trying to relate it to his story; but the wily shepherd was non-committal.

Strangely enough, the Sergeant Davis case was suspended and no further enquiries were made into the movements of Clerk and MacDonald, the men accused by Macpherson; something which strongly suggests collusion at a high level.

In September 1753, however, Clerk and MacDonald were arrested on charges of rebellious behaviour and were imprisoned in Edinburgh's Tolbooth Prison in June 1754. During their resultant trial (June 10 1754), it came out that Clerk's woman had been seen wearing Sergeant Davis' gold rings; and that Clerk, after Davis' murder, had suddenly become prosperous. Witnesses too came forward to swear that Clerk and MacDonald were on the hill with guns near to where the murder was committed. Indeed, one Angus Cameron attested that he had seen the two kill the soldier and strip the body. Although the testimony of the witnesses greatly impressed the jury, they returned a verdict of not guilty. The reason for this was that the ghost of Sergeant Davis had spoken in Gaelic, a language it did not know in life! Sir Walter Scott's own conclusion to the story, dated 'Abbotsford, 18 March 1830', set out that the whole tale was a conspiracy to cover Jacobite activity, using the traditional superstitions of the Highlanders.

Chapter 9

Ghosts which soldier on

The spectral rider

In 1854 a British Army officer, Major-General R. Barter, was a young subaltern in the India service. During his spell of duty Barter was witness to a curious set of apparitions. He saw not one ghost but three, simultaneously; and the Society for Psychical Research thought the story important enough to publish in their *Proceedings* (Vol V, 459, 1888).

On this particular occasion Lieutenant Barter was ordered to duty at the station of Murree in the Punjab. Here in the magnificent hill country, 7,000 feet above the steaming plains of southern India, he was able to rent a bungalow which had been built in 1852 by another officer, whom he identified in his testimony as Lieutenant B. This officer had died at Peshwar in January of 1854, and Barter arrived at Murree in the early summer of the same year.

One evening, shortly after Lieutenant Barter and his young wife had moved into the bungalow (which they called 'Uncle Tom's Cabin'), he entertained a fellow officer and his wife. These guests left around 2300 hours and Barter strolled with them to where the footpath to his bungalow joined what was known as the bridle-path. His friends had to clamber up this path to reach the newly built road leading round the Punjabi hills; a road that the soldiers nicknamed 'the Mall'. It was a beautiful, clear, moonlit night and Barter stood for a while smoking a cigar and watched his friends climb the zigzag trail. Nearby Barter's two dogs snuffled noisily in the undergrowth.

With a final wave of his hand as his friends disappeared over the hilltop, Barter turned and made his way back to the bungalow. When he called his dogs, however, he heard the ring of a horse's hoof as its iron shoe struck a stone on the bridle path. At length, above him, there appeared a man on horseback attended by his two *syces* (grooms). The man wore full evening dress, with a white waistcoat and a silk tophat. The horse the man was riding Barter later described as 'a strong hill pony, dark brown in colour with a black mane and tail'. The rider sat his mount with a strangely listless air, the reins hanging loosely from his hands, and on each side of the pony's head walked a *syce*.

'*Koi hai?*' ('Who is it?'—in Hindustani) called out Barter. But there was no reply. The party kept on in silence. Barter shouted again, and once more there was no response, but the strange group halted. To his horror Barter recognised the rider as Lieutenant B, the former owner of 'Uncle Tom's Cabin'. Strangely enough Barter noticed that Lieutenant B was stouter than when he had known him and now sported a rather unfashionable fringe of sidewhiskers.

Barter ran forward to get a closer look at Lieutenant B, but the instant he did so the rider, horse and grooms disappeared. Puzzled, Barter turned again towards the bungalow, and then for the first time noticed that his two dogs, which never before had strayed from his heels, were cowering in the undergrowth. At length he coaxed them out and returned to the bungalow. He told his wife what he had seen (his testimony was later substantiated in letters by his wife and brother officers), and next morning called on a friend, Lieutenant Deane, who had served in the same regiment as Lieutenant B. At first Barter did not reveal that he had seen Lieutenant B's phantom; he confined himself to general questions.

'How stout he had become lately,' remarked Barter, 'and what possessed him to allow his beard to grow into that horrid fringe?'

'Yes,' said Deane, 'he became very bloated before his death; you know he led a very fast life, and while on the sick list he allowed the fringe to grow in spite of all we could say to him'.

Then Barter asked where the dead lieutenant had obtained the pony, describing the beast in detail. Deane turned a startled look at him: 'Why, how do you know anything about that? You hadn't seen B for two or three years and you certainly never saw the pony. He bought the pony at Peshwar and killed him one day riding in his reckless fashion down the hill to Trete'.

Only at this point did Barter tell Deane of his strange encounter.

Barter and his wife remained at 'Uncle Tom's Cabin' for a further six weeks. During that time, they testified, they repeatedly heard the sound of someone galloping down the path leading to the bungalow. Once, when the clattering hoofs sounded louder than usual, Barter rushed out onto the veranda. There he found one of his Hindu servants with a *tattie* (screen) in his hand.

'Why do you stand there?' asked Barter.

'A strange figure came riding down the hill,' the man replied in Hindustani. 'It passed me like a typhoon and went round the corner of the house.' The servant said he was determined to waylay the thing, whatever it was, adding under his breath: '*Sharitan ka ghur hai*' ('This is a devil's house').

Major-General Barter's story is of interest to psychic researchers because his descriptions are clear and precise. Also the ghosts that he saw were not in nondescript 'white garb', but in identifiable costume. Further it was an 'amalgam sighting', not only were there three identifiable ghosts but an animal ghost also. For this reason this story is something of a psychic classic.

British military activity in India has produced a number of interesting cases*, of which this one related by Robert Dale Owen (1801-77, Scottish-American social reformer and Congressman) in *Footfalls on the Boundary of Another World* (1859: Third English Edition, London, 1875) is another classic tale.

Captain Wheatcroft of the 6th Dragoons

Robert Dale Owen wrote: 'In the month of September, 1857, Captain German Wheatcroft, of the 6th (Inniskilling) Dragoons, went out to India to join his regiment.

'His wife remained in England, residing at Cambridge. On the night between the 14 and 15 November 1857, towards morning, she dreamed that she saw her husband, looking anxious and ill; upon which she immediately awoke, much agitated. It was

* See for instance, 'Ghosts of the Mutiny' by Michael and Mollie Hardwick in John Canning's collection; and, the Sepoy story in Elliot O'Donnell's *Ghostly Phenomena* (T. Werner Laurie, London, 1910).

bright moonlight; and, looking up, she perceived the same figure standing by her bedside. He appeared in his uniform, the hands pressed across the breast, the hair dishevelled, the face very pale. His large dark eyes were fixed full upon her; their expression was that of great excitement, and there was a peculiar contraction of the mouth, habitual to him when agitated. She saw him, even to each minute particular of his dress, as distinctly as she had ever done in her life; and she remembers to have noticed between his hands the white of the shirt-bosom, unstained, however, with blood. The figure seemed to bend forward, as if in pain, and to make an effort to speak; but there was no sound. It remained visible, the wife thinks, as long as a minute, and then disappeared.

'Her first idea was to ascertain if she was actually awake. She rubbed her eyes with the sheet, and felt that the touch was real. Her little nephew was in bed with her; she bent over the sleeping child and listened to its breathing: the sound was distinct, and she became convinced that what she had seen was no dream. It need hardly be added that she did not again go to sleep that night.

'Next morning she related all this to her mother, expressing her conviction, though she had noticed no marks of blood on his dress, that Captain Wheatcroft was either killed or grievously wounded. So fully impressed was she with the reality of that apparition, that she thenceforth refused all invitations. A young friend urged her soon afterwards to go with her to a fashionable concert, reminding her that she had received from Malta, sent by her husband, a handsome dress cloak, which she had never yet worn. But she positively declined, declaring that, uncertain as she was whether she was not already a widow, she would never enter a place of amusement until she had letters from her husband (if indeed he still lived) of a later date than the 14 November.

'It was on a Tuesday, in the month of December 1857, that the telegram regarding the actual fate of Captain Wheatcroft was published in London. It was to the effect that he was killed before Lucknow on the *fifteenth* of November.

'This news, given in the morning paper, attracted the attention of Mr Wilkinson, a London solicitor, who had charge of Captain Wheatcroft's affairs. When at a later period this gentleman met the widow, she informed him that she had been quite prepared for the melancholy news, but that she had felt sure her husband could not have been killed on the 15 November, inasmuch as it was during the night between 14 and 15 November that he appeared to her.*

'The certificate from the War Office, however, which it became Mr Wilkinson's duty to obtain, confirmed the date given in the telegram: . . . "No 9579/1 War Office, 30 January 1858. These are to certify that it appears, by the records in this office that Captain German Wheatcroft, of the 6th (*Inniskilling*) Dragoons, was killed in action on the 15th November 1857. Signed, B. Hawes."

'Mr Wilkinson called at the offices of Messrs Cox and Greenwood, the army agents, to ascertain if there were no mistake in the certificate. But nothing there appeared to confirm any surmise of inaccuracy. Captain Wheatcroft's death was mentioned in two separate despatches of Sir Colin Campbell, and in both the date corresponded with that given in the telegram.

'So matters rested, until, in the month of March 1858, the family of Captain Wheatcroft received from Captain GC†, then of the Military Train, a letter dated

* Owen added this footnote: 'The difference of longitude between London and Lucknow being about five hours, three or four o'clock AM in London would be eight or nine o'clock AM at Lucknow. But it was in the *afternoon* not in the morning . . . that Captain Wheatcroft was killed'. Thus his ghost would have appeared before his actual death if he had died on the 15th.

† Owen did not reveal this soldier's name.

near Lucknow, on the 19 December 1857. This letter informed them that Captain Wheatcroft had been killed before Lucknow, while gallantly leading on the squadron, not on the 15 November, as reported in Sir Colin Campbell's despatches, but on the *fourteenth in the afternoon*. Captain GC was riding close by his side at the time he saw him fall. He was struck by a fragment of shell in the breast, and never spoke after he was hit. He was buried at the Dikoosha; and on a wooden cross, erected by his friend, Lieutenant R of the 9th Lancers, at the head of his grave, are cut the initials GW, and the date of his death, 14 November 1857*.

'The War Office finally made the correction as to the date of death, but not until more than a year after the event occurred . . .'.

Robert Dale Owen went on: 'This extraordinary narrative was obtained by me direct from the parties themselves. The widow of Captain Wheatcroft kindly consented to examine and correct the manuscript and allowed me to inspect a copy of Captain GC's letter, giving particulars of her husband's death. To Mr Wilkinson, also, the manuscript was submitted, and he assented to its accuracy so far as he is concerned. I have neglected no precaution, therefore, to obtain for it the warrant of authenticity.

'It is perhaps', concluded Owen, 'the only example on record where the appearance of what is usually termed a ghost proved means of correcting an erroneous date in the despatches of a Commander-in-Chief, and of detecting an inaccuracy in the certificate of a War Office'.

A stranger in the fog

The following ghost story came to me from the grand-daughter of the ex-soldier who underwent the experience. The soldier was called Harry Kirkup and he lived for many years at Blaydon, near Newcastle. Harry Kirkup was a man fond of his pint of beer and a bet on the horses. He did not believe in ghosts. Any of his acquaintances who admitted to having seen ghosts, or said they had psychic powers, met with Harry's scorn. He was a complete sceptic, not to say a cynic. But after his ghostly experience he was a changed man and no longer laughed at ghost stories.

Late one winter's evening in 1917, Harry Kirkup, then a sergeant in a northern regiment, was hurrying down Westgate Road towards Central Station at Newcastle. It was foggy when he started out from his sister's house in Westgate Road yet, although he knew his way, the fog was so thick that he lost his bearings. He was groping around trying to find Westgate Road again, when a voice came to him from out of the gloom: 'Are you lost mate? Follow me', said the voice.

'I want to get to the Central Station,' replied Harry.

'That's all right,' the voice encouraged. 'I'm going there myself. Keep close and follow me.'

Harry did not need to be told twice. He fell in beside the stranger, who had now fully materialised out of the fog.

Westgate Road was very quiet. The only sound came from distant workshops on 24-hour shifts. The air was damp and cold, and it penetrated the clothes. The fog made talking a painful business, so the two fell silent. As they passed through the pools of light etched in the fog by the gas lamps, Harry Kirkup ventured a glance at

* Owen noted: 'It was not in his own regiment, which was then at Meerut, that Captain Wheatcroft was serving at the time of his death. Immediately on arriving from England at Cawnpore, he had offered his services to Colonel Wilson of the 64th . . . he joined the Military Train then starting for Lucknow.'

his companion who was now revealed, by his flashes, to be a sergeant in some southern regiment. But curiously enough, Harry noticed, the soldier's uniform was of the kind worn in the South African War, now some 16 years past. Harry was just going to ask the soldier why he was wearing an outdated uniform, when the stranger broke the silence: 'Are you going back to your unit?' Harry said he was.

'So am I,' said the stranger. 'I have to catch a train from Newcastle to London.'

'I have, too,' Kirkup replied. 'It would be great if I might travel with you. For company you know.'

'Sure,' replied the fellow sergeant. 'I shall be glad of the company too.'

On arrival at Newcastle's Central Station the two soldiers got into an empty carriage. By now the fog had begun to clear a little and a few faint stars showed themselves.

'The night is very similar to what it was one night in 1899,' the stranger remarked as the train pulled out of Newcastle.

'You recollect a night 18 years ago?' Harry Kirkup asked somewhat puzzled.

'I have good reason to,' the South African War veteran replied. 'I was congratulating myself that night, as we started from Newcastle station. I had a compartment to myself. Just then a man got in. He sat opposite to me just as you are now. I did not like his looks one bit. He had a low, sloping forehead, a receding chin, a long bony nose and protruding eyes. It was an ill-balanced face. And he was an ill-looking man. He wore a shabby loose-fitting black suit. For all the world he looked like an undertaker.

'I was tired. I had been recruiting for my regiment in Newcastle. As I searched my pocket for a cigarette to try and keep myself awake, I inadvertently pulled out my wallet and my month's pay spilled out onto the compartment floor. I picked up the money, and all the time I was aware that the man opposite was watching my every move.

'Minutes later I was nearly dropping off with the monotonous rumble of the train wheels when the movement of the man opposite roused me. He was holding a knife in one hand and made a lunge at my chest. I grabbed his wrist and deflected the knife and we fell to the floor.'

'Did you win the scrap?' interrupted Harry Kirkup.

'No' replied the strange soldier. 'Although my assailant was very wiry, he was stronger than me. I tried to get at the window cord communicating with the guard's van, but the man pulled me back and plunged his knife into my chest.'

'But you were fortunate—his blow missed the vital spot?' Harry Kirkup said, averting his eyes, feeling rather sick at the scene so graphically described.

'No' said the stranger. 'The blow did not miss. It killed me.'

'It did what?' gasped Harry, looking up again not believing his ears. There was no reply. The strange South African War sergeant had completely vanished. Harry Kirkup was alone in the compartment, and the train rattled on through the darkened outskirts of Newcastle.

One soldier ghost plays billiards

One of the most remarkable accounts of a military phantom was publicly related some years ago by Lieutenant-Colonel The O'Doneven of Gold Mead, Lymington, Hampshire. He attested that he once played billiards with a ghost, which he beat 100 up. He described the experience thus to his friends:

'It happened after I had taken two batteries up to the Midlands in 1943. We were billeted in a lovely old house, surrounded by park lands. All the furniture and pictures were covered with dust-covers, and two old retainers of the family, one of whom was the butler, had been left in charge for the duration. I formed a small mess and retained the services of the butler to help us out, and to emphasise that we were guests and not just intruders. Our frugal dinner was timed at 7.45 pm each evening.

'One cold night my watch must have gone wrong for, as I turned down the stairs into the hall where we dined, I saw by the clock that it was only 6.45 pm. I was on the point of sitting in front of the fire when I heard the sound of billiard-balls being clicked about.

'I pushed open a door and found myself in a long room. At the table was a youngish man, in a sort of Kitchener Army Blues' uniform knocking balls about. He was humpbacked. He said nothing, but smiled when I asked "Want a game?". So we began. We were 98-all when I heard my officers moving about in the hall. The shot was mine, a sure pot of his ball, or the gentlemanly cannon shot off red to white. As I took my shot, he quietly walked through another door, into what I afterwards discovered was a bathroom.

'Halfway through dinner, I asked "Any of you seen the little chap in blues?", but none of my officers had and I was on the point of letting the matter drop, when I added, "A nice lad, with a hump. I've just beaten him at billiards."

'The butler, on the point of handing me some apple tart, froze and went pale. "You've seen Master Willie, sir," he said. I waited sensing, as a Celt, what I already knew. The butler went on: "Master Willie, sir, was her Ladyship's brother. He had managed to join Kitchener's Army, in 1915, but the authorities threw him out on discovering that he was deformed. He came back here, Christmas 1916. He played a good game of billiards and shot himself in the room where he loved to play. We see him sometimes . . ." '

Eugénie and the violet perfume

Charles Louis Napoleon Bonaparte, Napoleon III (1808-73), was the son of Louis Bonaparte, King of Holland, and of Hortense de Beauharnais, daughter of the Empress Josephine. After unsuccessful attempts to secure the French throne in 1836 and 1840, and years of imprisonment, he took advantage of the revolution of 1848 to return to France and, following the famous *coup d'état* on December 2 1851, emerged as master of France and was proclaimed Emperor in 1852. During the next year he married Marie Ignace Augustine de Montijo, who consorted him as Eugénie. Dictatorial and discredited at home, unsuccessful in his foreign adventures, Napoleon III's surrender at Sedan in the Franco-Prussian War of 1870 brought ruin to the second Empire, and France once again became a republic.

After this *débâcle* Napoleon and Eugénie, with their son Louis, fled to England where they were hospitably received by Queen Victoria. The son Louis (or 'Lou Lou', as his mother called him) was eventually commissioned in a British regiment which ultimately served in South Africa. There, in the jungles of Natal during a skirmish with Zulus in 1879, Louis was killed. The young prince's body was recovered and given temporary burial. Eugénie vowed that she would retrieve her son's body and bury it in the vault she had had constructed on Napoleon III's death at Farnborough.

Eugénie set out on her quest in 1880 accompanied by Sir Evelyn Wood and Dr Scott. On arrival in Africa the party set out into the tropical jungle to find the young man's grave. By 1880, of course, the shrubs and grass had grown thick, and even the Zulu guides hired by Eugénie could not find the grave. Sir Evelyn Wood tried to persuade the former empress to return to England. But the lady was adamant, she was not going to return to England without her son's body. '*Mais votre Majesté*', supported Dr Scott, '*La jungle est trop impénétrable; cette tâche est au-dessus de vos forces*'. (But Your Majesty, the jungle is too impenetrable, this task is too much for you.) The Empress waved aside all obstacles, and at length astounded her companions one morning by exclaiming: '*Par ici! C'est la route*'. (Through here. This is the way.)

Instantly she dashed into the jungle, her companions followed as best they could. On she plunged, never swerving from her chosen path. She stumbled over fallen logs, holes and rocks, through grass so high that it struck her face. At last her exhausted companions heard her exclaim: '*C'est ici. C'est ici. Oh, mon petit brave, je te trouve!*'. (Here it is. Here it is. Oh my little one, I have found you!) There, so completely overgrown with brush as to be completely hidden from any angle of approach, was the cairn marking the young prince's grave.

Afterwards she answered the inevitable question: 'Your Majesty, how did you know where to go?' She explained that, as they all stood in the jungle looking at each other hopelessly, she suddenly became aware of a strong scent of violets. The first whiff was so unexpected and so overpowering that she almost fainted. She said that her '*pauvre petit garçon*' had had a passion for violet perfume, and it was the only toilet scent that he ever used. As she breathed the fragrance, it seemed to draw her along. The odour had faded at the cairn!

The ghost from Spion Kop

Amelia Raynham, the prominent operatic soprano of the 1890s, had been a firm friend of our family for many years before my kinsman Thomas met her in the 1920s. Even though she was an old lady then, she had an active mind and a needle-sharp wit. At 80 her memory was sharp as ever and her Chelsea apartment was a popular musical and literary salon. Knowing that Thomas was at the time collecting more strange ghost stories for a further private dossier, she invited him to tea, to tell him of her ghostly encounter on the Isle of Wight.

For the Raynhams, All Saints Church, Ryde, had many family associations. Amelia Raynham's mother had attended Princess Christian, when on behalf of Queen Victoria the princess laid the church's foundation stone in 1869. And in 1872 the Raynham's had been present when the church was consecrated by Bishop Wilberforce.

During the Easter of 1900 Amelia Raynham was staying with friends at Appley Park. Normally her visits to the Isle of Wight were a matter of great pleasure to her, but on this occasion personal grief spoilt her vacation. It was then almost nine months since the Boer War in South Africa had broken out and her brother George had been reported missing. The last the family had heard of him was that he had been seen at 8.30 pm on January 23 1900 among the advance column attacking the Boer positions at Spion Kop, where his superior officer Major-General E. R. P. Woodgate was in command. The ensuing battle of Spion Kop was perhaps the bloodiest, and certainly the most futile engagement of the whole South African War; so the Raynham's believed the worst.

For solace in her grief Amelia Raynham visited familiar All Saints Church, and it was there that she encountered the strange phantom. Throughout, her story was corroborated by her friend Marjorie Banks, who had come over for the day from Newport. It was mid-afternoon when Amelia Raynham and her friend entered All Saints Church, and for a few minutes they walked round the outer aisles admiring the architecture, which all considered the best specimens of Sir Gilbert G. Scott's work. At length they sat in one of the pews near the high altar and began to discuss what might have happened to George.

As they were quite alone in the church they turned their heads to see who had come in when the church door clanked open. To their surprise they heard the door close again, but no one appeared. Strangest of all was that the sound of footsteps was heard proceeding down the nave, past them and right up to the altar; but no one was to be seen. There the footsteps stopped. Puzzled, the two girls went to investigate but could find no one. The church was entirely empty but for themselves. They stood for a moment in the sunshine which slanted through the church windows, and wondered at the footfalls which appeared to be made by heavy cavalry, or army boots, for there had also been a clear clinking sound like spurs jingling.

Just as the two women were making to leave, the invisible boots sounded again and near the altar they saw an officer with head bowed facing the main window. The soldier turned and Amelia Raynham saw that it appeared to be her missing brother George. With echoing footsteps her brother walked down the aisle towards her, his arms outstretched. She ran to meet him, but as she came close she saw that his face was covered with blood from a terrible head wound and that his jacket was soaked in the gore and stained with mud. In a moment the figure of the soldier disappeared right in front of her.

Marjorie Banks had been watching this all the time and she ran to where her friend was standing sobbing. Carefully Miss Banks searched all the nearby pews, but could find no trace of the phantom soldier. For a few minutes in broad daylight the ghostly officer had seemed flesh and blood to the two young women.

Instinctively Amelia Raynham knew that she had seen the ghost of her brother, who must now be declared dead. The strange story was later discussed by members of the Society for Psychical Research, whose theory on the phenomenon ran as follows. Because of the close attachment between Amelia Raynham and her brother there would be a positive telepathic rapport. In this way brother and sister would be 'in tune', on the same wavelength of thought vibrations. Again, because he was already in her thoughts, said the psychics, Captain Raynham's spirit was able to communicate with her in surroundings which brought back such happy memories for both of them. All Saints Church, Ryde, meant happy memories of childhood holidays spent together. Thus, even in spirit form, Captain Raynham remembered that the church would be a place to which his sister would always return and therefore he chose that place to materialise and show her his fate. The materialisation was so powerful as to be visible to a third, and telepathically unconnected witness.

Companion on the march

A successful New York author, who had served as a major in the Canadian army during World War I, once startled guests at a dinner party by retelling this strange story, which he swore on oath as being true.

'It was in 1915, and we were stationed at Ypres. I was then a captain, and my company and its battalion were in the front line trenches for a prolonged stretch of duty. For nine days we were in that trench without relief. All that time we had been under constant fire, we had lived on sparse rations, and we were worn out. Finally, on the evening of the ninth day, the relief showed up in the communications trench, and we filed out for a rest billet, cold, hungry and dog-tired. As it was we had ahead of us a march of about nine miles, following a roundabout route to our destination. First we had to take a road that ran parallel to our trenches for a considerable distance until it came to "Suicide Corner", a right-angle junction with another road leading back to the rear. This was a spot which the Germans shelled every night in the hope of catching troops or supplies in movement.

'We reached the Corner and were lucky enough to make the turn without suffering any shell fire. In order to diminish the number of casualties in case a shell burst on the marching column, the battalion was spread out thinly, with spaces between the platoons. The commanding officer of my company was up with the forward ranks, and my duty was to bring up the rear.

'On each side of the road and parallel to it ran a line of ditch with water in the bottom. Men had been known on these roads to drop out of ranks from sheer fatigue, fall into a ditch and drown there. The fields on either side were then mere wallows of soft mud, so it was my special duty to see that none of the men straggled or fell on the march.

'As we slogged along mechanically, we could hear shells bursting on Suicide Corner behind us, and we congratulated ourselves on our luck in missing them. We quickened our pace because the next burst might fall upon our route of march. Soon a man in the rear rank of the platoon in front of me gradually dropped back until he was abreast of me. I recognised him as Private Burke.

' "Tired?" I asked.

' "No, sir, not very," he answered.

' "Cold?"

' "No, sir."

'I had eaten so little that day that I took out of a pocket a bottle of milk tablets and shook out four or five into the palm of my hand and put them in my mouth.

' "Hungry?"

' "Yes, sir."

' "Have some?" I offered the milk tablets to the man tramping along beside me.

' "Yes sir, thank you," he replied, and he held out his palm while I shook out some tablets for him. I steadied his hand so as to be sure not to spill any of them. I was miserably cold myself, but when I touched his hand it felt like a piece of ice.

' "You *are* cold," I said to myself. Then we marched along in silence for a while, keeping together. Gradually he began to lag until he was about half a pace back of me. All at once, I realised that he was behind me. I knew I must not let him do that, and turned sharply to order him up. But there was no one there. Fearing that he had dropped into a ditch, I took out my pocket flashlight and walked back playing the light on the ditches on each side of the road for some distance, but there was no trace of him. I was bewildered and worried. I was responsible for allowing no man to fall out on the march, and this man dropped behind me for only an instant to disappear completely!

'Suddenly it came over me that Private Burke had been killed three days before and I had seen him buried. I knew him well, as I was bound to know the men in my company with whom I had served for months. Was it possible that in the poor light my eyes had deceived me and I had mistaken another man for Burke? But whoever he was, he had dropped behind me and vanished. I was worried, as I had good reason to be. But when our long march was ended at the rest billet and the muster roll was called, not a man in the battalion was missing.'

American law researcher John D. Colby first told me this story; the soldier-author was his cousin.

In time of need

For as long as men have fought each other there have been stories of remarkable escapes from death. No less are there stories of phantoms returning to help their

The Tower of London is the well-established haunt of many ghosts, to the discomfiture of the percipients. One sentry died of shock after being attacked by a phantom bear!

An unknown Roundhead haunts the paths around Noseley Hall, Billesdon, Leicester.

The assassination of Archbishop Thomas Becket on December 29 1170 had many psychic repercussions.

Ghostly soldiers whirl this table at Ann of Cleves' House, Lewes, Sussex.

The ghost of Geoffrey de Mandeville appears on horseback in East Barnet (above) once every six years.

Roman sentries still ride the bounds near the Chapel of St Peter-on-the-Wall (right) at Bradwell in Essex.

The sound of ghostly soldiers locked in battle are heard around Mersea Barrow, Essex (below).

Blythburgh Church, Suffolk, is troubled by the moans of a phantom negro drummer, Black Toby, executed for murder in 1750.

Stones in the ruined north aisle of Kilmallock Abbey, Co Limerick, exude the ectoplasmic tears of the ghostly White Knight, Sir Maurice Fitzgerald.

relatives cheat death in time of war. George Wilson, an American serving in Russia at the time of the Red Revolution, was convinced that the ghost of his sister helped him avoid violent death twice.

At the time of his ghostly sister's first materialisation, Wilson was commanding a machine-gun crew in Vladivostok, placed to guard American property. There were some five minor rebellions in Siberia following the 'White-Red' conflict, which caused the overthrow of Czar Nicholas II's government, and it was during one of the Japanese sponsored revolts (prelude to the Siberian Expedition 1918-22) called the 'Gaida Revolution' that the incident occurred.

The Reds, who were in power, were shooting at the rebel troops under General Gaida from sniper positions. It was evening as Wilson and his gunners sat watching the gunfire from the emplacement. Near to the gun carriage Wilson watched the spectre of his sister materialise, and she appeared to be pointing to his feet. Without thinking Wilson bent down to see what she was pointing at but saw only a spent match. At that moment a shell passed over where his head and shoulders would have been and it exploded directly behind the gun. Wilson's entire gun crew were killed. Again, Wilson testified that his sister's ghost saved him from death when a coal bag eccentrically swayed on a hoist above his head, while he was on duty at Vladivostok docks.

The spectral 'army chaplain'

The Reverend Dr Harris was not an army chaplain in the true sense of the word. His large number of military friends and his keen, if not obsessive, interest in military affairs, however, earned him the nickname of 'Army Chaplain' among the Bostonian aristocracy of Massachusetts. The ghostly appearance of Dr Harris is interesting for the following reasons: it had no vestige of the 'cold horror' usually associated with ghosts; its appearance was recorded by an avowed sceptic, with professional sang-froid; and the ghost appeared not at night, but in 'the brightest noontide'.

Testimony for the appearance of this ghost comes from the papers of Nathaniel Hawthorne (1804-64), the American novelist and author of *The Scarlet Letter* and *House of Seven Gables*. Educated at Bowdoin College, Maine, Hawthorne was of an intelligence and character which was of great use in describing ghostly phenomena. At the time of his sighting he was US Consul at Liverpool. Among his circle at Liverpool were John Pemberton Heywood and his wife. One evening, while dining at their home, Hawthorne retold the story of his ghostly confrontation with Dr Harris. So impressed was Mrs Pemberton Heywood that she asked the celebrated author to write it down for her. This he did, and the following is his personal testimony. It is interesting to note that the manuscript of the story eventually came into the possession of Mrs Pemberton Heywood's sister, the Honourable Mrs Richard Denman. Some years later Mrs Denman sent the manuscript to the *Nineteenth Century* magazine, which published it in the issue of January 1900.

'To: Mrs John Pemberton Heywood Liverpool, 17 Aug 1856

'I am afraid this ghost story will bear a very faded aspect when transferred to paper. Whatever effect it had on you, or whatever charm it retains in your memory, is perhaps to be attributed to the favourable circumstances under which it was originally told.

'We were sitting, I remember, late in the evening, in your drawing-room, where the lights of the chandelier were so muffled as to produce a delicious obscurity through which the fire diffused a dim red glow. In this rich twilight the feelings of the party had been properly attuned by some tales of English superstition, and the lady of

Smithills Hall had just been describing that Bloody Footstep which marks the threshold of her old mansion, when your Yankee guest (zealous for the honour of his country, and desirous of proving that his dead compatriots have the same ghostly privileges as other dead people, if they think it worth while to use them) began a story of something wonderful that long ago happened to himself. Possibly in the verbal narrative he may have assumed a little more license than would be allowable in a written record. For the sake of the artistic effect, he may then have thrown in, here and there, a few slight circumstances which he will not think it proper to retain in what he now puts forth as the sober statement of a veritable fact.

'A good many years ago (it may be as many as fifteen, perhaps more, and while I was still a bachelor) I resided at Boston . . . In that city there is a large and long-established library, styled the Atheneum, connected with which is a reading-room, well supplied with foreign and American periodicals and newspapers. A splendid edifice has since been erected by the proprietors of the institution; but, by the period I speak of, it was contained within a large, old mansion, formerly the town residence of an eminent citizen of Boston. The reading-room (a spacious hall, with the group of the Laccoön at one end, and the Belvidere Apollo at the other) was frequented by not a few elderly merchants, retired from business, by clergymen and lawyers, and by such literary men as we had amongst us. These good people were mostly old, leisurely, and somnolent, and used to nod and doze for hours altogether, with the newspapers before them . . .

'One of these worthies, whom I occasionally saw there, was the Reverend Doctor Harris, a Unitarian clergyman of considerable repute and eminence. He was very far advanced in life, not less than eighty years old, and probably more; and he resided, I think, at Dorchester, a suburban village in the immediate vicinity of Boston. I had never been personally acquainted with this good old clergyman, but had heard of him all my life as a noteworthy man; so that when he was first pointed out to me I looked at him with a certain speciality of attention, and always subsequently eyed him with a degree of interest whenever I happened to see him at the Atheneum or elsewhere. He was a small, withered, infirm, but brisk old gentleman, with snow-white hair, a somewhat stooping figure, but yet with a remarkable alacrity of movement. I remember it was in the street that I first noticed him. The Doctor was plodding along with his staff, but turned smartly about on being addressed by the gentleman who was with me, and responded with a good deal of vivacity.

'. . . His especial haunt was the Atheneum. There I used to see him daily, and almost always with a newspaper—the *Boston Post,* which was the leading journal of the Democratic party in the Northern states . . . There his reverend figure was accustomed to sit day after day, in the self-same chair by the fireside; and, by degrees, seeing him there so constantly, I began to look towards him as I entered the reading-room, and felt that a kind of acquaintance, at least on my part, was established . . . this small, white-haired, infirm, yet vivacious figure of an old clergyman became associated with my idea and recollection of the place. One day, especially (about noon, as was generally his hour), I am perfectly certain that I had seen this figure of old Doctor Harris, and taken my customary note of him, although I remember nothing in his appearance at all different from what I had seen on many previous occasions.

'But, that very evening, a friend said to me, "Did you hear that old Doctor Harris is dead?" "No", said I very quietly, "and it cannot be true, for I saw him at the Atheneum today". "You must be mistaken", rejoined my friend. "He is certainly dead!" and confirmed the fact with such special circumstances that I could no longer doubt it . . .

'The next day, as I ascended the steps of the Atheneum, I remember thinking within myself, "Well I never shall see old Doctor Harris again!" . . . as I opened the door of the reading-room, I glanced toward the spot and chair where Doctor Harris usually sat, and there, to my astonishment, sat the grey, infirm figure of the deceased Doctor, reading the newspaper . . .

'The apparition took no notice of me, nor behaved otherwise in any respect than on any previous day. Nobody but myself seemed to notice him . . .

'From that time, for a long while thereafter—for weeks at least, and I know not but for months—I used to see the figure of Doctor Harris quite as frequently as before his death. It grew to be so common that at length I regarded the venerable defunct no more than the other old fogies who basked before the fire and dozed over the newspapers . . .

'After a certain period . . . I began to notice, or fancy, a peculiar regard in the old gentleman's aspect toward myself. I sometimes found him gazing at me, and unless I deceived myself, there was a sort of expectancy in his face. His spectacles, I think, were shoved up, so that his bleared eyes might meet my own . . . Being a ghost, and amenable to ghostly laws, it was natural to conclude that he was waiting to be spoken to before delivering whatever message he wished to impart . . . In the reading-room of the Atheneum, conversation is strictly forbidden, and I could not have addressed the apparition without drawing the instant notice and indignant frowns of the slumberous old gentlemen around me. I myself, too, at that time, was as shy as any ghost, and followed the ghosts' rule never to speak first. And what an absurd figure should I have made, solemnly and awfully addressing what must have appeared, in the eyes of all the rest of the company, an empty chair! . . .

'For such reasons . . . and reflecting, moreover, that the deceased Doctor might burden me with some disagreeable task . . . I stubbornly resolved to have nothing to say to him. To this determination I adhered; and not a syllable ever passed between the ghost of Doctor Harris and myself . . .

'To the best of my recollection, I never observed the old gentleman either enter the reading-room or depart from it, or move from his chair, or lay down the newspaper, or exchange a look with any person in the company, unless it were myself. He was not by any means invariably in his place. In the evening, for instance, though often at the reading-room myself, I never saw him. It was at the brightest noontide that I used to behold him, sitting within the most comfortable focus of the glowing fire, as real and lifelike an object . . . as any other in the room . . .'

For the rest of his life, Nathaniel Hawthorne, at the back of his mind, secretly wished that he had spoken to the ghost and questioned this apparition he described as 'the sober statement of a veritable fact', but fear and foreboding stopped him. What if the ghostly 'army chaplain' had involved him in distasteful circumstances? Hawthorne just couldn't take the risk, but this did not lessen his belief in ghosts!

Chapter 10

Ghostly sentries & men-at-arms

According to experts in psychic phenomena, some ghosts are doomed by fate to wander the earth for a specific period. Maybe they walk the earthly plane to expiate a crime they committed in mortal life, or to pay for an error of remission. Sometimes ghosts are deemed to appear as a warning, or perhaps in order to tell someone of their terrible experiences in life. Such might be the case of the ghostly sentry who runs a lonely lane in Hampshire.

Ghost of the running sentry

On the elevated ground west of Aldershot Town is famous Beacon Hill, which for years was used to warn London, 38 miles away, and the garrison towns in between, of victory or impending war. In 1815 the bonfire on Beacon Hill blazed out the news of Wellington's success over Napoleon at Waterloo; and immediately a sentry was ordered to carry the good news to the local people of Aldershot. In those days the region was wild and as the sentry ran down the rough track, today known as Alma Lane, he was waylaid and murdered by unknown assailants. Locals say his ghost is still running.

Particularly on winter nights the sentry's heavy studded boots and the clanking of his musket are clearly heard as he hurries along. One person who testifies to having heard the phantom run is Major Hampden Morris of Telford, Surrey. He and his wife stayed at Beam Cottage, Alma Lane, from 1946-49 and during the winter of 1948 they heard the runner no less than three times a fortnight*.

More sentries at Windsor

The ghostly sentry at Windsor Castle, Berkshire, pays penance for a personal sin. In the 1920s a young guardsman shot himself while on sentry duty at the part of the castle known as Long Walk. Some weeks later another guardsman, an 18-year-old grenadier called Leake, was patrolling the Long Walk in the early hours of the morning, when he saw a dim figure walking towards him. At first the young grenadier thought it was his relief, until he saw the figure's face beneath the bearskin cap. It was the face of the guardsman who had shot himself while patrolling the same eerie beat.

* Two more cases of murdered soldiers are of interest. One is the case of the murdered French dragoon (he was on the run from Sissinghurst Castle), who haunts the Chequers Inn at Smarden, Ashford, Kent. The other is the ghost of Private Edward Dobson who was murdered at the Globe Inn, Ludlow, Shropshire, while garrisoned at Ludlow in 1553.

Long Walk of Windsor Castle, the largest inhabited castle in the world and one of the oldest in England, is the haunt of another ghost which patrols from time to time. This is the ghost of Herne the Hunter, once a warden of Windsor Great Park under King Henry VIII. Herne was suspected of witchcraft and hanged himself from the branches of a great oak, which was thereafter known as Herne's Oak, until it was destroyed in 1863. For centuries Herne's ghost has accosted the sentries at Windsor and finally he has become a sort of military cult hero. William Harrison Ainsworth (1805-82), the English historical novelist, popularised Herne in his *Windsor Castle* (1843); and old prints of the ghost of Herne show him with antlers on his head (like some wild huntsman from Norse mythology) leading a band of ghostly warriors. Sentries at Windsor were quick to give the alarm whenever Herne appeared, for his coming was thought to bring an unknown blight to nearby crops, foliage and trees, and death to cattle. Shakespeare refers several times to Herne and his oak in *The Merry Wives of Windsor*.

Phantoms of the Tower of London

The Tower of London also has both ghosts of dead sentries and phantoms which have been seen by sentries while on duty. Even on the brightest day in summer, when the sun sparkles on the dome of St Paul's Cathedral and the trees by the twinkling River Thames are almost garish in their greenery, the Tower of London is a forbidding place. The stones of the gateways are cold to the touch, and the huge walls of the central White Tower cast a chilly shadow. 'There is no sadder spot on earth', wrote the brilliant Victorian historian Thomas Babington, Lord Macaulay (1800-59), and the sense of melancholy he noted is as oppressive today.

On the dark morning of February 12 1957—the 403rd anniversary of the execution within the Tower of Lady Jane Grey, Queen of England for only nine days—a young Welsh Guardsman called Johns shivered in the wet and stamped his feet as he listened to the clock on Waterloo Barracks chime 0300 hours. He was just settling himself at attention again, when stones rattled on the roof of his sentry box. High on the battlements of the Salt Tower, 40 feet above, Guardsman Johns saw a 'white shapeless form'. He made the usual challenge and, thinking the figure a felon, shouted for help. A search party could find nothing, though later another sentry reported seeing 'a strange white apparition with no shape at all' at the same position on the Salt Tower. the place where the ghost was seen was only some 100 yards from the house of the Yeoman Jailer who had held custody of Lady Jane Grey.

'I thought I was seeing things', said Guardsman Johns. 'The ghost stood between the battlements. I went to tell the other guard and as I pointed to the battlements the figure appeared again . . .' A Welsh Guard's officer later said: 'Guardsman Johns is convinced he saw a ghost. Speaking for the regiment, our attitude is: "All right so you say you saw a ghost. Let's leave it at that" '. Even today sentries at the Tower do not dismiss the ghost stories, for the phantoms have been seen so many times.

The Beefeaters (the nickname given both to the Yeoman of the Guard and the Yeoman Warders of the Tower), who were founded by Henry VII as 'protectors of the Royal Person', play down the instances of ghosts when recounting all the gory details of the executions on Tower Green. Even the present Resident Governor and Keeper of the Jewel House, Major-General William D. M. Raeburn, CB, DSO, MBE, and his staff courteously parry all requests for information about the ghosts but past governors have not been so reticent.

Col E. H. Carkeet Jones, a former Constable of the Tower, once related the story of the soldier of the 60th Rifles who, in 1864, was court-martialled for having been found unconscious by the Captain of the Guard, at the door of the King's House (then called the Lieutenant's Lodgings). Above this door, incidentally, was the little room where Anne Boleyn, Henry VIII's second wife, passed her last night before going to the scaffold in 1536.

At the court martial, the soldier's main defence was that a figure in white came towards him and didn't stop when challenged. He charged the figure with fixed bayonet, but met with no resistance. When he realised that he had been trying to stop a ghost he fell in a faint. Two other sentries corroborated the soldier's story—they saw the whole thing from a window of the Bloody Tower—and the sentry was acquitted.

Unfortunately, a sentry on duty near the Jewel Tower during the early 1800s did not escape as easily. Standing at the door of the Jewel Room, which lay shadowed beneath an archway, the sentry heard the clock strike midnight. As the echoes died away, the sentry saw an enormous black bear, rearing up on its hind legs, yellow fangs bared, ready to strike. The sentry raised his musket which had a bayonet attached, and lunged at the red-eyed beast. The bayonet passed straight through the animal, which completely disappeared. The bayonet and musket were later found embedded in the oaken door. Underneath, the sentry lay in a faint!

The next morning the Keeper of the Crown Jewels, Edmund Lenthal Swifte, visited the sentry in the Tower's sick bay, and ascertained that the man had not been drunk, nor asleep on duty. Indeed the soldier, a man of good conduct and exemplary character, was still trembling in a state of shock; a few days later he died.

Edmund Swifte was one of the few senior officers in the Tower who have had sympathy with those who had seen ghosts at the Tower; for he had seen the ghosts in the Tower buildings and grounds many times himself and until he retired in 1852 the subject of supernatural phenomena in the Tower was under constant review*.

During World War II, a sentry was continually posted at the Spur Tower. Shortly after one sentry had come on duty, he saw a party of ghostly sentries approach him and in their midst walked two others carrying a stretcher. On the stretcher lay the corpse of a headless man, whose decapitated head was tucked under his armpit. What the sentry reported seeing at the subsequent enquiry tallied in every detail with an old execution procedure at the Tower. The condemned prisoner (if he was to be executed at Tower Hill) was handed over to the Sheriffs of London by the Lieutenant of the Tower at the Bulwark Gate. After the execution the headless body and the severed head were borne by a guarded stretcher party to the Tower for burial.

Again, in February 1933, a sentry reported seeing a ghost not far from the Bloody Tower. This time it was the white phantom figure of a headless woman, which seemed to float towards him. As one newspaper of the day reported: 'Confronted by such an apparition, the sentry fled, making his way to the guardroom, greatly unnerved'.

Of the ghosts in full armour which walk their phantom way in the Tower of London, the following have been the most frequently seen: a former Duke of Northumberland, who walks the battlements between Martin Tower and Constable's Tower muttering to himself; Robert Devereux, 2nd Earl of Essex, who is continually seen wiping his brow; Lord Guildford Dudley, the unfortunate husband of Lady Jane Grey who sheds a ghostly tear; and the Duke of Monmouth who curses all in sight. Sometimes the ghost of the Jacobite soldier-nobleman Lord Lovat has been seen by Tower sentries, but he is a jovial spectre. Lord Lovat went to the block for his part in the

* In the 1860 issue of *Notes and Queries* Swifte described in full his strange sighting in 1917 at the Tower, of a ghostly 'cylindrical tube . . . about the thickness of my arm, and hovering between the ceiling and the table'.

Jacobite rebellion roaring with laughter after seeing a stand occupied by his Whig enemies collapse, killing a dozen of them who had come to see him die!

Wandering souls

Sir John Gates, a great favourite of Henry VIII and Captain of the Guard to his son Edward VI, was another who lost his head in the Tower for his support of Lady Jane Grey. Henry VIII had allowed Sir John to have Beeleigh Abbey, near Maldon, Essex, and it is here that his ghost walks. On August 22, the anniversary of the day he was beheaded in 1553, Sir John is reputed to walk in true ghost textbook fashion, with his head under his arm. He strides through the lovely beamed Jacobean bedroom, but disappears near the magnificent four-poster bed that was made for James I.

Picturesque Beeleigh, by the way, originally built in the 12th century for the White Canons, was the home until his death in 1936 of William Foyle, the founder of the world-famous bookshop. More than once his house-guests were disturbed by Sir John's ghost.

The ghost of Henry Grey, the soldier Duke of Suffolk, who took part in the insurrection against Queen Mary, also began to haunt the family home at Astley Castle, near Coventry, after his execution in the Tower. The haunting continued even after the house he knew was dismantled and reconstructed. Incidentally, a head, believed to be the duke's, was found in 1849 in the vault of Holy Trinity Church in the Minories (an unattractive thoroughfare leading southward to the Tower of London), where it was preserved in a glass case until the church was pulled down. The red tinge of his beard could still be seen and the facial skin was intact. A gash on the neck of the severed head showed where the executioner failed to sever it with the first blow. The head is thought to be among the vestry relics of St Botolph's Church, Aldgate, London. Poor Suffolk, however, has never caught up with his head and still walks without it at Astley Castle!

Not every military ghost, however, was male in mortal life. The ghost of the beleaguered lady of Old Wardour Castle, Tilsbury, Wiltshire is but one example. With a garrison of only two dozen trained soldiers, Lady Blanche Arundell held her castle for five days against the Puritan siege of May 1643. Try as he might with cannon, mines, petards and fireballs, the Roundhead commander, Sir Edward Hungerford, could not dislodge Lady Blanche. Today the ghostly lady-at-arms walks on the terrace at Wardour, then strolls beneath the massive yews and oaks which shade the crumbling ruin. Once the ghost was seen by the headmistress of a nearby village school, while she was walking at dusk in the castle grounds. The ghost vanished by the edge of the lake which lies opposite the castle.

Cromwell's contemporaries

As will have been seen in a previous chapter, the English Civil War produced many a phantom soldier. But apart from ghosts on battlefields there are more 'personalised' hauntings, like that of the Roundhead Colonel William Morton, who is said to patrol in East Wellow from the site of the Manor House where his family once lived to the parish church. Another Roundhead haunts Noseley Hall, Billesdon, Leicester. He was last seen a short while ago on the gravel path by the lake beneath the trees in front of the house, by Mrs Robert Hazlerigg, sister-in-law of the present owner, Lord Hazlerigg.

Prestbury, near Cheltenham, Gloucestershire, and Salisbury Hall, near St Albans, however, have a ghost phenomenon in common: they are both haunted by Royalist messengers of Civil War vintage. At Prestbury the phantom cavalier was a despatch rider who still gallops with the news of the Roundhead victory at Worcester. The beat of his horse's hooves has been heard round the corners of Burgage and Mill lanes, and past the cottage called 'Crossways'. This phantom also gallops along Shaw Green Lane, pausing to turn into Bow Bridge Lane and thence disappears into the night.

Salisbury Hall's cavalier walks at night along an upstairs passage. During the Civil War, this soldier in the King's army was carrying secret despatches when he was ambushed by Roundheads. He was chased into the moated manor and there shot himself when he found no way of escaping. The passage along which the sound of his ghostly footsteps are heard leads nowhere.

Cavaliers too are said to haunt the following inns: 'The Who'd Have Thought It' at Melton Coombe, near Yelverton, Devon; 'The Ring O'Bells' Middleton, near Manchester; 'The Reindeer', Banbury, Oxfordshire; and the 'Crab and Lobster', Sidlesham, near Chichester, Sussex—the ghost here is thought to be Sir Robert Earnley. John Hampden (1594-1643), the English patriot who opposed Charles I's 'Ship Money' tax, incidentally, is said still to roam the rooms at 'The Plough' at Clifton Hampden, Oxfordshire. But Roundhead Sir Henry Rich prefers to walk his own rooms at his former home of Holland House, Kensington.

At Pluckley, near Charing, Huntingdon, one of the famous resident 'Twelve Ghosts' is that of a Civil War colonel. He regularly strides among the trees of Park Wood, a mile and a half from the present railway station. Oliver Cromwell himself is said to haunt Old Basing House, but the most famous location for his personal haunting is Apsley House, situated at 149 Piccadilly, Hyde Park Corner, London*.

Apsley House, the town residence of the first Duke of Wellington and his home until his sudden death in 1852, was built between the years 1771-8, from designs by Robert Adam, for the second Earl Bathurst. The house takes its name from Earl Bathurst's title held before he succeeded his father. Originally of red bricks, the house itself is built on the site of the old lodge of Hyde Park, which in turn had followed the 'Pillars of Hercules', the inn at which Henry Fielding's Squire Western, in *Tom Jones,* stayed when pursuing his daughter.

At present in the shadow of the skyscraper Hilton hotel, Apsley House now houses the Wellington Museum, but once its small paned windows saw the front line of political revolution and violence. Although a military hero, the Duke of Wellington who served in turn as Prime Minister and leader of the Tory Opposition, was opposed to parliamentary reform; so much so that public adulation turned sour and he became the most unpopular man in Britain. Regularly angry mobs gathered outside Apsley House, yelling for the Duke's blood. Twice they stormed the place, hurling stones and bottles, but the Iron Duke had special shutters fitted to his windows and remained recalcitrant behind them.

During the winter of 1832, however, the Reform Bill crisis took an ugly turn and the mob constantly screamed outside Apsley House. On Christmas Eve 1832, as Wellington prepared for bed, he met a ghostly figure walking down one of the corridors in Apsley House. Wellington immediately recognised the burly phantom in antique armour as Oliver Cromwell, who seemed to be pointing a warning finger towards the seething crowd outside the house. During his lifetime Cromwell had had good cause to fear mobs. Wellington only saw the ghost for a short time and said nothing to anyone until long after the Reform Bill had become law.

* He is also said to haunt The Golden Lion Inn at St Ives, Cornwall, where once he had his district headquarters.

St Thomas' assailants

England has many a curious tradition concerning penances and penitential gifts to the Church, especially during the Middle Ages. Bovey Tracey, Devon, for instance, has a fine church dedicated to the canonised Archbishop of Canterbury, Thomas à Becket. Legend says that it was founded as an act of penance by William de Tracey who, along with Reginald fitzUrse, Hugh de Morville and Richard le Breton, murdered the rebellious cleric at five o'clock on the afternoon of December 29 1170. The assassination of Becket, however, left more intriguing psychic repercussions than the many miracles reported at his tomb.

A few years ago an American school-teacher visited Kent for the first time, and stayed with some friends near Bridge, some three miles outside Canterbury. As this particular December day was sunny she decided to take her dog for a walk, and enquired of her host which way she might take without getting lost. She was directed to a deeply rutted lane on which, if she kept turning left, she would come out onto the main road and find her way back easily to the cottage.

She set off down the lane with her dog at her heels, and presently came to a fork; here a grass-covered byway branched off. Being of a pioneer New England spirit, and loving to explore the country of her 18th century ancestors, the American school-teacher thought she would walk down the other lane for a short distance. The byway appeared to have been an old coach road at one time.

The dog raced ahead of her enjoying his freedom, when suddenly he stopped short and looked ahead into the damp and misty greenness beyond: there the lane was thickly overhung with trees. The dog slunk to the hedgeside and cowered, trembling. The school-teacher talked soothingly to the dog in an attempt to coax him out of the way-side undergrowth. As she was kneeling she felt a strong blast of air behind her which pushed her over, as if someone has passed at great speed. She spun round, but no one was there and in a second or two her dog was back on the road again barking happily.

When she returned to her friend's cottage, she related the happenings of her afternoon's walk, explaining her dog's behaviour in detail. Her host and hostess were not even mildly surprised at her story, for it was not the first time they had heard of the ghost of William de Tracey.

On the accomplishment of the barbarous deed, inspired by Henry II's fatal outburst against Becket, the troublesome low-born clerk, the four men-at-arms had taken different directions to avoid capture. De Tracey had made for Dover, down the road that was to become a grass-covered lane some 800 years later. Other people have seen, or rather have been knocked down by de Tracey before, and they will respectfully step aside next time!

Kemsing, near Sevenoaks, Kent, also has a phantom man-at-arms connected with the Becket slaughter. Once a year, the locals say, at the end of December, a phantom knight on a spectral horse dismounts at the door of Kemsing church, which is on the old pilgrim's road to Canterbury. Several times he has been seen kneeling in prayer inside the church. Many think he is one of the four murderers, but no one knows which knight.

Knights of the whirling table

While on the subject of Thomas à Becket's assailants, it is interesting to note the famous 'Knights' Table' at the museum in Anne of Cleves' House, Lewes, Sussex. Carved from a solid slab of Petworth Marble, the table and its occult associations are thus described in Arthur Penrhyn Stanley's *Historical Memorials of Canterbury* (London, 1855). Referring to Becket's murderers he says: '. . . they rode to South Malling Deanery, near Lewes. On entering the house they threw off their arms and trappings and placed them on the table which stood in the hall and after supper gathered round the blazing hearth. Suddenly the table started back and threw its burden on the ground. The attendants replaced the arms. But soon a still louder crash was heard and the various articles were thrown farther off. Soldiers and servants then searched in vain underneath the *solid table* to find the cause of its convulsions, till one of the conscience-stricken Knights suggested that it was indignantly refusing to bear the sacrilegious burden of their Arms.'

Sometimes, it is said, on December 29, the table whirls rapidly of its own accord making weird noises; if you listen carefully you can hear the whine of a distant voice saying 'Remember poor Thomas! Remember poor Thomas!'

Gatcombe's crusader

The ghostly influences of another man-at-arms still obsess the people in the tiny village of Gatcombe, in the Isle of Wight. This time it concerns a girl who fell in love with a crusader in the Middle Ages. Gatcombe's beautiful church, dedicated to St Olave, was built by the Normandy family of Estur in 1290. On the shadowy north side of the sanctuary, set in a recess of the thick walls, lies the effigy of the courageous crusader Edward Estur. Of solid oak and time-polished by many curious fingers, the effigy has a small winged angel at the crusader's helm and a little dog at his sollereted ankles. Legend says of this little dog that it comes to life every 100 years to dance on its hind legs on Midsummer Eve. But the mystic power of the crusader takes precedence in the superstitious gossip of the folk of Gatcombe.

Strange happenings began in the 1800s when the beautiful young woman called Lucy Lightfoot fell in love with the effigy of the dead crusader. A pious worshipper at St Olave's, the lonely, raven-haired, dark-eyed girl came daily from her father's farm at Stoney Meadow in the Bowcombe Valley. Hitching her mare to the church porch, Lucy spent an hour or two in mystic communication with her lover, dead some 600 years.

Lucy's passion for the effigy became the talk of the neighbourhood. Yet, as she set out on the morning of June 13 1831 to visit her friend Marjorie Braithwaite of nearby Chillerton Green, no one cast a curious eye as she broke her journey at Gatcombe for her daily visit to the crusader. Locals saw her ride up to the church porch, tether her horse and disappear inside. Moments later a violent storm broke out and for two hours the rain lashed down with tropical intensity. Local records verify the force of the storm in which the damage ran into hundreds of pounds. But worst of all, to the complete terror of the inhabitants, shortly after 11 o'clock, a total eclipse of the sun was experienced which lasted for 40 minutes.

When the storm had abated, a farmer called George Brewster was assessing the damage to his property, when he noticed that Lucy Lightfoot's mare stood by the church drenched and whimpering. The steam rose from its flanks as it desperately tried to break its tether. Brewster comforted the horse for a while and then went in search of Lucy. She was nowhere to be seen; she was never found, for she had completely disappeared from the island.

There were no signs of a struggle, but the steel misericord (a dagger used by medieval knights for despatching fallen opponents) which had formed a part of the crusader's effigy had been torn from the right arm. Shattered fragments of the weapon were found on the altar, but the chrysoberyl set in an engraved lodestone, which had adorned the hilt of the dagger, had vanished as completely as Lucy herself.

Lucy's strange disappearance might have been forgotten for ever had it not been for the diligent scholarship of the Revd Samuel Trelawney, pastor of St Mary's Methodist Church in the Isles of Scilly. Trelawney, a student of the crusades, discovered in 1865 an ancient manuscript written by Philippe de Mézières, Chancellor to Peter I, King of Cyprus, between 1359-69. Peter, apparently, had raised an army in 1364 to fight in Palestine and de Mézières had acted as chronicler. Among the volunteers listed was one Edward Estur of the Isle of Wight. But most curious of all, in Edward's company was a brave and beautiful woman from Carisbrooke called Lucy Lightfoot!

According to de Mézières, Lucy had travelled with Edward Estur, but the latter had prudently persuaded her to await his return from the conflict in the Holy Land at Cyprus. After the war they had planned to return to England together and marry. Before Estur left for Palestine, Peter made him a 'Companion of the Order of the Sword'. Among the insignia of the Order, the Revd Trelawney noted, was a short-bladed misericord, with a chrysoberyl set in a lodestone upon the hilt.

King Peter's knights had a successful campaign, and after sacking Alexandria in 1365, attacked the coast of Syria and the armies of the Sultan of Egypt. During this campaign Edward Estur received a blow which split his helmet and shattered his skull. For four months he lay in a coma, but was finally shipped back to England. His wound damaged his brain so badly that he had no recollection of Lucy Lightfoot.

De Mézières' manuscript mentions that Lucy Lightfoot waited in Cyprus for three years for Edward Estur to return. When rumour reached her, however, that he had died she bore her grief and married a fisherman called Lionello Momallino from Terra Vecchia, now Bastia, a small Corsican fishing-village. Her marriage was apparently happy and she settled down to fruit-farming on her own account.

Trelawney was fascinated that the two Lucy Lightfoots could have loved the same man, for his researches entirely ruled out coincidence. As the de Mézières manuscript was not discovered until over 30 years after Lucy's disappearance it is unlikely that she knew the story of her namesake. No tradition was extant on the island from which she could have learnt the story.

Why indeed did the 19th century Lucy Lightfoot fall in love with an effigy? Its bland, flattened, stylised features are certainly not handsome. Trelawney was completely baffled, but today those who believe in reincarnation are less so. Was the original Lucy reborn, with the same name 500 years later, near her old birthplace, they might ask? In the effigy of the crusader did the reborn Lucy see the likeness and living body of her long dead love? Scientific research however, suggests another explanation.

For some considerable time now, the present Rector of St Olave's, Gatcombe with Chillerton, the Revd James Evans, has been intrigued by the Lucy Lightfoot story and he believes that the true explanation lies along complicated scientific lines of research as yet not entirely explored. Perhaps the theories set out by Dr Alan Bruce-Barton of Connecticut University in the *Journal of Scientific Studies* may offer a logical explanation. Bruce-Barton suggests 'that in the four dimensional space-time continuum in which we live, according to Einstein's theory of relativity, matter itself is a kind of "kink" in the time-space manifold and, where "kinks" occur, space is warped or distorted and even time itself becomes curiously mixed up, as it were. Such "kinks" become very much accentuated *when a sudden alteration of natural forces occurs*, and they can produce strange and fascinating results leading to all kinds of radiation discharges'.

The abnormal events then (storm—electrical force; eclipse—outpourings of radiation from sun spot effects) of June 13 1831, may have set up a powerful chain reaction which swept through Gatcombe church and involved Lucy Lightfoot, quite unwittingly, in its consequences. Furthermore we know from the properties of chrysoberyl ($BeAl_2O_4$—a beryllium aluminate crystallised material generally of a green colour, translucent and having a vitreous lustre and conchoidal fracture) that, when grains of it explode, their inner energy acts as an extra booster to its discharge power. Likewise we know that when the crystals of lodestone (Fe_3O_4—an ore of iron, consisting of the peroxide and protoxide of iron in a state of combination) disintegrate under pressure they give off magnetism many millions of times greater than that discharged under similar circumstances by other substances. Add all this power of the chrysoberyl-lodestone-natural forces to the passionate, almost insane desire of a pubescent girl for the object of her desire then in front of her, and there is a force of mental-chemical power so potent as to bend time and space—or at least this is what Einstein's line of thought suggests.

Did time become distorted on June 13 1831? If so it is possible that the reborn spirit of Lucy Lightfoot stepped off the plane of the present into that of her dead lover no longer dead at that moment when time was 'bent'. In his arms the second Lucy Lightfoot might have been trapped and left marooned in the early 1360s, or projected into some future time.

Scientific research into such time sequences is only in its infancy, but one day the answer may be found for Lucy's disappearance. Certainly, after she had gone, the phantom figure of the man-at-arms often observed near St Olave's church was never seen again.

A tale from Washington Irving

In his famous *Sketch Book* (New York, 1819), Washington Irving (1783-1859), the American short story writer, essayist and historian, tells the story of a haunted picture at Bracebridge Hall, Yorkshire. The picture, said to be that of a crusader ancestor of the squire of Bracebridge, has never been academically identified. An old porter's wife, however, at Bracebridge Hall affirmed to Elliott O'Donnell that she had often heard in her youth tales concerning the crusader, who was deemed to descend from the picture, mount his white horse and visit his tomb in the neighbouring village church. On such occasions the church door swung open without any visible agency. One of the dairymaids of the estate actually attested that she had seen, while quite sober, the man-at-arms ride through the great park and through the closed churchyard gate.

Another villager declared that she had seen the crusader pace the aisles of the church on moonlit nights. It was believed that some wrong had been left unredressed, which kept his spirit in a state of permanent unrest. There was a story current in the local village that a sexton, who believed that the crusader was guarding treasure, endeavoured to break open the crusader's tomb. He had hardly begun his task when the marble hand of the recumbent knight's effigy dealt him a blow on the head, which stretched him senseless on the ground. When the sexton recovered consciousness he fled from the church in terror, and never dared to enter it again!

What ails Earl Geoffrey?

East Barnet, the modern urban district and parish of south Hertfordshire, two miles south-east of Barnet, has its own ghostly puzzle. Why does the ghost of Geoffrey de Mandeville still patrol this part of rural England? Geoffrey de Mandeville, Earl of Essex, succeeded his father William as constable of the Tower of London, c 1130. Only when King Stephen, Count of Blois (1105-53), created him Earl of Essex in 1140, did Geoffrey de Mandeville play any conspicuous part in history.

Eventually de Mandeville fell from favour and, during 1143-44, he maintained himself as a rebel and a bandit in the fen country, using the Isle of Ely and Ramsay Abbey as his headquarters. As J. H. Round points out in *Geoffrey de Mandeville, a Study of the Anarchy* (London, 1892) de Mandeville's career as outlaw exemplifies the worst excesses of English anarchy between 1140-47. When he rode high de Mandeville held concessions of great wealth and was virtual viceroy for the King in Essex, Middlesex, London and Hertfordshire. Geoffrey died of head-wounds received in a skirmish at Mildenhall, Suffolk, September 1144.

In truth Geoffrey de Mandeville had only a slight connection with East Barnet, which was only a small part of his vast administration. Nevertheless, tradition has firmly linked his wraith with the village, as has the legend of Trent Park, Cockfosters. The legend states that at Christmas Geoffrey de Mandeville can be seen striding around in full armour, with red cloak and scarlet plume. Some say that his earthbound spirit still searches out the modern site of treasure he buried in the 1140s.

Geoffrey de Mandeville's ghost was given further credence and prominence in 1925, when rumours spread that strange things had been seen and heard in stables at East Barnet. The rebel knight had crossed the boundary of death once more, the people averred. In 1926 the district council decided to demolish the stables and utilise the bricks thereof as infilling for a new road. Scarcely had this work commenced when the ghost of de Mandeville clanked around a neighbouring house in protest! The ghost was heard no less than four times in unaccountable circumstances, and some of the roadmen testified to their foreman that 'things started to go wrong'. Another caught a glimpse of a man-at-arms in a red cloak, passing the haunted stables at midnight.

During the period 1926-32 various newspaper reporters and psychic researchers investigated the case of wandering Geoffrey de Mandeville, but no conclusions were reached. On December 1 1932 a group of people actively involved in psychic matters decided to track down the errant ghost, and gathered in East Barnet valley. The group waited patiently for a long time in the valley. Then, just before the rising of the moon, they heard an uncanny noise like the clanking of armour. At first it was a distant sound, but then it came near, only to fade away. The people decided to walk in the direction of the fading sound and moved off towards Oak Hill; and there in the faint moonlight they saw the ghost in full armour of Geoffrey de Mandeville. As their report later stated: 'The glance was a fleeting one, but very distinct, and the sight is fixed in the minds of those who saw it as plainly as if it had been revealed in the midday sunlight'.

Another group scouring the area from the junction of Brookside and Cat Hill to Pymms Brook, saw Geoffrey de Mandeville again on December 25 1932. In the locality of Monk Frith they also saw the shadowy form of a long-legged, headless hound, the phantom dog which legend said often accompanied Geoffrey de Mandeville. A report appeared in the *Sunday Despatch*.

As far as can be seen Geoffrey de Mandeville appears in six-yearly cycles (1926, 1932, 1938, 1944, 1950, 1956, 1962, 1968) and is due to materialise again in 1974. Perhaps a party of ghost-hunters will see him once more as they wait cold and apprehensive among the gathering mists on Oak Hill!

Chapter 11

Romans, rogues & refugees

In 58 BC Caius Julius Caesar (c 101-44 BC), the famous Roman general, began his invasion of Gaul. Three years later he was mounting his first British expedition. To the people of Rome distant Britain was almost legendary: it was at once a source of mineral wealth and a mythical land. Its very size was in doubt, and its name, Britannia, offered the Roman imagination a new world of awesome isolation and uncharted risk. Hence the excitement with which Rome received the news of the invasion of Britain by Caesar. Indeed the *vox populi* judged the campaign as an exploit of unrivalled enterprise and daring, which proffered new laurels to their member of the triumvirate who had conceived it, and new prestige to the name of Imperial Rome.

Around 0900 hours on an autumn morning in 55 BC, 80 ships appeared off the cliffs of Dover not far from Walmer Beach. Ranged along the white cliff-tops thousands of charioteers, spearmen and horsemen looked down on the Roman flotilla as it pitched and rolled in the Channel swell. 'I saw the enemy forces standing under arms along the heights', wrote Caesar in his *De Bello Gallico*. 'At this point of the coast precipitous cliffs tower above the water, making it possible to fire directly onto the beaches. It was no place to attempt a landing, so we rode at anchor until 1530 hours awaiting the rest of the fleet. I summoned my staff and company commanders, passed on to them the information obtained by Volusenus*, and explained my plans. They were warned that, as tactical demands, particularly at sea, are always uncertain and subject to rapid change, they must be ready to act at a moment's notice on the briefest order from myself. The meeting broke up; both wind and tide were favourable, the signal was given to weigh anchor, and after moving about eight miles up channel the ships were grounded on an open and unevenly shelving beach.'

Thus was recorded the curtain-raiser to the first Roman attack on the British Isles; the prelude to the full scale invasion which was not to follow until nearly 100 years later. Nevertheless Britain remained a Roman province for over three centuries and was willed a civilisation whose relics and occultism remain.

The phantom legionaries

The Scottish Border Country known by the Roman soldiers and artisans has changed little although the oak, ash and birch trees covered more of the Border hill slopes in the days of the Romans. A relic connected with the Romans and with ghostly occurrences is to be found on the crest of a hill at Newstead, on the road to Melrose,

* Caius Volusenus—a trusted subordinate who acted as a military spy.

Roxburghshire. Here the Roman soldiers of Gnaeus Julius Agricola (AD 37-93) constructed a camp which they called *Trimontium* (the three mountains) after the three neighbouring Eildon Hills. The camp retained importance as a strategic post for defence and as a posting link for the road from *Bremenium* (High Rochester) to *Curia* (Borthwick Castle) and far beyond. Nowadays buses containing parties of tourists slow down to examine the plaque commemorating the camp, not far from which the ghosts of the Roman legionaries take on unusual tasks. The sounds of soldiers marching have been heard both by tourists and locals during the evening and early morning. Again farm-workers returning home have heard the mysterious sound of hammering and sawing. Occasionally sounds of trumpets and the clashing of cymbals have been heard.

Several years ago, in the courtyard of Barrow Farm on Mersea Island, near Colchester (Roman *Camulodunum*), a huge earthmound was excavated. The mound was found to contain the human ashes, funeral urn and personal possessions of a Roman centurion. Many who live in this sparsely populated part of Essex believe that these were the mortal remains of the Roman soldier whose ghost is said to have patrolled the salt marshes for centuries. The late Ted Allen, a wildfowler, who used to live in the Pyefleet Channel area, often reported seeing a Roman centurion wading this waterway. Many too of those who have been on their way home from the venerable little pub at the crossroads, the Peldon Rose, have affirmed hearing 'marching footsteps' with no soldier to be seen. A former rector (1871) of East Mersea, the Revd Sabine Baring-Gould (1834-1924), used to tell that on some nights one could clearly hear the clash of swords and the clang of breastplates as the ghostly Roman soldiers battled their way ashore at Pyefleet.

The gaunt Saxon chapel of St Cedd stands on that grassy mound at the end of the Roman way from Bradwell-juxta-Mare, Essex. This second oldest English Christian shrine was built in 654 from the stones and bricks of the Roman shorecastle of *Othona,* where the powerful *Comes Litoris Saxonici* (The Count of the Saxon Shore—who was in command of the coastal forts from the Wash to the Solent) had kept his garrison of Stablesian Horse. Near here a mounted Roman soldier has been repeatedly seen galloping from Bradwell, through the farmyard of Eastlands Farm and thence down the deeply rutted farmtrack (the last remnant of the Roman road) towards the chapel.

James Wentworth Day noted that a birdwatcher from one of the cottages near by once told him: 'I have been in bed . . . more than once and heard a horse come galloping down the road, without let or stop for gates. The hoofbeats were so loud in the night that the first time I thought the horse had run away from the farm. Then it got onto the grass field between the chapel and the cottage and I heard it go thundering by the garden gate, but the hoofbeats were muffled by the grass. I rushed out to see who it was . . . It was bright moonlight, as bright as day . . . there wasn't a horse in sight, yet I could still hear hoofbeats.'

In more recent times two priests from the Christian Community of Othona heard the centurion, and notes in the local historical society's archives record sightings in 1967 and 1968. Other locals report that the centurion also patrols from the direction of the Estuary, near Weymarks Farm, through the site of the Othona Community and towards St Peter's Chapel. Incidentally Roman legionaries are said to haunt the Grand Pump Room, Bath, and the George and Dragon Inn at Chester and The Castle Inn, Chichester.

A phantom legion is said to patrol still the ramparts of Flowers Barrow, Purbeck Hills, Dorset. The ghosts were seen in 1678, 1939 and 1970.

Stone Age refugees

Avebury, the enchanted village within the sacred circle of stones, the oldest temple of the ancient capital lands of England, has produced its own phantom horsemen. These fleet-footed ghosts have been said to haunt the green heart of the Wiltshire Downs since the days of the Romans; but Cranborne in Dorset can offer a spectral horseman which certainly predates the Roman legions.

Atop Cranborne Chase the wind sighs in the branches of the isolated clumps of pine and beech. As you walk by, sheep nibble unconcerned at the springy turf which has grown among the flints of the old Roman road. On some nights you run the risk of accosting a phantom traveller on this ancient highway. While motoring on the road between Cranborne and Handley one evening, a Fellow of the Society of Antiquaries encountered this ghost. Not far from where the remains of the Roman road to Old Sarum crosses the newly metalled highway, the scholar saw a horseman approach at a gallop. As horse and rider drew nearer, the man saw that the warrior had bare legs and, as he rode along, a grey cloak streamed out behind him. In his hand the mysterious rider carried what looked like a war axe.

For about 100 yards this phantom soldier thundered along by the side of the archaeologist's car, then vanished close by an ancient burial mound. Psychic researchers are not quite sure whether this is the phantom of a Roman mercenary, or the ghost of one of the Romans' enemies, the Ancient Britons, but several people have seen the ghost. One shepherd who saw the spectre emerge from a clump of trees near the site of a prehistoric camp says: 'I asked him for a light for my pipe, but he vanished as soon as I spoke!'

Many of the early European ghost stories of phantom soldiers spring undoubtedly from that racial remembrance of times past which is known as race memory. A traditional Welsh story fits this definition. It was long said that a burial barrow near Mold, Flintshire, was haunted by a soldier in golden armour. In the neighbourhood there was no historic story to account for his frequent appearances at the barrow's entrance, but the sepulchre's name *Bryn-yr-Ellylon* (Hill of the Fairy), would suggest that those in the locality considered it a place of the 'good people'. The barrow was excavated in 1832 and inside was found the skeleton of a tall man wearing a corselet of bronze which had been overlaid with gold. In his work on early man in Britain, Professor Sir William Boyd Dawkins states that the corselet is of Etruscan design and probably dates from Romano-British times. So this ghost, or at least a dim memory of the entombed man, must have persisted in the area of Mold for some 1,400 years.

Elliott O'Donnell recorded that an armoured phantom chieftain of Mynyddislwyn has been seen from time to time, right up to the early 1900s. Again, Rudyard Kipling, the creator of *Puck of Pooks Hill,* believed that the pre-historic vallums of Pook's Hill near his house at Burwash were haunted by contemporary spirits. He admitted as much to R. Thurston Hopkins, the psychic researcher and President of the Society of Sussex Downsmen, who organised a ghost hunt at Glad Wish Wood.

Tramping footsteps

Christina Hole, the prominent British folklorist and Honorary Editor of the magazine *Folklore,* once told me that in her experience the most recurring psychic phenomena concerning military phantoms was tramping feet! To support her opinions she quoted several cases including that of the tramping footsteps of a heavily booted man at Ford House, near Newton Abbot, Devon. These footfalls, thought to be those of

A menacing grenadier glowers at customers in the aptly named public house at 87 Wilton Road, London SW1.

A wartime photograph of Field Marshal Erwin Rommel. His unhappy ghost is said to stalk the sand ridges of Jarabub Oasis.

There is evidence that ghostly soldiers re-enact this historic raid. The Dieppe raid of World War II.

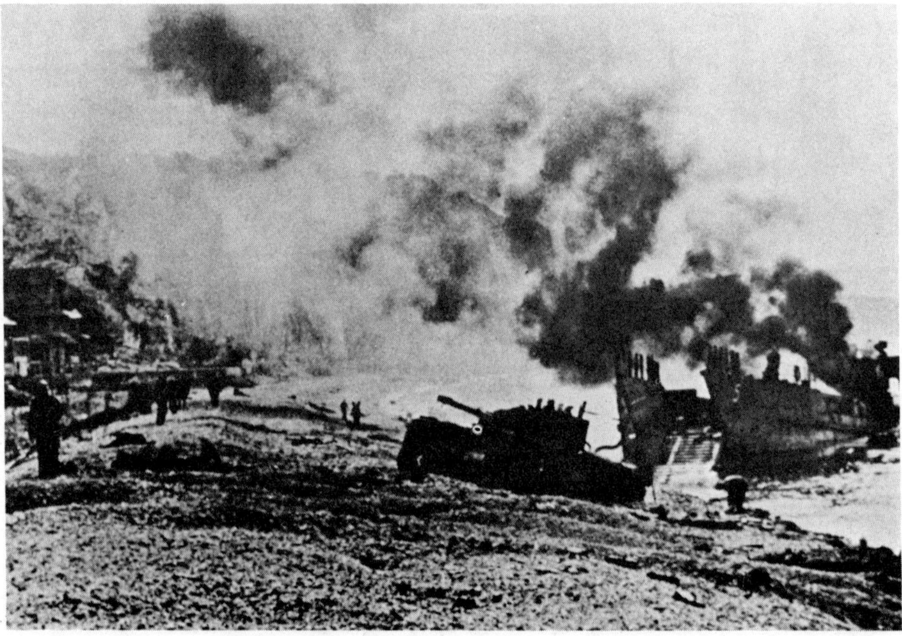

'Cruachan' mascot of the Argyll and Sutherland Highlanders (above left).

HRH Prince Philip (above right) presents leeks to the Welsh Guards.

The US Military Academy at West Point, New York (below), is the scene of a modern military phantom.

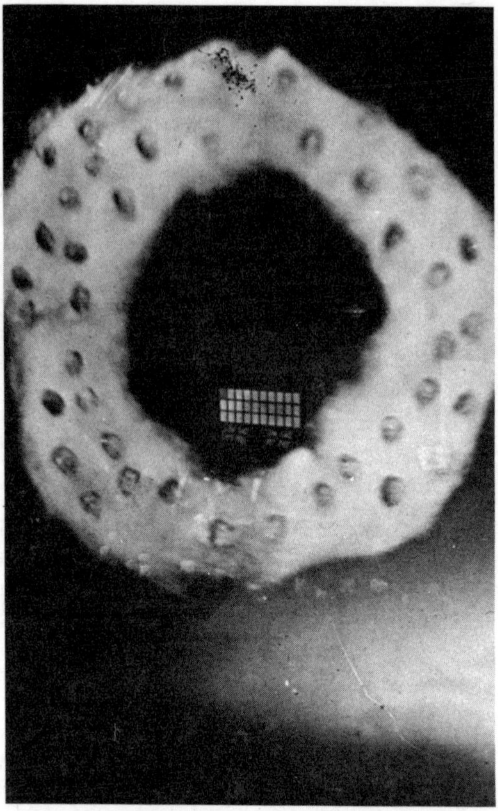

Two examples of 'spirit photography'. Phantom soldiers appear at the Albert Hall (left) and the Cenotaph (below).

William III (ruler of England from 1689-1702), who slept here on his first night in England, are heard passing hurriedly down corridors and through several of the rooms.

At Smarden, by the river Beult, Kent, there is a 14th century village inn called 'The Chequers'. Here, where sheep smugglers used to gather, walks the ghost of the soldier who was murdered soon after his return from the Napoleonic wars. His boots are heard slithering over the boards of the inn's two oldest bedrooms.

'Chappie O'Houndwood', however, is a ghost who actually showed off his boots. The old mansion of Houndwood lay on the north bank of the river Eye, about four miles south-west of Coldingham in Berwickshire. Since before the days (1856) of its owner, Mrs Sarah Coulson (who first recorded the happenings), this house has been reputedly haunted. No one has been able to recognise the ghost, but down the decades he has acquired the nickname of 'Chappie' (derived from the local dialect word 'chap', to knock). 'Chappie' is a peculiar ghost in that he only materialises his lower legs. From his knee he sports worn riding breeks and his feet are shod in blood-stained cavalry boots. As he strides up and down, he is accompanied by the sounds of steel on steel and the heavy breathing of a man *in extremis*.

Dover Castle battlements still ring, some say, to the footsteps of the little drummer boy who was murdered in the early 19th century. He was on his way, carrying the garrison's wages for the weekly pay parade, when he was waylaid and robbed of his wallets. His murderers decapitated him at a blow and his ghost still obligingly materialises headless: sometimes he drums his own funeral roll, sometimes he just paces up and down, presumably looking for his money and his head! In Wiltshire, on the other hand, ghostly drumming took on a more sinister role.

The drummer of Tedworth

To occult bibliographers the Revd Dr Joseph Glanvill, chaplain to Charles II and a Fellow of the Royal Society, is known for his works on witchcraft and also for his examination of two military phantoms. The first was his investigation of the spectral battle of Edgehill (see pp 19–23) and the second the curious case of the Tedworth Drummer, the earliest of well-attested poltergeist cases in England. From Glanvill's papers the story may be built up as follows.

It appears that, in March 1662, John Mompeson, a magistrate of North Tidworth, Wiltshire, ordered the arrest of an ex-military drummer turned vagrant called William Drury. It was said that Drury had used forged civil documents to defraud people of money. Mompeson tried the drummer, but set him free after confiscating his drum. He apparently promised Drury that if further enquiries into his character proved in his favour then the drum would be returned to him. In the meantime the drum was to be lodged with the Bailie of Ludgershall. For some reason the drum came into the possession of Mompeson himself a few weeks later (April 1662).

Whilst the magistrate was away in London strange occurrences were enacted at his home. Drumming was heard over the house, children were knocked off their feet and thrown into the air by invisible forces, a Bible was hidden in a cold grate, shoes were hurled at their owners, and some suffered the indignity of having their brimming chamberpots emptied into their beds; while a horse had one of its feet forced into its mouth.

Such occurrences were repeated for a month, usually for five days in succession, followed by three nights of silence, when the procedure began again. And then: 'after a monthe of peace, it came into the room where the Drum lay, four or five nights out of seven, within half an hour after they were in bed, continuing almost two hours.

The sign of it just before it came was, they still heard an hurling in the Air over the house, and at its going off, the beating of a Drum, like that at the breaking up of a Guard. It continued in this room for the space of two months, which time Mr Mompeson lay there to observe it'.

The drummings continued even though the drum was finally destroyed. Early in 1663 Drury was apprehended at Gloucester for stealing pigs and although clearly guilty, he escaped hanging. While he was in Gloucester gaol he idly boasted that he had 'plagued' Mompeson for taking his drum. As a result of this public indiscretion Drury was tried at Salisbury for witchcraft and sentenced to transportation. Glanvill reports that the phantom drumming ceased while Drury was out of England, but began again when he somehow managed to escape to return to England. It is not recorded how or when the phantom military tattoos ceased, but they went on for some time at intervals of several years. Some said that Drury was aided by the spirits of his fellow Cromwellian drummers, who had been killed in the Second Civil War (1648).

By way of comparison it may be remembered that there is also the case of the drummer of Cortachy. According to local superstition a drummer is heard in the vicinity of Cortachy Castle, north-west Angus, Scotland, whenever one of the Ogilvys (the Earls of Airlie) are about to die. The cases of phantom drumming preceding the deaths of Walter the 14th earl in 1819, the 15th earl David in 1849 and the 17th earl David Stanley William in 1900, are particularly well attested in family diaries and memory.

Yet another drummer, however, was to make his mark in British occult military history.

Black Toby's crime

On Monday June 26 1750, the village of Blythburgh, Suffolk, was crowded with soldiers from Sir Robert Rich's regiment of dragoons. These men, who had fought alongside their monarch George II (the last British king to command his army in the field) at Dettingen in 1743 against the French, were billeted for a time on the unwilling inhabitants of Blythburgh, and one of these soldiers was a particular nuisance. Tobias Gill, a constantly drunk negro drummer, was forcibly expelled from the White Hart inn three times on that black Monday.

Besotted with rum, Black Toby, as he was known, lurched across Blythburgh heath looking for a fight. As he stumbled over the bracken he caught sight of Ann Blakemore, a girl from Walberswick. Lust glinting in his red-framed eyes, Toby chased and caught Ann. Although she fought him, Toby overpowered her and raped the terrified girl, knotting his kerchief around her neck to stifle her screams. Black Toby pulled too hard and Ann Blakemore was strangled. All that night Toby Gill lay in a drunken swoon beside the body of the dead girl, and at dawn two farmers came across him there. They roused Toby, who put up a fight, but eventually he was dragged to the local magistrate and was subsequently tried for murder.

Toby was found guilty and was sentenced to hang. From the prison at Bury St Edmunds, he was marched to the crossroads at Blythburgh and was hung in chains on September 14 1750. For months his rotting carcass swung in the breeze and, in time, carrion crows, magpies and herring gulls stripped the flesh from his bones and pecked out his brains through the eye sockets. Although he was dead no one would venture past his chain-hung corpse; in death people feared Toby as much as they had when he violated their property in life. Even today his ghost is said to be seen moaning near the site of his execution. Sometimes, the old folk say, he can be seen furiously driving a hearse drawn by four black horses with flames coming from their nostrils. But no one dare stay long enough to obtain a good look at the awful sight.

For some reason drummer boys seem to have got themselves into all kinds of occult trouble. For instance, in the winter before the battle of Waterloo, a drummer boy home on leave fell in love with a girl from Potter Heigham, Norfolk. Though she returned his love, her father refused to accept a soldier as a son-in-law, and the two lovers were compelled to meet secretly at a place called Swim Coots on the Heigham side of Hickling Broad. Every February evening the young drummer would skate across the ice-covered Broad to meet her; then one night the ice gave way and the boy drowned, but his ghost skated to keep his tryst with his sweetheart. Sometimes still, at around seven on misty February evenings, the roll of a drum is heard across Hickling Broad. Then the phantom skater appears through the gloom, beating a tattoo as he tries to summon his long lost love.

Whenever the head of the St Quinton family (lords of Harpham) was about to die, a ghostly drumming is said to have sounded from a well in a field near the church (now known as the Drumming Well). Local legend has it that this was prophesied by the mother of a drummer boy who was accidentally knocked into the well by one of the St Quinton family.

Another version of the story is that William the Conqueror, after taking part in the battle near Harpham, promised to give the village and surrounding lands to the first person to reach Harpham. This was a drummer boy, but a knight named St Quinton knocked him into the well and claimed the village instead.

Drummer boys seem, indeed, to have a great proclivity to get themselves murdered! Matchem Bridge—now buried under the Great North Road near Brampton Hut Hotel, Huntingdonshire—was named after Gervase Matchem, a sailor who murdered a drummer boy in 1780. As R. H. Barham relates it in his *Ingoldsby Legends,* the boy's ghost appeared drumming to Matchem on Salisbury Plain and forced him to confess. The sailor was hanged at Huntingdon and afterwards gibbeted at the scene of his crime. The ragged corpse swung in its cage for many years and, one freezing night, a group of village lads drinking at Brampton Hut dared another lad to offer the corpse of Matchem some hot broth, and climbing a ladder, put the broth in the corpse's lips. As he did so a sepulchral voice intoned 'Cool it! Cool it!' The horrified lad fell off the ladder, and was said to be an idiot ever after.

Soldier spectre at Leith Hall

While I was in Aberdeen recently at a session of 'Meet the Author', I met American-born novelist Elizabeth Byrd, who told me her particular soldier ghost story. Her sighting had taken place on July 16 1968 when she was living at Leith Hall, Aberdeenshire. Dating from 1650, when its nucleus was constructed on the site (it is believed) of medieval Peill Castle by James Leith, the old house is now a National Trust property, having been donated by the Honourable Henrietta Leith-Hay in 1945.

Elizabeth slept in the east wing of Leith Hall and awoke early one morning to see a strange man looking at her across the bedroom. She saw him quite clearly for about two minutes as a solid ghost, as he stood between the dressing table and the foot of the bed. Seeming to be some six foot tall and massively built, the man was darkly bearded and wore a shirt and tight, dark-green trousers. Although she cannot swear to it, Elizabeth believes he was carrying a sword in his left hand: but his head was clearly bandaged. Slowly, though hesitantly, the ghost dematerialised as Elizabeth shouted in horror, 'Go away! Go away!'

With the help of Henrietta Leith-Hay's book *Trustie to the End* (Oliver & Boyd, Edinburgh, 1957), Elizabeth Byrd pieced together the possible identity of her uninvited ghostly visitor. Mrs Leith-Hay wrote: 'On the 21st December (1763), John Leith (the laird of Leith Hall) went to dine with some friends and neighbours at the tavern of Archibald Campbell, Vintner, in Castle Street, Aberdeen. There were fifteen of them, most of whom sat late over their wine. That was not a temperate age, though it was hard-headed. It took a deal of wine to put a man under the table . . . it did not take so much to make him quarrelsome . . .'

Apparently John Leith and a man called Abernethy of Mayen quarrelled, and Lord Forbes tried to make the peace. In the resultant confusion John Leith was shot in the forehead by Abernethy. 'John Leith was found lying in the Castlegate', wrote Mrs Leigh-Hay, 'and [*was*] carried to a house where his wife and eldest son were summoned'. Leith suffered for three days, and died on December 25 1763. Mrs Harriot Leith sued the Abernethy's and was granted £150 in 1769.

A verse of a ballad about the John Leith 'murder' intrigued Elizabeth Byrd and helped her with the possible identity of her ghost:

'Leith's servant bound the bleeding head
And bore him to his bed
And covered him with blankets warm
And due attention paid.'

Elizabeth Byrd mentions the encounter in her engrossing book *A Strange and Seeing Time* (Robert Hale, London, 1969); (see also her *Ghosts in my Life*, 1967), with the note that her husband Barry Gaunt also saw the soldier phantom on November 4 1968 and in 1967.

Wandering spirits in Ireland

In his entertaining book *The Lively Ghosts of Ireland* (Wolfe Publishing, London, 1968), American psychic researcher Hans Holzer mentions how he, with the aid of medium Sybil Leek, laid IRA (Irish Republican Army) ghosts near Listowel. These Irish guerrilla soldiers dated back to the 1920s, but there are far older soldier ghosts than that in Ireland. During the early 1800s this pamphlet was circulating in Ireland: *Apparitions which were seen at Portnedown Bridge after the Irish Massacre*. The massacre mentioned referred to the great rebellion which had broken out in Ireland in 1641, supported by the 'old Irish' and by the Norman Irish. It was inspired by hatred of the rule of Thomas Wentworth, Earl of Strafford (see p 92), who had been sent to Ireland by Charles I as Lord Deputy in 1631; and by the fear of what would happen under Puritan rule. Thousands of Protestants perished. The ghostly 'evidence' was claimed to have been originally supplied by Sir John Temple, once Master of the Rolls in Ireland.

'James Shaw, of Market Hill, in the county of Armagh, innkeeper, deposeth, that many of the Irish rebels, in the time of this deponent's restraint, and staying among them, told him very often, and it was a common report, that all those who lived about the bridge of Portnedown were so affrighted with the cries and noise made there, as that they durst not stay, but fled away thence, so as they protested, affrighted to Market Hill, saying, they durst not return thither for fear of those cries and spirits, but took grounds and made *creaghs*, in or near the parish of Mulabrac. Jurat 14 Aug 1642.

'Joan, the relict of Gabriel Constable, late of Durmant, in the county of Armagh, gent, deposeth and saith, that she often heard the [*rebel soldiers*] Owen O'Farren,

Patrick O'Connellan, and divers others of the rebels at Durmant, earnestly say, protest, and tell one another, that the blood of some of those that were knocked on the head and afterwards drowned at Portnedown bridge, still remained on the bridge and would not be washed away; and that often there appeared [*soldier phantoms*] . . . breast-high above the water, at or near Portnedown, which did most extremely and fearfully screech and cry out for vengeance . . . and that their cries and screeches did so terrify the Irish thereabouts, that none durst stay nor live longer there, but fled and removed farther into the country, and this was common report amongst the rebels there; and that it passed for a truth among them, for anything she could ever observe to the contrary. Jurat 1 Jan 1643.'

The ghosts of other soldiers were seen in the area of Portnedown by Katherine Coke and Elizabeth Price, and in the same pamphlet Arthur Azlum of Clowargher attested that he saw rebel soldiers drown several of their opponents in the river Belturbet. Some weeks afterwards the ghosts of the drowned were seen by himself and one Rurmore O'Reby 'the then sheriff'.

Irish folklore contains many instances of ghosts. From time to time the pile of stones in the ruined north aisle of Kilmallock Abbey, county Limerick, exudes the ghostly tears of Sir Maurice Fitzgerald, the fabulous White Knight. Once the occupant of grim Michelstown Castle, County Cork, this knight earned his name from the light coloured armour he wore: but he perpetrated many unchivalrous acts. For his penance for killing Elgiva O'Rourke, daughter of the Prince of Brefni, Sir Maurice was made by fate to weep forever. Thus many testified that however dry the day there was always moisture on the White Knight's marble effigy. Even when the tomb was smashed by acts of vandalism the stones still wept the penitential tears.

Oscar Wilde's mother, Jane Francesca Agnes Lady Wilde (1824-98) known as 'Speranza', also told of a 'watery ghost soldier', who plagued fishermen who were out on the Shannon. This was the ghost of a deserter from Athlone barracks, who committed suicide by cutting his throat while perching on the parapet of a bridge.

A daughter of the regiment

Barracks are a set of buildings with all conveniences for human habitation generally used for the accommodation of units of fighting forces. The nature, site and construction of barracks are, of course, usually determined by the strategic or other employment of the troops concerned. So, soldiers of the British sovereign's bodyguard were billeted in barracks which were built in London, and at places suitably near royal palaces and residences. Barracks in England situated near the coast are usually constructed more in the nature of forts while those in the country were chosen more for health reasons. In Britain there is a fine collection of regimental barracks providing many examples of architecture (particularly 18th century), but strangely enough few barrack archives record hauntings.

During the early part of 1804, a woman's ghost was seen by several Coldstream Guard sentries, who were serving at Wellington Barracks, London, then known as Recruit House. The sightings caused so much alarm that some of the soldiers were called upon to make signed declarations on oath before magistrate Sir Richard Ford, who had been engaged for the purpose by the Commanding Officer on the permission of the Secretary of War (two Secretaries of War took an interest in the case, Robert Hobart, the 2nd earl of Buckingham and his successor, John Jeffreys, 2nd earl of Camden).

One statement, dated January 15 1804, made by Welshman George Jones (b 1785), is of particular interest: 'I do so solemnly declare that when on guard at Recruit House on or about the 3rd inst., about half-past one in the morning, I perceived the figure of a woman, without a head, rise from the earth at a distance of about two feet before me. I was so alarmed at the circumstance that I had not the power to speak to it, which was my wish. But I distinctly observed that the figure was dressed in a red striped gown, with red spots between each stripe, and that part of the dress and figure appeared to me to be enveloped in a cloud. In about the space of two minutes, whilst my eyes were fixed on the object, it vanished from my sight. I was perfectly sober and collected at the time, and being in great trepidation, called the next sentinel, who met me half-way, and to whom I communicated the strange sight I had seen'. This phantom walked between the canal, which then ran through St James' Park, and the Cockpit.

Sir Richard Ford collated his evidence but produced no rational account for the odd occurrences. Knowing the archives of the Footguards well, he searched through the histories and found a note that around 1785 a sergeant in the Guards had killed his wife. In an attempt to make identification of her corpse difficult, the soldier had hacked the head off and had then thrown the corpse into the canal. Witnesses described the body's clothes as cream satin with red stripes and red spots between the stripes!

During the night of January 18 1804, another sentry saw the headless ghost whilst at point No 3. He fainted and was found in that state by an orderly officer and the sergeant of the guard. The incident was duly reported by the laconic sergeant in the daybook. Later a Church of England clergyman obtained permission to investigate and spent the night at point No 3. He recited prayers for the dead for many hours, but saw nothing. The headless ghost was not seen again, but the sentry posts were moved just in case she should return.

Not long afterwards another sentry, Richard Donkin, swore that whilst he was on guard behind the Armoury House at midnight, he heard a loud noise coming from an empty house near the post. He later testified: 'At the same time I heard a voice cry out, "Bring me a light! Bring me a light!" The last word was uttered in so feeble and changeable a tone of voice that I concluded some person was ill, and consequently offered them my assistance. I could, however, obtain no answer to my proposal, although I repeated it several times, and as often the voice used the same terms. I endeavoured to see the person who called out, but in vain. On a sudden the violent noise was renewed, which appeared to me to resemble sashes of windows lifted hastily up and down, but that they were moved in quick succession and in different parts of the house, nearly at the same time, so it seemed to be impossible that one person could accomplish the whole business. I heard several of my regiment say they have heard similar noises and proceedings, but I have never heard the calls accounted for'.

The house was officially searched by representatives of the Coldstream Guards, but as it had been empty for years nothing was found of recent human habitation. The incident and that of the headless woman remain open mysteries.

Yarn of the jolly grenadier

Knowing that I was collecting stories of phantom soldiers, Joseph Braddock of Wadhurst, whose book *Haunted Houses* is still eagerly sought in antiquarian bookshops, brought this yarn to my notice.

A step or two away from St George's Hospital The Grenadier inn stands at 18 Wilton Row, London SW1. In George IV's day the inn was called The Guardsman and tradition has it that it was used as a billet for some of the Duke of Wellington's officers. This might very well be true because the inn is actually situated at the junction of Wilton Row and Old Barrack Yard: the latter was once part of old Knightsbridge Barracks which L.T.Stanley attests in his *The Old Inns of London* (Batsford, London, 1957) was pulled down long ago. Apsley House, the Duke's own residence (see p 116) is close at hand.

There is a small card room at the inn which once formed a part of the officers' mess and it was here one September in the early 1800s that a Guards officer was caught cheating. Angry and ashamed the officer's brother subalterns are said to have flogged him unintentionally to death, and legend claims that the ghost of the officer walks on the anniversary of his death.

Successive landlords have reported unusual happenings at the inn and today staff are reluctant to sleep at the hostelry, particularly during September. Both guests and staff have seen the ghostly grenadier who seems jolly in aspect. The ghost has not been seen during recent years, but the staff believe that the regular occurrence of minor mischiefs is his work; such as the sound of footsteps in unoccupied rooms, the switching on and off of electric lights, the apporting of objects from one room to another, and the strange tendency for beer bottle tops to fly spontaneously in a horizontal direction! The ghostly grenadier does not confine his activities to his familiar inn: residents at nearby houses in Wilton Row often complain that taps, switches and levers are manipulated by unseen hands! Yes, the mysterious happenings at The Grenadier inn have all the makings of a classic poltergeist case.

The unhappy German field marshal

Sheik Ami ben Yosef has a favourite yarn concerning the unhappy German field marshal who walks the desert on certain nights. The ghost was first seen by the sheik's guards one night on the sand ridges above Jarabub Oasis. Rough hands awoke the sheik from his slumbers and a terrified guard garbled that he had just seen a ghostly soldier outlined against the sky among the dunes. The sheik spat his disgust at the man, but followed to see for himself. Sure enough, there was the ghostly soldier walking up and down along the line of dunes. Occasionally the figure stopped, booted feet apart with hands behind his back. Over his garrison cap, set at a jaunty angle, a pair of goggles glinted in the desert moonlight.

Sheik Ami ordered his guard to fire a round over the figure's head, but this had no effect. The men, having fetched a holy man just in case a quick prayer of exorcism was needed, padded nearer across the warm sand; and then the sheik saw for himself the outline of the man he had feared all those years before; he whispered the name of the man to his followers.

Field Marshal Erwin Rommel (b. 1891) was probably the ablest German general engaged in World War II. His conduct of the war during the North Africa campaign won him high praise and brought the redoubtable Afrika Korps nearly to Alexandria. But Rommel's involvement in politics, and his collusion in the attempted assassination of Hitler on July 20 1944 brought his downfall. Rommel was given the choice of trial or suicide and he chose the latter. But why does his restless spirit walk the sands of Libya, striking terror into the hearts of the Bedouin nomads? Does the 'Desert Fox' brood over the mistakes of El Alamein? Or is it happiness which locks his earthbound spirit to the dunes? Does his spirit dwell fondly on the memory of the Afrika Korps' finest hour, when the German tanks moved relentlessly down the road from Tobruk to Alamein? No one knows as yet, for no one has had the courage to remain long enough to ask the ghost!

Chapter 12

American tales

General Garfield's experience

James Abram Garfield (1831-81), 20th President of the United States, gave little publicity during his lifetime to his psychic experiences. A native of Orange, Ohio, he was forced by the death of his father to earn his own living at an early age. Around the year 1837 Garfield began to have 'strange ghostly visitations' of his father's wraith, which advised him on what to do. The early advice was to follow a pattern in which he was to go to Hiram College, Ohio, and from there to Williams College, Massachusetts, from where he graduated and later became a professor.

Garfield told several of his close friends that on the outbreak of the Civil War he was appointed to command a volunteer regiment; an appointment he was advised to accept by his dead father.

As a leader of the Republican party he stood for the presidency and was elected in March 1881. He later identified himself, on occult advice, with the movement for the reform of the civil service and in this way alienated many of his supporters. In July 1881 he was shot by a disappointed fanatic who had unsuccessfully sought office. Garfield did, however, publicly admit that he had a premonition that he was going to be killed; he told all this to a close aide who was able to testify to its veracity later.

Garfield, incidentally, was one of those Presidents who were deemed to be assailed by occult bad luck, especially that connected with numbers. All Presidents of the United States, it is said, who are elected at 20-year intervals will die in office. Garfield was one, the others were: William Henry Harrison (1840); Abraham Lincoln (1860); Garfield in 1880; William McKinley (1900); Warren G. Harding (1920); Franklin D. Roosevelt (1940); and John F. Kennedy (1960). One might imagine that the Presidential candidates of 1980 will feel a trifle uneasy!

President Abraham Lincoln, of course, admitted to having a certain premonitory dream which occurred three times in relation to important battles of the Civil War, and a fourth time on the eve of his assassination.

The embarrassing ghost at West Point

The spectre first appeared on All Hallows' Eve (October 31 1972) as a shimmering and luminous shade wearing a neat down-turning moustache and a US Cavalry officer's uniform of circa 1830. The ghost appeared through a door in the bureau area of Room 4714 of the 47th Division Barracks at the US Military Academy in West Point, New York, frightening two 'plebs' who live there.

Army upper-class men kept watch in Room 4714 and the ghost obligingly returned to waft to the bathroom, ruffle a bathrobe and turn on a shower. The ghost appeared again in November 1972 in room 4714 making the room turn cold.

Since then four cadets have seen the ghost and one has felt its presence. Since December 1972 room 4714 has been 'Off limits'. 'It's a damned embarrassment to the Point', said the CO!

Help from the soldier-priest

During a still evening in the spring of 1893, Dr Herman Hilprecht, famous Assyriologist of the University of Pennsylvania, was working at his desk. He was getting bogged down with his translations. Behind his desk was a statue of the Babylonian god Nebo, and Dr Hilprecht was staring at this as he pondered over the difficult translations he had in hand. The pressure was building up as Dr Hilprecht had to translate the Assyrian inscriptions by the next day; but somehow he just couldn't get it right. The Doctor was talking aloud: 'I cannot say more than that they are the fragments of ancient writing belong to the Cassite period of Babylonian history'. Thinking hard all the time Dr Hilprecht sat back in his chair and closed his eyes. Before him evolved a mental picture of his desk, the fragments he was working on and the statue of the god Nebo. In this state of mind the learned man dropped into a slumber, yet all the time the picture of his study remained in his conscious mind. Suddenly in Dr Hilprecht's trance-dream there appeared a priest of old pre-Chistian Nippur. From his clothes Dr Hilprecht was able to recognise him as one of the soldier-priests.

The figure beckoned to him and Dr Hilprecht felt himself get up out of his chair. Now he was no longer in his study but was being led into another room of impressive proportions.

'I have brought you here', Hilprecht heard the priest say, 'in order to help you'.

'*Asipu*—Where am I?' the Doctor said, using the old Babylonian form of address.

In his low, smooth tone the priest replied: 'You are at Nippur, in the treasure chamber of the Temple of Bel, king of heaven and earth and father of the gods. It is called *E-Kur,* signifying "mountain house". The staged tower above us is built in imitation of a mountain. The sacred shrine of the god is on the very top.'

'*Asipu,* will you tell me where this treasure chamber is located—which side of the chapel?' asked the scholar.

'On the south-east side,' replied the priest. Hilprecht now realised that he seemed to be back in the exact location where the fragments he was trying to translate had been found, only they were discovered in a different time sequence—thousands of years on! 'Tell me priest, of the words I am trying to translate?'

The soldier-priest directed Dr Hilprecht to a white wall of the temple, and on this wall he traced with dye one of the translations which had been puzzling Dr Hilprecht:

Dingar Ninib du mu
Dingir en lil
Luga l-a-ni ir
Ku-rigalzu
Patesi dingir Enib
In-na ba

'The inscription which puzzles you dates from 1780 before the coming of your Christ', said the priest, 'and means in the language of your country and era: "To the god Ninib, son of Bel, his lord, has Kurigalzu, pontifex of Bel, presented this".

In a moment they were back in Hilprecht's study and the priest was pointing to the manuscript on the Doctor's desk. The manuscript, for which Hilprecht was doing the translations, was for a book which was the joint effort of himself and the brilliant German Assyriologist Professor Frederick Delitzsch, professor of Semitic languages at Berlin. 'Let us look at the second piece which puzzles you'. The priest pointed with his baton: 'See here. Both you and your colleague have suggested that *Nebuchadnezzar* means "Nebo protect my mason's mortar board"—This is not so. The word means: "Nebo protect my boundary".'

The next instant the soldier-priest vanished.

The Doctor opened his eyes, and before he forgot he jotted down the answers the soldier-priest had given him. Later he told of the strange 'visitor' to his wife who advised him to say nothing about the incident to his colleagues. Dr Hilprecht would have nothing of this however, and went on record as saying that he owed the answers to a soldier-priest of old Babylonia.

The last Civil War veteran

On December 19 1959 Walter Williams died, only a month after celebrating his 117th birthday by eating barbecued pork while a band played 'Dixie'. Williams was something of a character in his lifetime and is famous as the last survivor of the American Civil War of 1861-5, in which he fought as a cavalryman under the banner of the Confederacy. During his later years Williams delighted in re-telling campaigns of Terry's Texas Rangers and of general Civil War exploits. Among his many interests, too, was the collecting of occult phenomena concerning the Civil War, like superstitions, omens and ghost stories concerning its combatants. One story in particular fascinated him for he had known the participants, and it is taken from a battered old notebook once in Williams' possession. Under the title 'Ghost's Testimony in Court' is the inscription in pencil 'William Hughes and Thomas Blondie were known to WW'.

William Hughes was congratulating himself as he rode his black mare home on a moonlit November night in 1867. 'There's not a better mare to be had for the money in Abiline,' he meditated, 'nor in the whole of Texas for that matter.'

Then he fell to thinking about his good friend Thomas Blondie, who had died in the Civil War. He had bought the mare that day from Peek Blondie, Thomas' brother, who was administering his estate. Peek was a good friend of his, too, and he certainly had given him a bargain in that mare.

Hughes and Peek Blondie had been soldiers together in the Civil War, and had been initimate friends for many years. Thomas had died in battle, and Hughes had been with him when he breathed his last. Thomas had made many mistakes, but was a good man and a good soldier—always he could be depended upon to keep his word, Hughes reflected.

The black mare was going along in the moonlight at a good steady pace. As he was getting sleepy, Hughes was glad that home was less than a mile further on. They were alongside the graveyard, and that was scarcely a mile from home.

He thought of the tombstones looking awfully white and tall, but maybe it was because the moonlight was so bright. He thought of Thomas' grave—they had brought him there from the battlefield in a tarpaulin—and he hoped that Peek would erect a tombstone one day. Surely there'd be enough money. Thomas had been well-off, what with his Texas stake, livestock and everything. Suddenly the mare jumped—half across the road—and neighed loudly. Hughes jerked the bridle, but the mare pranced around in a semi-circle and stopped against the graveyard fence.

To his amazement Hughes saw Thomas Blondie standing in uniform at the other side of the fence, looking at him. For a full minute he stood there looking at rider and horse, and then he appeared to melt into the moonlight. The horse shivered and Hughes stared. He was cold and speechless with terror. He had waited for his old friend to speak but Blondie had just stood there, looking. Hughes, on regaining his wits, spurred the mare home; and with a sigh of relief slid into his comfortable bed beside his sleeping wife. He decided to stay nothing to anyone about his encounter.

Weeks went by and Hughes followed the local gossip about Thomas Blondie's affairs. Peek Blondie was handling everything, but one aspect intrigued most folks.

'Well, I'm thinking about Thomas' four illegitimate kids,' intoned Rich Chesterton of the Merifold store. 'What are they a'goin' to get. Thomas always provided for them well. I hope he fixed it in his will so they'll get somethin'. He's got no wife and reg'lar children to leave it to, and Peek and Sadie Blondie have no children, and they're well fixed. Yes, I say the children should have it.'

The gossip went on and at last a legal tangle was discussed in all the saloons. Because they were illegitimate Thomas Blondie's four children could inherit nothing, and that Peek was keeping the lot for himself. A day after he had heard all this William Hughes was ploughing in his far field when Thomas Blondie's ghost appeared to him again in broad daylight; the ghost made no communication.

A few nights later, when he was in bed with his wife, Hughes distinctly heard the discharge of cannon far away, and heard the voice and groans of Thomas Blondie just as it had been before the soldier's death. This time there was a witness: Mrs Hughes heard the groans, so they both got up and searched the house carefully. All was quiet.

The Hughes were just dropping off to sleep again when William felt a painful blow on his forehead; he cried out and both he and his wife sat up in bed. No one was in the room, but Hughes' temples were running with blood from a small wound in the hairline.

From that time on the shade of Thomas Blondie never left Hughes' side for more than an hour or two. It said nothing to him, just stared. After a while the ghost did speak.

The ghost of the old soldier instructed William Hughes to go to Peek Blondie and remind him of a conversation Thomas Blondie had had with him before he went to the war. Apparently Thomas had told his brother that he wanted to provide for his four illegitimate children and that Peek was to see to it in the event of Thomas' death.

William Hughes told Peek Blondie of seeing the ghost and the conversation he had had with it. Peek laughed in Hughes' face and ran him off his land. Strangely enough, however, two days later Peek Blondie was found by the river impaled to a tree with a short sword which had been in fashion during the Civil War; beside Peek on the ground were the deeds of his inherited property torn into shreds. The murderer of Peek Blondie was never found and the case remains open.

Peek's widow Sadie was left in charge of the estate, and she was in the same mind as her husband: no shrift for the four illegitimate children. In time, on the strength of the ghost's message relayed to them by William Hughes, the four illegitimate children brought a suit against Sadie Blondie.

Because of the conspicuous part played by the ghost in the case, it became one of the most sensational legal battles in American legal history. The purpose of the trial was mainly to get the facts of the ghost's appearance on record; this object was accomplished.

Everyone knew well, law or no law, that Sadie Blondie would never withold from Thomas' children a fair share of the proceeds from the estate after William Hughes' testimony. No lawyer would have dared to advise her to do that after the publicity, and no one connected with the case was willing to incur the displeasure of the soldier's ghost. So, in due time, the children of Corporal Thomas Blondie of the 14th-15th Texas Brigade were provided for.

Chapter 13

Supplement on the Dieppe Raid

During August 1952 Mrs Dorothy Norton, 32, with her two young children, and in company with her sister-in-law Mrs Agnes Norton, went for a holiday to Dieppe. This French seaport and watering place in the Département Seine-Maritime, on the English Channel, lies 33 miles north of Rouen. Although by no means a spectacular holiday resort, Dieppe has a 15th century castle and a fine church dating back to the 13th century. One time a lair of Norman pirates, the town was occupied by the English during 1420-35 (Hundred Years' War). In the wars of religion, Dieppe was a Huguenot stronghold, but its prosperity declined after the revocation of the Edict of Nantes in 1685 in particular, and after the English and Dutch bombardments of 1694 in general. Dieppe with its trade in wine, fish and fruit still has a quiet charm of its own. It had indeed plenty to enable the two Norton women to relax, and for the children to enjoy. The Nortons wanted and sought a quiet holiday but, for reasons quite beyond explanation, they did not achieve this.

Today the name Dieppe conjures up for the average Briton the famous raid of the Second World War: the Combined Operations raid carried out on the night of August 18-19 1942 by a force of 5,000. Canadian troops, a detachment of the US Ranger Battalion and approximately 1,000 officers and men of No 3 and No 4 Royal Marine Commandoes took part; they were embarked in naval vessels and transports and were protected by warships and by a continuous fighter plane 'umbrella' of the RAF. The purpose of the raid was to get information about German defences in the west, and on conditions to be expected in a large-scale assault on a strongly held Channel port. Among the objectives were, of course, the two powerful German batteries of 5.9 coast defence guns at Berneval on the right, and at Varengeville-sur-mer on the left of Dieppe; and a radio-location station which was used in German attacks on British Channel convoys.

Basically the plan for the landings was to beach men at half a dozen points, preceded by an intense naval bombardment, followed by quick action fire from Spitfire and Hurricane aircraft on the main defences. Tanks were to be put ashore to support the infantry and to destroy selected objectives.

For their *pension* in 1952, the Nortons chose a pleasant three-storeyed house facing the sea at Puys near Neuville-Dieppe. This house was supposed to have been used by German troops as a headquarters around the period of the raid. Dorothy and Agnes Norton shared a bedroom on the second floor, and the children shared a room two doors away. From the windows of the *pension* the beach (code-named Blue Beach) could clearly be seen, the site of the part of the famous raid of 1942 which did not go according to plan.

The approach to the French coast by the raiders was betrayed through certain transport ships running into some enemy-armed trawlers. At Varengeville-sur-mer (about 5 miles out of Dieppe), No 4 Commando landed at Orange Beach according to plan, storming the Hess and Vasterival batteries, taking prisoners, destroying their guns and ammunition dumps. At the same time, Canadian troops (South Saskatchewan Regt) and the Queen's Own Cameron Highlanders landed at Pourville, and men of the Royal Regiment of Canada landed at Puys—the hamlet where the Norton's chose their *pension*—but a delay in attacking upset their plans and they were met by heavy German firing. The Royal Regiment of Canada suffered heavy casualties. Despite the losses valuable lessons were learnt at Dieppe which were to assist the Normandy invasion. But the slaughter and acts of gallantry were to leave a psychic aura over the Dieppe beaches which were to affect the Nortons ten years later.

At the time of the strange happenings the Nortons' pleasant and, up to then uneventful holiday was drawing to a close. At 0420 hours on Saturday August 4 1952, Agnes Norton got out of bed, went out of the room, and returned to say to Dorothy: 'Did you hear that noise?' Dorothy had! For during a period of 20 minutes both had heard quite clearly the rattle of machine-gun fire, cries, shouts and words of command (in English). Together the women went out onto the balcony and listened: above a general hubbub they could hear the crash of guns and the whine of dive-bombers.

It seemed extraordinary to the Norton women as they stood and listened that the children had not been awakened—indeed, why was it that none of the *pension's* other guests had been aroused?

Looking at their watches at 0450 hours the women were able to log exactly when a lull came in the noise, But at 0505 hours it started up again. louder than ever. Another lull came at 0540 hours, and the noise recommenced at 0550 hours with an intensity of aeroplane engines; by 0620 hours the sounds seemed to have drifted away a little.

Carefully the Nortons made a note of the times of these extraordinary noises, and it was later possible to confirm that they coincided with the sequence of events of the Dieppe Raid:

0347 hours: The gun-boat leading No 3 Commando runs into armed trawlers, and is disabled. The Commando landing craft disperse. No 4 Commando lands and destroys the Hess battery. Canadians land but are pinned down by heavy and accurate fire. (A period of comparative silence, because of the delay in landing.)

0450 hours: Delay in landing.

0507 hours: Landing effected. (All hell breaks loose.)

0512 hours: Bombardment of Dieppe by destroyers.

0513 hours: Hurricanes swoop. (Increased aeroplane engine noise.)

0520 hours: The main Dieppe force under intense fire, beginning of heroic attack.

0540 hours: Pause in naval bombardment. (Lull noticed by Nortons.)

0550 hours: Increased air attacks.

0600 hours: The force commander decides to commit his reserve—the Fusiliers Mont-Royal—but they too are pinned down.

Some time later, after the Nortons had returned from holiday, Guy W. Lambert, CB, President of the Society for Psychical Research 1956-58, investigated the Nortons' story. He notes: 'Apart from the coincidence of the times, showing an analogy between the noises of the original Dieppe raid and those heard by the Nortons, the obvious explanation of what they had heard could be ruled out. For instance, they could not have been listening to wind-borne noises from some war films being shown at a cinema—there was no cinema in Puys, nor was any radio programme of such a character being broadcast.' Could the Nortons have read up the times of the various attacks and landings in some official account, and recounted them afterwards? Today the answer is still no. They could not have done this for the official account of the Dieppe Raid was not published until early 1953, some five months after their experience.

Recently, it seems, another World War II location has provided a psychic mystery. Are wartime manoeuvres being psychically re-enacted on the site of the famous Maginot Line? This question was posed by the *Worcester Evening News*, after testimony from half-a-dozen witnesses describing unaccountable activities near the crumbling remnants of what were the world's greatest fortifications.

The Maginot Line was the French system of fortifications along the whole of the eastern frontier of France, from Belgium to Switzerland; the greatest part of which was situated in Alsace-Lorraine. The fortifications were built during 1927-35 under the direction of André Maginot (1877-1932), the French Minister of War in 1922 and 1929, and the French President Painlevé. The scheme consisted of thousands of forts—of several storeys—set deep in the earth, containing complete underground towns, railways, power stations and so on. It cost more than £30,000,000 to build and was outflanked by the Germans in 1940.

For 33 years the formidable defence works have been silent, but recently psychic researchers have discovered data which would lead to the belief that the Maginot Line is by no means dead. Early in 1973 two spinsters, Marie and Brigitte Larousse, were walking through fields containing some of the derelict emplacements when they both heard simultaneously 'what sounded like heavy lorries in the vicinity. Then we heard shouting and what appeared to be troops on the march'. The two women assumed that it was a military exercise somewhere near, but on a closer examination of the area from an elevation could see nothing; the overgrown roads were empty. The commanding officer of a local garrison denied that there had been any troop movements in the area when similar reports were published in a French newspaper.

Then came the statement of farm-worker Pierre Chalmain: driving his tractor near the Maginot Line he claimed he heard 'the sound of soldiers singing as they worked'. When he investigated he claims to have seen a battalion digging trenches in front of a blockhouse. Going back to the same area the following week he found that the ground had been untouched for 'at least thirty years'.

New evidence came to light soon afterwards from two schoolgirls from the village of Trente. With two friends, they said they watched an army convoy driving across the fields to the Maginot Line. It was loaded with troops and equipment. The route was an old supply run, which since 1947 had been so farmed as to be impassable.

No more than a week later insurance agent Charles Bonet was driving from Metz to Luxembourg, when his car broke down in an isolated spot. As he waited for a *garagiste* to arrive he listened to some pop music on his car radio. Suddenly the frequency changed and a military play appeared to be broadcast. Two officers were discussing an underground ammunition store. Then an urgent voice broke through, announcing that it was General Maxine Weygand (1867-1965, appointed chief of the French general staff in 1940 and a member of the Vichy Government), and that the Maginot Line was to be abandoned as part of a plan to withdraw French troops. The programme then returned to pop music. Puzzled, Bonet asked the local radio station to confirm their programme for that day: there was nothing in their transmissions to match what Bonet had heard. Could Bonet have inexplicably been tuned into events which had been first enacted 30 years ago? No one knows, nor can anyone offer a rational explanation; but there seems to have been more occult action on the Maginot Line since it was abandoned than during all the years it was France's main defence system!

Chapter 14

Some military traditions

Some customs, cults and ceremonies

A great deal of the military ceremonial which once appertained to the armies of Europe has died out. In Britain, however, a few remain. One of the most interesting ceremonies is the Tattoo, or Beating the Retreat, which takes place wherever soldiers are stationed. The Retreat is by far the oldest custom, which first appeared in the 16th century as the 'Watch Setting'. This consisted of prolonged drum beating at sunset to warn the night guard to mount, and to give notice to soldiers beyond the confine of camp (or town, or city walls) to return, for the gates were to be closed. The Tattoo (derived from a Dutch word to turn off beer taps!) originated in the 17th century, when drummers were sent out to beat through the streets at dusk to rout the soldiers out of the inns and brothels and back to billet. This in time developed into a musical performance—as did the Retreat. In the case of the Tattoo a bugler sounds the 'Last Post', to signify that the day is at an official end. (NB: in theory, a bugler does not mark the end of the Retreat, as there are a few more hard drinking hours left!)

Beating the Credits is another old military 'sound ceremony'. By an Act of Parliament of 1696, regiments leaving billets were ordered to warn 'by sound of trumpet and beat of drum' local merchants so that they could make sure that soldiers who owed them money paid up before leaving. Today this ceremony takes the form of a ceremonial march through a town as a gesture of friendship.

The military cult of the Champion is still alive in Britain: this cult has its origins in chivalry, although it dates from earlier times. In the judicial combats of the Middle Ages, the Champion was the hired combatant who took the place of women, children, aged persons, or any incapable of fighting their own battles. These Champions were not of noble birth, rarely were they dubbed knights, and in general they were regarded as disreputable persons. Later, in the age of chivalry, the name acquired a higher meaning and was applied to a knight proper who challenged or defended on behalf of an injured nobleman, lady or child.

The office of the Sovereign's Grand Champion was begun by William the Conqueror in England, and was inherited by the Dymoke Family of Scrivelsby, Lincolnshire. It was the champion's duty to ride on a white charger—fully clad in armour—into Westminster Hall during the coronation ceremony. There, throwing down his gauntlet, he challenged any person who dared to deny the sovereign's right to the throne. The custom was discontinued in this form at the coronation of William IV. The Dymoke family still retain the privilege of Sovereign's Grand Champion, which is symbolised by the carrying of the Royal Standard.

The cult of Britannia

Of all the symbolism used in military occultism, for the British soldier down the ages the 'Spirit of the Country'—epitomised by Britannia—has been the firm favourite. Soldiers from every regiment have attested the 'good luck' factors behind Britannia, and if a soldier was not lucky enough to buy a charm with a Britannia symbol—or was not artistic enough to scratch one on metal himself—then he kept a coin showing Britannia somewhere in his pack. Contrary to popular belief, Britannia has a long history as a military cult emblem.

Whenever the Romans conquered a nation they did not ride rough-shod over the beliefs and superstitions of their new subject people. Instead, they often set up their own altars alongside those of the vanquished so that the whole mystic pantheon of gods was thus placated at one and the same time.

Each wood, valley and mountain in the part of Europe conquered by the Romans would be deemed by the legionaries to have a native Genius, or a good or evil spirit, which would have to be propitiated as soon as possible after the arrival of the legions. Thus, altars with inscriptions like the one found at the junction of the Leader Water and the River Tweed, Scotland, are quite common: DEO SILVANO PRO SALUTE SUA ET SUORUM C. ARRIUS DOMITIANUS C(ENTURIO) LEG(IONIS) XX V(ALERIAE) V(ICTRICIS) V(OTUM) S(OLVIT) L(IBENS) L(UBENS) MERITO (To the God Silvanus, Caius Arrius Domitianus, centurion of the 20th Legion, Valeria Victrix, has paid his vow willingly, gladly and deservedly for his own safety and that of his household.)

Domitianus set up several altars in the area of Newstead, Roxburghshire, Scotland, the site of the Roman fort of Trimontium, to the wild life around and to the goddess Diana in particular. In the same spirit of mysticism the Roman Emperor Hadrian (76-138 AD), whose famous wall straddles England from the River Tyne to the Solway Firth, first introduced to coins minted in Britain the figure of a woman with spear and shield, her right foot resting on a pile of hewn stone (to represent his wall?). This slim, long-legged woman, with slender forearm supporting a meditative chin, he called Britannia, but there is more than a hint that the figure was inscribed to honour his own protector, the goddess Diana.

Hadrian certainly took seriously the mystic potency of Britannia, his new ally the Genius of Britain, for he also incribed coins ADVENTUI AUG. BRITANNIAE, where he as Emperor and the Genius are shown giving sacrifice to the Roman gods.

Antoninus Pius (86-161 AD), Hadrian's successor, who built another wall from the Forth to the Clyde in Scotland, issued two commemorative coins with Britannia figures, one of which shows a sad woman with shield laid aside, hand on cheek.

Several centuries were to pass before Britannia appeared again on British coin issue, this time as a figure on the copper halfpennies and farthings of Charles II. The model for this Britannia, it has been suggested, was Frances Stewart, Duchess of Richmond, who has survived in history as the woman who successfully resisted the king's wooing. One of Charles' farthings, representing Britannia, should be available today to collectors at around 50 pence ($1.20).

Over the years it may be noted that Britannia's hemline has been a bone of contention between minter and monarch. On Charles II's series, Britannia's legs are bare to the knee, but the tin halfpennies with the copper plug of James II show her draped to the ankle. With the coming of William III's halfpenny the hem has been raised again to the knee, to be dropped again on Queen Anne's copper farthing (now valued at around ten pounds—$24.00).

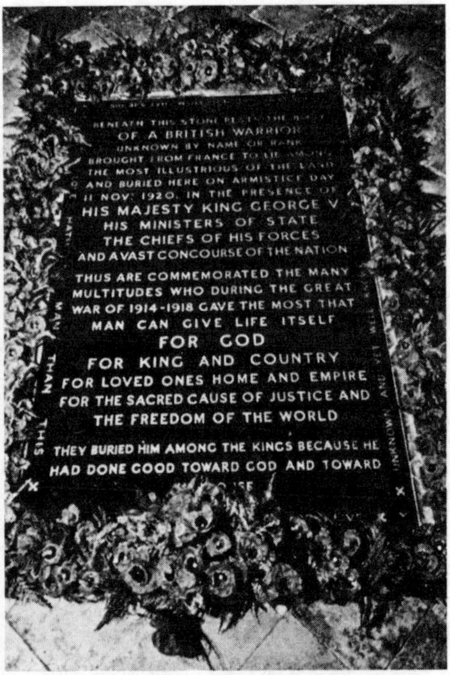

The coffin (above left) and the tomb (above right) of 'The Unknown Soldier'.

In ancient times, after a great battle, the victors used to set up a trophy of weapons and armour, or an empty tomb, to symbolise the even older sacrifice of thanks to the gods of war. Today the idea of burying an unknown soldier with honour is a direct link with the occult practice of prehistoric days.

Perhaps the most famous of all 'Unknown Soldier' tombs is that in Westminster Abbey, London. The idea for this particular national memorial came to an army chaplain, Revd David Railton, MC, during his service in Armentières in World War I.

On the night of November 7 1920, the bodies of four British soldiers were disinterred with the utmost secrecy from the battle areas of Aisne, Somme, Arras and Ypres, and were then taken to the Chapel at St Pol. The corpses were not identifiable and Brigadier-General L. J. Wyatt, DSO, Director of the War Graves Commission, selected one for reburial in Westminster Abbey.

The body was placed in a coffin of Hampton Court oak and was conveyed under escort aboard HMS Verdun *to Dover. From here it was taken by train to London, and via the Cenotaph in Whitehall to the Abbey. The coffin was sealed in a tomb following a service witnessed by representatives of the British and Continental governments.*

King Robert the Bruce of Scotland epitomises the cult hero.

The Romans propitiated their spirits of war, led by Mars, with both human and animal sacrifices.

Celtic gods of war (right) were thought to protect the graves of warriors.

Monumental brasses (below right) were once the most popular symbol of military hero worship.

The Romans often appealed to the spirits of war on their grave slabs (below) by the symbolism of the warrior triumphant.

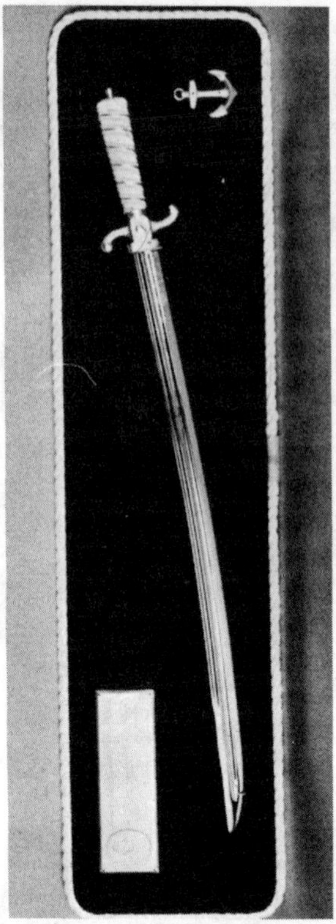

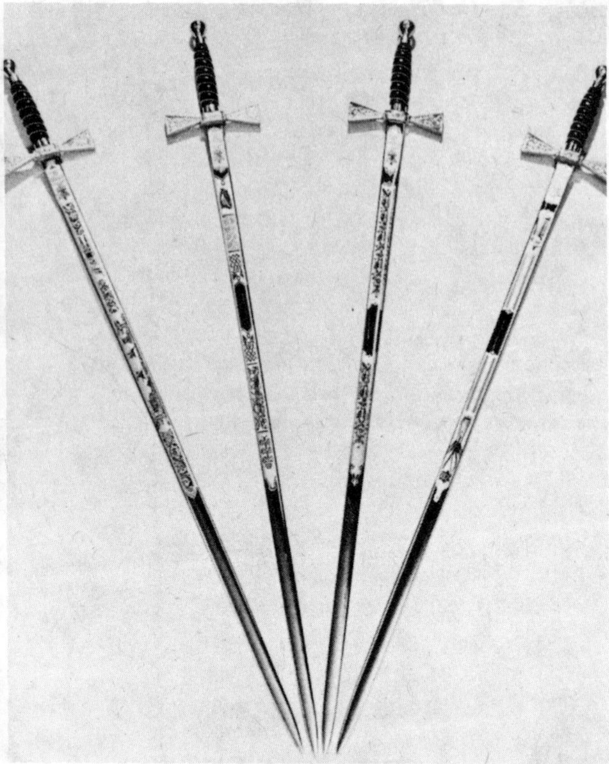

A replica of the sword carried by Captain James Cook (above left) and a selection of modern commemorative swords.

More than any other weapon the sword has become a magic cult symbol. Because of its cruciform shape the sword became a religious and magic emblem and so, from time immemorial, it has taken a prominent place both in magic ritual and as an instrument of healing. Indeed, one touch with a sacred sword was once considered enough to cure a wide range of maladies, from leprosy to the plague. One country above all in which the sword is still thought to have magical properties is Japan, where it is still considered to represent the soul of the samurai *(warriors). In Japan it was once a regular custom to tell fortunes from the markings on a sword blade.*

Swords as a defensive weapon have a long history; from the Ancient Egyptian examples of 2000 BC to the foil, épée and sabre of modern fencing. Swords first appeared in Europe in the Bronze Age, developed from an earlier short dagger of copper. The earliest known examples are leaf-shaped and two-edged, with a point for thrusting. The sword of the Iron Age was not tempered, and so was easily bent.

Although the Romans had two serviceable swords called the gladius *and the* sparta, *carbonisation-formed steel swords came with the Vikings. Their swords were two-edged with a cross-bar, or quillons, and had a pommel as a counterpiece. The medieval sword developed from the Viking sword, and was two-edged and cruciform in shape.*

In the East the single-edged weapon was a favourite, and was brought to Europe to be developed as the cleaver-like falchion. Armour began to be discarded in the 16th century, so sword hilts became more complex, and bars were used to protect the hand which had formerly been covered with a gauntlet. The rapier and court sword were relics of the ancient blades.

To make their swords powerful instruments of magic, soldiers of all ages have decorated their blades with magic emblems.

George III's incused cartwheel twopenny piece depicts a noticeable change; his Britannia sits sedately holding a trident instead of a spear. A helmeted Britannia appears on the penny, halfpenny and farthing of George IV, William IV, the coins of Victoria and issues to the present day.

The pose of Britannia altered when Edward VII came to the British throne. This time the model was Lady Susan Hicks-Beach, daughter of Sir Michael Hicks-Beach, Chancellor of the Exchequer and Master of the Royal Mint, and Britannia was depicted standing, with shield, trident and flowing cloak; the engraver was G. W. de Saulles. The florin Lady Susan graced (she obtained her title by virtue of her father's elevation to the peerage as Earl St Aldwyn) can be bought today for about 1 pound 50 pence—($3.60).

Three other coins are of interest to the Britannia researcher/collector. The first is the pattern for a standing Britannia, engraved in 1788 by L. Pingo, which showed the figure with a wand in the left hand, a laurel branch in the right, and a globe and oval shield device. This never appeared. The second is a restrike nude Britannia which also never appeared, and thirdly, the much circulated 1895 Trade Dollar which first saw the light of day at Bombay Mint for use in Hong Kong, the Straits Settlement and throughout the Far East, to replace the long-current Mexican Dollar.

Down the centuries the figure and name of Britannia has served her country of origin as a vital propaganda symbol (also found on medals, used as ship names and the name of metal), for underlying all was the feeling: 'Britain will always rule the waves'.

Flags

Because of the Cult of the Standard, which went back to primitive times, and the semi-sacred character of flags, regimental colours are still treated with reverence. On being taken into service, they are presented with ceremony and are blessed by a chaplain (shaman of primitive times). On parade, infantry colours are carried by junior officers, and escorted by an armed bearer party. This party, in wartime, was expected to fight to the death to protect the colours, thus the casualty rate of this group was abnormally high. For the same symbolic reason, the colours are paraded in the centre of the regiment when on the march and not at the head. When a colour is replaced, the old colour is 'laid up' with ceremony in a church, or a public building, being marched off these days in parade in slow time, to the tune of 'Auld Lang Syne.'

'Touching the flag' as a symbolic act of martial brotherhood was a ceremony much used by Adolph Hitler at rallies. Today some British and American regiments carry on the occult representations of the colours. For instance, in 1969, when the new Royal Regiment of Wales was formed by an amalgamation of the South Wales Borderers and The Welch Regiment, its colours were presented by Prince Charles. The Queen's Colour bore a silver wreath. In 1879, the Borderers were serving in the Zulu War, being then the 24th Foot. Five companies of the 1st Battalion, fighting around the Queen's Colour, were wiped out at the battle of Isandhlwana. The victorious Zulus swept on to a nearby farm, Rorke's Drift, which was being used as a hospital, and was defended by one company of the 2nd Battalion. Against vastly superior and fanatic groups of warriors, the 24th held out all night, and in the morning the Zulus drew off. Later, the Queen's Colour was found in the nearby river, having been carried that far around the body of a senior lieutenant. The Colour was brought back to England and Queen Victoria placed a wreath of immortelles on the spike, and commanded that a silver replica be carried on this Colour for ever. The original Colour and the wreath are laid up in the Regimental Chapel in Brecon Cathedral; and so it is that the tradition continues with the new regiment.

Incidentally, the last colours to be sent forward into action were those of the 58th Foot, later the 2nd Battalion, the Northamptonshire Regiment, which fought the Boers at Laing's Nek in 1881.

When soldiers salute the colours they are in fact saluting the memory of brave men who lost their lives in action; a direct occult relic of saluting the totem (flag) of primitive times, around which the souls of dead tribesmen were thought to gather.

The Trooping of the Colour is a much loved 'Colour ritual' among visitors to Britain, and certainly the most famous British flag ceremony internationally. For this enactment, the Colour of one of the regiments of the Guards is trooped annually on Horse Guards Parade, London, on the Queen's Birthday. Years ago, at the end of the day's activities, the Colour used to be taken to the billet of a junior officer, or ensign responsible for its safety; this developed into the ceremonial Lodging of the Colour. During the 18th century the Lodging Ceremony was added to the Guard Mounting parade in London—and because the music played during the Lodging was known as 'a troop', this gave the name to the combined event.

Badges

As a form of human occult communication, badges started out as plain scratches on stone and bark, made by primeval man to identify groups and tribes. In time, badges developed a mysticism all their own, and in military terms incorporated (with flags) the 'good luck' of the regiment. The surrender of such insignia to an enemy was considered a slight to the gods and a failing of the heroes of the past. The following badges give some indication of the modern relics of the old military cults.

1

2

3
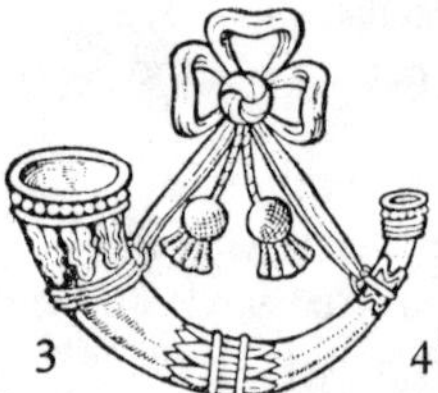

4

5

6

7

8

9

10

11

1—6th Foot—Royal Warwickshire Regiment. Cult of Animism.
2—The badges of the 16th/15th The Queen's Royal Lancers. The 16th were the first British cavalry regiment to use the lance in action. Cult of Weaponry.
3—The Light Infantry. Cult of Heroes.
4—The cap badge of the former Royal West Kent Regiment. Bore the White Horse of the ancient kingdom of Kent: this custom dates back to the Jutish invasion of England in 449 AD, led by Hengist and Horsa (landed Pegwell Bay, Ebbsfleet) under the banner of the prancing white horse. The horse and motto were also worn by Kent's two Yeomanry regiments. Cult of the Horse.
5—The badge of the Devonshire and Dorset Regiment. Bears Exeter Castle motif and the battle honour of the Sphinx. Cult of the Standard. (The oldest battle honour in the British Army extant is 'Tangier 1662-80', granted to the Royal Dragoons and the West Surreys.)
6—The badge of the Royal Armoured Corps. Cult of Might.
7—The Gordon Highlanders. Crest of the Marquis of Huntley (4th Duke of Gordon) who raised the regiment in 1794. Cult of Tribes.
8—One of the earliest forms of mystic symbol to distinguish between friend and foe was the wearing of a twig or sprig from a particular tree (totem) on the head-dress. The cap badge of the Cheshire Regiment bears an acorn and oak leaves (dates from the 18th century). Cult of Flora.
9—The badge of the former Wessex Brigade. The Wyvern—the ancient badge of the Kingdom of Wessex. Cult of Mythical Beasts.
10—The badge of the Royal Wiltshire Yeomanry. Some badges worn by the Pembroke Yeomanry. Cult of Chieftains.
11—The badge of the former Royal Norfolk Regiment—now a part of the 1st Royal Anglian Regiment. It is claimed that the Norfolks were granted this for service in Spain in 1707. The Cult of Britannia (see above).

Uniform badges, by contrast with regimental badges, have a shorter history, yet they still bear the ritual of regimental traditions. Probably the cult of the regimental tradition as we know it today has its roots in the 18th century. Then, grenadiers and drummers, for instance, of regiments which had badges awarded as battle honours, wore them on their caps—but it was the adoption of the shako which provided an opportunity of general badge wearing and the rise of the tradition.

Chapter 15

Military occultism

Facets of all psychic and ghostly phenomena have a basis in tradition and folklore. Thus the following study of the military aspects in occultism may offer some answers to the traditional belief in military phantoms.

In serried ranks assembled

One of the earliest armies of which we have any record is that of the great Ancient Egyptian pharaoh Rameses II. Although we know that he reigned for 67 years, and that his deeds are well attested on plinths and steles, and by the scholar Manetho, we can only guess that his reign occurred approximately in the first three-quarters of the 13th century BC. Rameses II is supposed to have conquered western Asia to the boundaries of India with an organised army of more than one million men. To him was also ascribed the formation of a warrior caste, the members of which had to serve in his army when necessary, had certain of their tax commitment refunded as a type of retaining fee, and were granted military fiefs. From Rameses' time, too, dates the first traceable evidence of an established cult of military occultism.

Ancient Egyptian documents testify that, when war came, officers of the pharaoh's army could mobilise 'the entire land'. Scribes had records of the soldiers, the priests, the artisans and the sources of food supply. So, when the pharaoh gave the order 'Bring forth equipment', the whole war machine cut across all social classes: common field labourers, temple youths, noblemen and pharaoh's advisers alike, all served together at the front. The soldiers of Ancient Egypt were all well equipped for war, but the lot of the infantry was hard. 'Come, I will speak to you of the ills of the infantryman', one ancient scribe wrote. 'He is awakened while there is still an hour for sleeping. He is driven like a jackass and he works until the sun sets beneath its darkness of night. He hungers and his belly aches. He is dead while he lives'. But, frightened and 'calling to his god, "Come to me that you may rescue me",' he fought, while his mystic cult symbols jingled at belt and banner head as potent occult symbols of protection. Thus from the earliest days of organised armies and warfare there was a definite cult of military occultism.

The gods of war

In all the well defined early cults of military occultism, a pantheon of gods was eminent, whether it were among the sophisticated cohorts of Persia, Greece and Rome, or among the ancient Teutons. The best known war-god is undoubtedly Mars, who was represented by an unusual variety of cult names: Mavors, Maurs, Mamers, Marmar, Marmor, Mamurius, and the honorific compound Marspiter. To the Romans the month *Martius* (our month March preserves the memory of his veneration, which was shared by most Latin and neighbouring communities) embraced the spring equinox and marked the oldest-known liturgical year at Rome. Its season, of course, reinforced this god's oldest function, that of bringing prosperity in agriculture. Chanting hymns and beating the ground, the state priests (usually the constant cult of Mars was entrusted to the Salian priests, whose title seems to derive from *salire*, 'to dance, to leap') prayed to Mars, in the form of Mamurius Veturius, to promote fertility. The Arval Brethren followed a similar cult.

Peculiar to Mars in Roman religion was the use of the horse, and special festival races (ie, the *Equirria*, March 14) were held in honour of Mars on the Campus Martius at Rome. Roman soldiers, it should be understood, only assembled on the Campus Martius and never within the city's sacred boundary *pomerium*. Known to the Greeks as Ares, Mars has been celebrated in word by such as the most famous of all Greek epic poets, Homer (c 700 BC), and in music by Gustav Theodore Holst (1874-1934), who depicted the war-god in his suite called 'The Planets'.

Probably derived from superstition concerning primitive war magic, Ares son of Zeus and Hera, was a divinity of Thracian origin, whose worship spread through Macedonia to Thebes, Athens and the cities of the Peloponnesus, especially Sparta. Homer tells us that Ares was detested by his parents. Generally he was hated by the other Greek deities, except his sister Eris (the evil goddess of discord), her son Strife, and Hades and Aphrodite. The latter fell in love with Ares and he with her: these two lovers were trapped together in a net which Hephaestus (Aphrodite's husband the limping fire god, Vulcan to the Romans) engineered for their downfall. This story is retold as a poem 'Lay of Demodocus' in the eighth book of the *Odyssey*.

Because of his unpopularity among his fellow gods, and his love of war for its own sake, Ares was a much abhorred and feared god; the Greeks, who disliked purposeless war, despised the Thracians for enjoying it. This attitude of the Greeks is reflected in the sparse myths concerning Ares. Homer, for instance, calls him murderous, bloodstained and the incarnate curse of mortals. Strangely enough, however, Homer also portrays Ares as a coward who bellowed with pain and ran away when wounded. Yet occasionally the heroes of the *Iliad* are deemed to 'rejoice in the delight of Ares' battle', but far oftener exult in having escaped 'the fury of the ruthless god'.

Ares, father of the warrior women, the Amazons, by the peace-loving nymph Harmony, was not always successful himself in battle: the two gigantic twins Otus and Ephialtes, bynamed the Aloeidae, conquered him and left him imprisoned in a brazen vessel for 13 months, until he was released by Hermes (Mercurius). Athene (Minerva) twice vanquished Ares, and Heracles also defeated him and forced him to return to Mount Olympus, at the summit of which dwelt the pantheon of Greek gods. According to late Greek tradition, Ares once defended himself before the gods in a trial where he was accused of murdering Halirrhothius, son of sea-god Poseidon (Neptune). Since he pleaded that he had saved his daughter Alcippe from being raped, Ares was acquitted, and the place of the trial became known as the Areopagus (a rocky promontory situated today west of the Acropolis at Athens).

Symbolically the bird of Ares was the vulture, and his animal the dog. Sometimes he was portrayed by the Greeks with the war-goddess Eryo (Latin: Belona) at his side, flanked by Terror, Trembling and Panic. Sometimes Alexander the Great is symbolised alongside Ares. Deified in his own lifetime for his successes in Egypt and India, Alexander was recognised as a war-god by the Greek cities of the League of Corinth.

Mars, whose sons by a mortal maiden were Romulus and Remus, the mythical founders of Rome, was certainly better liked by the Romans than Ares was by the Greeks. Mars never was to the Romans the whining deity of the *Iliad,* but was depicted magnificent in shining armour, redoubtable and invincible. The warriors of the great Latin heroic poem, the *Aeneid,* far from being jubilant to escape from Mars, actually rejoiced when they saw that they were to fall 'on Mars' field of renown': they 'rush on glorious death' and find it 'sweet to die in battle'.

Although Ares figured little in classical Greek mythology and was no more than a minor symbol of war to the Greeks; although he had no Greek cities in which he was exclusively worshipped, and was not a distinct personality like Hera, Hermes or Apollo, in the form of Mars the Romans made more daily use of him. He figures on Roman grave slabs usually alongside Hercules, and after Jupiter was by far the commonest of deities in Roman Britain. Contrary to the theories set out by A. von Domazzewski in the 19th century, in the second and early third centuries, Mars was the object of an official military cult not very different from the official imperial cult of *Iuppiter Optimus Maximus.* Furthermore, he showed in two distinct ways a closer contact with the life of the Roman people of Britain. Among the small rude altars on which private soldiers (generally anonymous) recorded their personal devotion, few bear the name of Jupiter, but many carry that of Mars. To the soldiers of Britain, at least, he was a living god.

Later the attributes of Mars were given to more localised gods. For instance, the Watling Street (the name of the old Roman road which ran from the Channel ports by way of London to Shropshire) shrines at Barkway, Hertfordshire, were dedicated to Mars Alator. At *Venta Silurum* (modern-day Caerwent, Monmouthshire) one of the local deities connected with a craft guild was Mars Ocelus Vellaunus ('Mars of the Hilltop'), equated with the Moselle valley god Mars Lenus, who was also closely allied with healing. Local gods bynamed Mars were thus not exclusively connected with war: Mars Silvanus, for instance, protected the forest.

In time Mars was freely identified with such Celtic deities as Belatucadanus, Camulus and Corotiacus, and was adorned with Celtic epithets like *Rigisamus*, 'most royal'. Furthermore one votary slab at Carlisle tells of the devotion of one IANUARIUS R to a bastard Mars deity suffixed Barrex; the latter is thought to be a Celtic epithet for 'supreme'. The full dedication runs: M(ARTI) BARREGI IANUARIUS REG. V(OTUM) S(OLVIT) L(IBENS) M(ERITO).

A prominent Celtic god Cocidius was, however, the favourite of the Roman soldiers in the north of England, particularly of the fort garrisons along Hadrian's Wall between Carlisle and Hexham. Here is one votary stone's inscription by way of example. It was found just to the south of modern Carlisle: MARTI COC(IDIO) M(ILITES) LEG(IONIS) II AUG(USTAE), CENTURIA SANCTIANA CENTURIA SECUNDINI, D(ONUM) SOL(VERUNT) SUB CURA AELIANI CURA(VIT) OPPIUS F(ELIX) OPTIO ('To the soldiers of the Emperor's own Second Legion, the centuries of Sanctius and Secundus, paid their vows to Mars Cocidius, Oppius Felix the sub-centurion took charge of the work').

Thus Mars 'went native' without compunction, and formed an important link between the Celtic and Roman elements of early British organised military occultism. In the latter stages of this process he ceased to be, in any special sense, a soldiers' god, for many of his Celticised avatars were not of the military sphere. Mars, in short, formed a point of contact between the occultism of the Roman occupying army and that of British civil life.

The Emperor Augustus, under whose reign London entered upon her career as the leading commercial port of the British Isles, greatly enhanced Mars' material condition at the end of the last century BC. Augustus made Mars responsible for the military victory over Caesar's murderers at Philippi, as well as for the revenge upon the 'invincible' Parthians. The temple of Mars in Augustus' forum thus attained such importance that the grand plaza gradually exchanged the name of the emperor for that of the god. Until the 1930s the street of Christian Rome which ran above the Forum Augustum was still called 'Via Marforio'.

Now that the £2,000,000.00 ($4,800,000.00) restoration of York Minster, one of the most famous ecclesiastical buildings in the world situated in the heart of Yorkshire, is completed, visitors are able to see the unique series of newly constructed underground chambers. The foundations of part of the perpendicular choir of this church were constructed on the site of the headquarters building (*principia*) of the Roman fortress. Known to the Romans as Eboracum, the military complex was rebuilt in stone by the XI Legion at the beginning of the second century AD. Here, in the centre of the great church, was the site (to be preserved for future generations) of the *sacellum*, the nearest approach the Romans had to a regimental chapel. The (current) emperor's statue was kept there, representing to the legionaries the fount of the occult potential necessary for military successes. The legions which were associated with York were not particularly devoted to Mars and imitated their fellows at such places as Bath, Lincoln and Chester, in worshipping the military 'genius of the place' as is described by R. G. Collingwood and J. N. L. Myers. Within a few feet of the *sacellum*, in the present eastern crypt of York Minster, is the traditional site of the baptism on Easter Eve 627, of the Northumbrian king Edwin. In this act Edwin recognised and acknowledged a source of military and civil occultism greater than the Roman *imperium* he so admired.

In the *sacellum* the Romans also kept their legionary standards (*vexillum*) so that the divine powers therein could bless them by inference. So, the environs of York Minster have been associated with military occultism for nearly 2,000 years, and today there are three regimental chapels (All Saints: Duke of Wellington's Regiment; St John's: King's Own Yorkshire Light Infantry; St George's: West Yorkshire Regiment) representing in modern terms the association the Minster has with the spirits of the men who suffered and died in the cause of justice.

Relics of this old military occultism are probably further represented in modern times by the number of regimental chapels to be found throughout Britain. The main centre of the modern 'cult of the war dead' is at Westminster Abbey, where is situated the 'Tomb of the Unknown Soldier'. A similar remnant of military occultism reflected in a 'cult of the dead' is to be seen at Arlington National Cemetery, Virginia, where America's 'Unknown Soldiers' of World War I, World War II and the Korean war are interred.

The Celts, of course, had a subsidiary pantheon of war-related gods and goddesses which was all their own. Of them Morrigu was perhaps the greatest, but most feared, war-goddess of the Celts. She probably originated in tribal memory from some pre-Celtic moon-goddess. Morrigu was deemed to hover over battlefields in the likeness of a carrion-crow. This latter belief may have been responsible for the modern superstitious classification of the crow (as well as the raven) as a bird of evil omen (see: *A Book of Superstitions*). Subordinate to Morrigu was the war quintet: Fea, the 'hateful'; Babd, the 'fury' (Cauth Bodva to the Celts of Gaul); Macha, the 'belligerent'; and Nemon, the 'venemous' (known around the Bath, Somerset area as Nemontana). The Gauls, incidentally, worshipped the war-god Teutates with human sacrifice, Teutates being akin to another Gaulish war-god Hesus.

There is still today a strong mysticism connected with Romano-Celtic objects found on British and Continental sites. Take, for instance, the case of Dr Anne Ross, the eminent Celtic scholar and author of *Pagan Celtic Britain* (London: Routledge). Dr Ross does a variety of research work for a number of museums, and late in 1971 she was asked to examine two carved stone heads which had been discovered near Hadrian's Wall. In a recent interview she said:

'Though there was nothing unpleasant about the appearance of the heads, I took an immediate, instinctive dislike to them. I left them in the box they had been sent in, and I put it in my study. I planned to have them geologically analysed, and then to return them as soon as possible to the North.

'A night or two after they arrived—I didn't connect this experience with the heads until later—I woke up suddenly at about 2 am, deeply frightened and very cold. I looked towards the door, and by the corridor light glimpsed a tall figure slipping out of the room. My impression was that the figure was dark like a shadow, and that it was part animal and part man. I felt compelled to follow it, as if by some irresistible force.

'I heard it, whatever it was, going downstairs, and then I saw it again, moving along the corridor that leads to the kitchen; but now I was too terrified to go on. I went back upstairs to the bedroom and woke Dick, my husband. He searched the house, but found nothing—no sign at all of any disturbance. We thought that I must have had a nightmare (though I could hardly believe that a nightmare could seem so real), and decided to say nothing about it.

'A few days later, when the house was empty, my teenage daughter Bernice came home from school at about 4 pm, two hours before Dick and I returned from London. When we arrived home, she was deathly pale and clearly in a state of shock. She said that something horrible had happened, but at first would not tell us what. But eventually the story came out.

'When she had come in from school, the first thing she had seen was something huge, dark and inhuman on the stairs. It had rushed down towards her, vaulted over the banisters, and landed in the corridor with a soft thud that made her think its feet were padded like those of an animal. It had run towards her room, and though terrified, she had felt that she had to follow it. At the door, it had vanished, leaving her in the state in which we found her.

'We calmed her down as best we could, and feeling puzzled and disturbed ourselves, searched the house. Again, there was no sign of any intruder—nor, in fact, did we expect to find any.

'Since then, I have often felt a cold presence in the house, and more than once have heard the same soft thud of animal's pads near the staircase. Several times my study door has burst open, and there has been no one there and no wind to account for it. And on one other occasion, when Bernice and I were coming downstairs together, we both thought that we saw a dark figure ahead of us—and heard it land in the corridor after vaulting over the banisters.

'The reason why I associate the heads with this haunting, if that's what it is, is this. Later, I learnt that on the night when the heads had first been discovered, the North-country woman who lived next door to the garden where they had been unearthed was putting her child to bed when a horrifying creature—she described it as half-man and half-animal—came into the room. She began screaming, and only stopped when her neighbours arrived. She was convinced that the creature had touched her, but what happened to it, she did not know. There was no sign that anyone had broken into the house, and the incident, like the incidents which have taken place in our house, is quite without any rational explanation. The strange thing is, the heads have gone now back to the museum. But this thing doesn't seem to have gone with them.'

Dr Ross sincerely believes that the stones have an occult link with the past, and so do other people connected with the discovery. Examination of the two heads showed that they were Romano-British and of Northumbrian stone; probably, say the experts, they came from a military shrine or temple dedicated to such a local god as Maponus, the 'Divine Son'. One must remember that the Celts of Britain were head-hunters, who believed that the severed human head had magical or divine properties. Similar powers were visited in stone heads; those sent to Dr Ross obviously stood guard over the shrine of a departed military god. Or has he departed?

Anhur, a human-headed deity and sun-god of Abydos, was probably the most prominent of all Ancient Egyptian war-gods. Also known as Onouris, this god was regarded as the son of Hathor, the horned cow-goddess of love, and dwelt at Sebennytus with Shu, the human-headed god of the air. The first prophet of this war-god's cult was Nebunenef, whose elevation to the dignity of high priest of Amun was ratified by Rameses II. Famous in Ugarit myth, however, Anthat (or Anahita, Anaitis, and Anthrathi), the goddess of love and war, was worshipped at Thebes during the reign of the warrior Thotmes III. Neith was the Ancient Egyptian war-goddess of Sais. Probably of Libyan origin, she may be equated with Pallas Athene, the Greek embodiment of wisdom and power.

By way of contrast, the Assyrians had a god who ruled both the moon and military matters. Known as Asshur, this war-god was invariably illustrated wearing a horned war-cap, and shooting an arrow from a gold bow. The whole picture was enclosed in a circle and displayed as an ensign for both Assyrian infantry and chariot divisions. Asshur replaced Marduk when the Assyrians dominated Mesopotamia. Another Assyrian war-god was Enurta of Nihib, who was represented mostly as a bird of prey. Atter (female counterpart Attar) was the male Venus god of war to the northern Semites, while Chemosh was the war deity of the Moabites in the wars against Israel: Chemosh was Shamash to the Babylonians. Some eastern goddesses including Ishtar of Mesopotamia and Anat of Canaan and Phoenecia, combined the roles of deities of fertility and war.

Among the war-gods of the Americas, Quahootze was perhaps the best known. He was the battle deity of the Nootka Sound Indians, and to him this great prayer was addressed on the eve of battle: 'Great Quahootze, let me live, not be sick, find the enemy, not fear him, find him asleep and kill a great many of him'. Epunamun was the war-god of the Araucanian Indians and was probably of Inca origin. Camaxtli was the Aztec war-god of Tlaxcala, and was sometimes merged with Mixcoatl. Teoyaomiqui, however, was the Aztec god of dead warriors, a military variant of Mictlantecuhtli, the death-god. Huitzilopochtli was the Mexican Indian god of war, whose feasts in May, July and December were scenes of great savagery: thousands of human victims were sacrificed in his honour.

In the East, Indra was the Vedic god of battle and rain, while in late Vedic myth the war-god Kartikeya was generally classed as a leader of the forces of good. To the Chinese, Kuan-Ti was the god of war who, contrary to other gods of his type, was mainly concerned with the averting of conflict and with the protection of the people from the horror of total war.

Hachiman is generally agreed by scholars to be the main Japanese god of war. Hachiman, the posthumous title of the Emperor Ojin, son of the Empress Jingu, was born in 270 AD during his imperial mother's war campaigns in Korea. While most records say that he died in 310 AD, Hachiman is deemed by many to have lived for

110 years. Hachiman's shrines are to be found all over Japan, but the most important are at Kamakura, Usa, and Otokoyama in Kyoto. Besides Hachiman, however, there are three other deities in the Japanese war pantheon, namely Marishiten, Bishamonten and Daikoku. The latter two are to be found among the *shichi fukujin,* 'The Seven Gods of Good Luck'. Bishamonten is furthermore the 'God of Riches' and is one of the Four Buddhist Kings of Heaven (*shitenno*). Daikoku has the Shinto name of *O-Kuni-Nushi-no-Mikoto,* 'Divine Master of the Great Island'. Fat, prosperous-looking, wearing a peculiar shaped cap, Daikoku is usually depicted sitting on two bales of rice with a sacred mallet in his hand (see: *Phantoms, Legends, Customs and Superstitions of the Sea*).

To the Polynesians the great war-god is still Oro, whose palace, legend states, may be found in the *Ao-Roa* (the clouds of heaven). To propel himself across the sky Oro uses the sacred canoe *Anuanua* (a rainbow). Identical with Oro is the rather unusual underground war-god Rongo sacred to the Mangaia of the Hervey Islands. Among the native population of Maui, second largest of the islands of Hawaii, glowering figurines of the war-god Ku are popular, and are much sought by American tourists and antique dealers alike.

Military cult heroes

The original meaning of the Greek word *heros* is 'a gentleman', a man of good family. Thus were the Homeric heroes, typified by Achilles in the *Iliad,* warrior-aristocrats, lovers of war, sport and feasting. But the word 'hero', used in everyday speech to mean an outstandingly brave person, or to designate the main participant in a literary work, may further be used in a more specialised sense, to refer to personages in so-called 'heroic' literature. Such tales, which have flourished in every age, deal with a race of men who are quite extraordinary in strength and courage, and who had dealings with supernatural beings; some of the heroes were deemed of supernatural parentage themselves. It should be noted that while it is quite possible for such cult heroes to become gods, it is rare for gods to become cult heroes. Throughout time gods have remained abstract conceptions and their relationship with mankind was through a medium/priest, who became identified with the god.

Heroes and outstanding military personages then, after their deaths have taken on supernatural auras. To many civilisations their individual military cult heroes have been deemed to reappear in phantom form, or in 'mystic essence' whenever a town, city, nation or community was in grave danger. This was the case with such military cult heroes as King Arthur. Among others most frequently mentioned are: Thomas of Ercildoune (c 1220-97), the Berwickshire poet and seer who Sir Walter Scott believed was the author of the poem *Sir Tristram;* Peredur, the Welsh knight trained by one of the nine witches of Gloucester; Alfatin, the Moorish hero who is still believed by the naïve to sleep, his green horse by his side, in a cave in the Sierra de Agner, whence he and his steed will emerge at the appointed time to avenge his people; the Holy Roman Emperor Barbarossa (Redbeard), Frederick I (c 1122-90), whose cult was particularly strong in Germany; Marco, the Serbian prince who in Slavonic myth is supposed to sleep on his horse in a cavern in Mount Urvinia; Earl Gerard of Mullaghmart, the Celtic nobleman who sleeps with his knights in the cellar of a castle in County Kildare; and King Wenceslaus (1361-1419) of Bohemia, the former western province of Czechoslovakia, who is now most celebrated in the carol 'Good King Wenceslaus' (folklorists have sometimes confused him with the Slavonic knight Stoymer, who is said to sleep alongside his companions under Mount Blanik in Bohemia).

Charlemagne, the great European ruler (742-814), and the central character of medieval legends, in which he is a superhuman warrior and the champion of Christianity against Islam, had perhaps the most persistent cult. He was said to have risen from the dead to fight in the Crusades, and was deemed by scholars to be alive but sleeping, till his peoples needed him. Incidentally the 'Seven Sleepers' often mentioned in folk chronicles as guardians of mankind against evil, are the Christian variant of the 'Sleeping Beauty' theme: these participants were the persecuted Christians who stayed for 200 years in a cave at Ephesus. Sometimes one military cult hero can appear in a variety of forms. Such is the case of Kaboi of the Karaya Indians, who was Kamu to the Arawaks, Tamu to the Caribs, Kame to the Bakairi Caribs and Zumu to the Paraguayans.

Even today, heroic legends spring up in societies which are engaged, for instance, in guerilla warfare. In some cases the military occultism of the old cult heroes is mirrored today among the young in their 'worship' of such figures as the Mexican revolutionary Zapata or the guerilla thug Che Guevara. During the 1930s in Germany an occult military cult was re-developed around the person of Adolf Hitler. Even a private life was 'manufactured' in myth form to strengthen Hitler's mystic role as saviour of his people, and as that essential leader-figure of Führer, who from earliest times in German politico-military occultism has always been a focal point for virulent dissatisfaction against social adversity. The great measure of the success of the aura of military occultism around Hitler as cult hero, however, as historian Joachim C. Fest has so clearly pointed out, was not due to outside aid; like the millions poured into Hitler's funds by industrialists and so on, or the votes cast in his favour by the populace (at no election did Hitler ever get more than 37.3% of the votes): it was due entirely to the lack of political sense and judgement on the part of millions of dissatisfied, embittered individuals, terrified of social levelling, who, under the pressures of the times, surrendered themselves even more fervently to the cult of occultism developed around Hitler.

It is interesting to note that the major significance today of the military orientated Germanen Order, which flourished during the period 1912-22, lies in the fact that some of its members had links with Hitler's early National Socialist Movement. Both cherished many of the military cult myths that were to prevail in extremist German nationalistic circles, particularly that of the true German master race (*Herrenvolk*) being descended from heroic Nordic warriors; those belonging to this race were fair-haired and blue-eyed, and represented the racial ideal. The two also embraced the obsessive belief in the existence of a 'Jewish peril' and had individual cults of military occultism expressed in hero worship.

The founders of the Germanen Order included Theodore Fritsch, publisher of the antisemitic periodical *Hammer,* Philipp Stauff, a journalist, Professor Heinrich Kräger and Hermann Pohl. Candidates for membership of the Berlin lodge of the Germanen Order, for instance, had their skulls measured with a 'platometer' to make sure that they conformed to the Order's Nordic racial ideals (some 30 years later Heinrich Himmler, Hitler's hated Minister of the Interior, organised a similar measuring operation on Russian prisoners). Furthermore their family backgrounds were exhaustively examined to assess whether or not they had Jewish blood in their veins. The initiation ceremony (for which see the only remaining records in the *Bundesarchiv,* Koblenz) was run on purely military occult lines and had as its guiding spirits the war-gods of the Teutons.

Inactive during World War I, the Germanen Order re-emerged in 1919 and Grand Duke Johann Arbrecht of Mecklenburg, a prototype German nationalist, became its

Grand Master. Many of the Order's members were to have close links with the German Workers' Party, which Hitler joined in September 1919 and transformed into the *Nationalsozialistische Deutsche Arbeiterpartei* (NSDAP—National Socialist German Workers Party). While Hitler had no use for the Germanen Order, its mystic rationale was akin to his and both included many facets of the German brand of military occultism which is not yet extinct today.

While the occultism surrounding military cult heroes is almost entirely dead today in the west, it still exists quite strongly in Japan, where the cult of the *chushingura* (47-*ronin*), for instance, is a fine example. The 47-*ronin* (or masterless *samurai*: see below) were the vassals of Asano Naganori, the Lord of the Castle of Ako, in the old Japanese province of Harima. In the spring of 1701 an Imperial envoy was sent to the *shogunate* (military government), and Asano and another *daimyo* (feudal lord), Date Mureharu, were appointed to receive and entertain him. As these two *daimyo* were young and inexperienced, the *Shogun* (generalissimo) delegated a further high official, Kira Yoshinaka, who was well-versed in the ancient court ceremonial, to assist them. Kira, however, a greedy and conceited old man, heaped insult after insult on Lord Asano who had failed to court Kira's favour by offering costly presents. No longer able to bear the insults, Asano drew his sword and attacked Kira. He succeeded in wounding Kira, but was prevented from killing him by an officer of the *Shogun's* guard. That same day the *shogunate* ordered Asano to commit *harakiri* (qv), while emissaries were sent out to confiscate the Asano domain.

Oishi Yoshio, the chief councillor of the House of Asano, resisted the confiscation but was forced to flee with the Asano family retainers. After several adventures Oishi and 46 of the retainers arrived at the mansion of the arrogant Kira Yoshinaka. A fierce fight followed their arrival on December 14 1701, and Kira was killed. Oishi and his brave band, however, immediately reported to the local magistrate what they had done, and awaited his orders at the Sengakuji Temple, Takarawa. All were sentenced to commit *harakiri* and were buried beside the grave of their beloved lord at the Sengakuji Temple. Their bravery and loyalty became a legend in Japan and the *chushingura* passed into Japan's cult of military occultism. Today the *chushingura* cult is still strong: thousands visit the graves of the 47-*ronin* every month to burn incense and to pray (the place was crowded 24 hours a day during World War II) and no day passes without fresh flowers adorning their graves.

Christians, of course, have been unable to acknowledge a cult of war-gods, so they have devoted their military cult allegiances down the centuries to a set of saints, who might be said to be remnant war-gods and military cult heroes. Popular saints among soldiers were the patron saints of their respective countries, and such as St George, St Michael, St Barbara, the patroness of the artificers of war (armourers, powder merchants and so on), and St Peter and St Paul, who, legend recounts, repelled Attila the Hun from the gates of Rome. The Immaculate Conception was given as patroness of American soldiers by Pope Pius XII on December 8 1942.

Name, rank and horoscope

From early times military strategists have tried to use the supposed mystic power of the gods and cult heroes to help their side win. The earliest attested example of the use of occultism in military strategy, however, is to be found in the documents relating to the recruitment and conscription of soldiers using astrological charts. Whenever he chose a new marshal or general, French commander Napoleon Bonaparte (1769-1821), for instance, paid no attention to college reports, or ability ratings. Instead he carefully assessed the subject's horoscope and asked the question: Is he lucky? In evaluating military acumen in this way Napoleon was not pioneering new methods of officer selection. Five thousand years before the Ancient Egyptians had chosen their soldiers by consulting star signs. The advisers to the mighty god-kings of Egypt found that men most likely to succeed in the army were those born under the signs of Scorpio, Aries and Leo. Traditionally the three fighters of the Zodiac, Leo was ruled by the forceful Sun, and the other two by the war-like planet Mars. Recently computer analysis has been made by statisticians in Europe and America of up-to-date army lists. The top five most successful classes of soldiers were found to be born under, in descending order, Scorpio, Virgo, Leo, Libra and Aries. So things have not changed much astrologically in 5,000 years!

Successful military leaders have been born under all the Zodiac signs, but the top four star signs have spawned the most: *Scorpio*, 'Blood and Guts' Patton, Field Marshals Rommel and Montgomery, and General de Gaulle; *Virgo*, Oliver Cromwell; *Leo*, Napoleon, Fidel Castro, Benito Mussolini, and T. E. Lawrence; *Libra*, Dwight D. Eisenhower, Lord Nelson and the French and German marshals Ferdinand Foch and Paul von Hindenberg. Nevertheless, the next four star signs in line also reflect acumen in military affairs, as the Duke of Wellington was born under Taurus, General Douglas MacArthur, and Major General Charles George Gordon of Khartoum under Aquarius. Way down at the bottom of the list come the gentle Piscean leaders like President George Washington. Awards for gallantry seem to be shared out in similar star sign analysis, although those born under Aries and Taurus seem to collect more than a normal share for successful soldiers.

The aspects of Mars in a soldier's horoscope, of course, are the most relevant to military occultism. By-named the 'rogue planet' by astrologers, too much influence from Mars seems to indicate a rather dangerous and violent temperament with character traits of impatience, tirelessness, excitability and irascibility. The true Mars subject is neither subtle nor profound. In manner the Martian is generally held to be rough and crude, lacking in refinement and uninterested in the arts. Nevertheless, both learned and religious people need a good deal of Mars in their astrological charts to sustain their unrewarding and often tedious studies. Mars subjects are, of course, as courageous as they are hasty and, although they do not take chances, they are never afraid to run risks and seem at times utterly fearless.

In the main Napoleon went further than most superstitious military leaders in the use of occult mechanics for officer selection. Not only did he devise his own form of geomancy, *L'Oracle de Napoléon*, using sequences of random dots, but he also based the fortunes of his senior officers on numerology (see: *A Book of Superstitions*). Numerologists say that in altering his name Napoleon changed his own destiny: when he dropped the u from Buonaparte, he changed his occult number from 1, standing for power and victory, to 4, the number of defeat and death! Strangely enough most nations give 4 the doubtful benefit of death, and nowhere is this more true than in Japan.

Bushido: the way of the warrior

A unique type of military occultism is to be seen in the *bushido* cult of Japan. As this is unique it is best assessed on its own. Yukio Mishima, the prominent Japanese novelist and commander of his own private army, died in a ritual suicide (*harakiri*—belly slitting, or more properly *seppuku*—ritual disembowelment) in 1970 after leading a raid on the headquarters of the Japanese Army. Almost aping the 1,400 troops of the Japanese Army's First Division, who on February 26 1936 tried to overthrow the government, Mishima and five of his uniformed troopers seized the army's commanding general after slashing eight guards with *samurai* swords. Having forced the army troops at the headquarters to assemble, Mishima harangued them for ten minutes concerning Japan's present day politics and the virtues of the ancient Japanese way; then he retired into another room and killed himself.

Mishima and his men, with the sentiments of traditional Japanese patriotism, had consciously acted in accordance with an ancient and much respected code, that of the *samurai** warrior of Japan's feudal past. Numerous people in Japan today abhor the complexities of modern life, and its stress on the material rather than the spiritual aspects of man's existence. They have an intrinsic nostalgia for the genre of society they consider existed in Japan before the intrusion of the West in the mid-1800s. Consequently they yearn for a return to its simpler virtues and values. But what exactly is the *samurai* tradition, which still appeals to so many in post-war Japan?

Mostly it refers to a behaviour pattern of that class of professional warriors who emerged from the Japanese provinces around the tenth and 11th centuries. Within 100 years or so, these warriors became the élite of Japan, and held that position up to the dawn of the modern era. In simpler terms the way of the *samurai* is a designation of the warrior spirit of Japan, which had its origins in a much earlier age.

As may be seen in historical references to the early Jōmon and Yayoi cultures, Japan has had a highly sophisticated martial orientation since before the dawn of fully recorded history. But the native warrior spirit seems to have been on the wane in the sixth century, probably because at that time Japan was coming increasingly under the 'civilising' influences of China. In time the imperial court became the centre of Japanese government: the court sat in the city of Nara during the eighth century, and in Heian at Kyoto, some 26 miles to the north, from the ninth century to the coming of the reign of Emperor Meiji (1868). Theoretically the power of the Japanese throne was absolute, but in practice others often took on the divine emperor's political prerogatives.

During the late seventh and eighth centuries this court caucus sought to rule Japan by employing a large officialdom and by maintaining a national army, conscripted from the peasantry. From about the end of this period the various ministerial families and Japan's aristocracy gradually carved up much of the land until the larger part of the territory which had been private domain was merged with the new estates. Over the ensuing centuries the court declined, but during Heian times rose to great heights as a cultural force. As more and more land fell into the hands of a few there was an obligation to curtail many of the once extant administrative services, including the responsibility of maintaining law and order, and provincial families were forced to take up arms to provide for their own policing and defence needs.

As provincial families (particularly the northern barons) continually flouted the court's will and tried to carve for themselves autonomous baronies, their new warrior retainers had extensive training in the martial arts. Leadership of this new warrior society, paradoxically as it may seem, was assumed mainly by distant relatives of the imperial family itself. From the two 11th-century wars ('Former Nine Years War' and the 'Later Three Years War'), the real story of the *samurai* in Japanese history begins, for in the chronicles of the age the true warrior held his life to be of 'no more value than a feather'. In battle no quarter was given and none was expected. Even in these

* The word *samurai* derives from the Japanese verb *saburau* 'to serve'. It was used in the earliest times for personal attendants, who appear to have been little better than domestic servants. Later the word became applied exclusively to members of the provincial warrior class.

early days the warrior code called for loyalty to a feudal lord and his family, and a retention of an exaggerated sense of personal pride. During the ensuing centuries the *samurai* rose to greater power, but it was not until the later years of history that the occultism of *bushido* became more prevalent.

The *samurai* of the Tokugawa period (1600-1868), who used their leisure to acquire a degree of education unknown among the Japanese fighting men of earlier eras, sought within their class mores to evolve an ideal code of behaviour for themselves. This code became generally known by the modern official term *bushido,* or the way of the *bushi* (an alternative to the word *samurai*), defined literally as 'military knights' ways', or 'precepts of knighthood'. One of the most striking differences between *samurai* code and western chivalry was the respective attitudes towards the enemy. In the West 'honourable' capture was possible, but in Japan surrender and capture were contemptible. If taken alive one could only anticipate brutal treatment according to *samurai* mores, so suicide was favoured. The brutal treatment of prisoners during World War II had much to do with the old Japanese attitude to surrender and capture. Although it is a modern term*, *bushido* therefore represents the Japanese equivalent of European chivalry. In the limited sense of a codified body of education and a particular view of life, *bushido* seems to form a part of the great movement quietly initiated by a group of 18th century scholars and men of letters of whom Hirata Atsutane (1776-1843), Kamo Mabuchi (1697-1769) and Motoori Norinaga (1730-1801) were the most prominent. *Bushido* reached an apogee with the Meiji Restoration and was broken up as a nationally-observed cult by the follies and violence of the 1930s and 1940s.

While saying that *bushido* is a modern term, the nucleus of ideas on which it was based is seen to be very old. From the earliest times the Japanese were a warlike race, and the whole *bushido* relationship of occult dedication between vassal and feudal lord really dates back to the patriarchal system of history. The spiritual content of *bushido* is to be encountered in the concept of *giri* (moral obligation), that duty which ties man to his superiors, inferiors and equals, and its nature in the concept of *chugi* (loyalty). As *giri* and *chugi* became the foundation stones of *bushido,* they both overlapped into every life situation to be reflected again in literature, the theatre and cinema as the basic plot conflicts. Contrary to Chinese teaching however, loyalty towards one's leader and lord (*chu*) was deemed imperative, to which filial piety (*ko*) always came second. In all things the *samurai* was guided by wisdom (*chi*), benevolence (*jin*), and valour (*yu*). In the *samurai* context, wisdom did not mean knowledge. The aim was to live according to what were considered to be the supreme and eternal ethical principles. Benevolence, however, implied pity (but not indulgence) for the conquered and the weak. The true *samurai* had to be magnanimous† as well as strong and courageous, but the supreme measure of personality was valour, which had to be combined with serenity and composure. This did not mean of course, that the *samurai* had to fling himself headlong into danger, rather, true courage was 'to live when it was right to live, and to die when it was right to die'.

The ideal *samurai* was expected always to maintain a perfect calm in the face of adversity, and most admired were those who could placidly read, recite or compose poetry shortly before drawing their last breath. Thus, every *samurai* was expected

* G. B. Sansom, *Japan, a short Cultural History* (1931) notes that *bushido* was known in the 18th century, while B. H. Chamberlain in *Things Japanese* (1927) says 'the very word appears in no dictionary native or foreign, before the year 1900.'

† The true *samurai* would not take life for its own sake. He would allow his defeated enemy a ritualistic death, while allowing the retainers mercy. The *ronin* (qv) of course, had a different system.

to be always ready to take his own life if events required it. Only in the most exceptional circumstances was one made a *samurai:* one was born into the mystique. A *samurai,* distinguished in appearance by his hair (top-knotted and shaven in front) and by the clan badge on his kimono, devoted himself therefore to living a pure, spartan life and perfecting himself as a fighting man. Socially he kept himself apart from polluted 'commoners', and it was unfitting for him to engage in any form of trade, or even to handle money. The *samurai's* education was consequently hard, and a part of his training was to learn never to betray the slightest emotion, whether of joy or fear. His word, *bushi no ichi gon,* was not only sacred, but lying and deception meant death. The *samurai* training included fencing, archery, wrestling, riding, javelin throwing, tactics, calligraphy and a deep study of ethics, literature and history—and of course, a vital petitioning of the gods and spirits who helped with these arts.

At 15 the *samurai* received his sword, for the chief of the martial skills in which he was expected to excel was swordsmanship. The two swords, one long and one short, that he carried at all times, were as much an occult protection and a badge, as weapons. The long two-handed sword, incidentally, was the one around which most of the legendary exploits grew; the short one was for decapitating a fallen enemy. The latter too was the suicide blade. The sword then was the visible weapon and *bushido* the unseen one. Dr Inazo Nitobe subtitled his volume *Bushido,* the premier source book on the subject, 'The Soul of Japan', and similarly the sword could be referred to as 'The Soul of the *Samurai*'. The Japanese sword was not only an efficient weapon without peer, but also a religious cult object symbolising the *samurai's* courage, prowess and knightly virtues. Passed down from father to son, the swords were deemed an actual part of the owner's personality, as one ancient Japanese poet recounted:

'Hush, listen! My soul, my sword!
Not molten with toil of days
Was the steel of your fashioning
But with labour of strenuous years
Till thy steel was a living thing.
Through your eager, thirsty veins
The red drops, hissing, ran;
Pure blood of fiery soul
Proud spirit of a man.'

Japan was forced to abandon her seclusion policy of more than two centuries with the arrival of Commodore Matthew Perry's American 'black ships' in 1853. This event foreshadowed 15 years of domestic and foreign crisis which the ruling Tokugawa *Shogunate* (excessively weighted by tradition) was increasingly unable to handle. In 1868 the *Shogunate* was overthrown by a group of lower-ranking *samurai* and the long shadowy figure of the emperor was restored to his 'rightful' tradition as ruling authority. These activist *samurai* led Japan into the modern world. But real governing power was not restored to the throne, instead it was assumed by a small group of men (chiefly these activist *samurai*) who in an enlightened oligarchy transformed feudal Japan into a strong modern nation. Other *samurai* were encouraged to become leaders of the new Japan, as they had been of old. It was soon realised however, that the retention of a feudal and privileged warrior class was incompatible with the needs of a modern society, and in the early 1870s the special rights of the *samurai* were abolished.

This does not mean that all *samurai* ethics were forgotten. Their discussion appears time and time again in the journals of the soldiers and sailors who took part in the Sino-Japanese War (1894-95), the Russo-Japanese War (1904-5) and the various

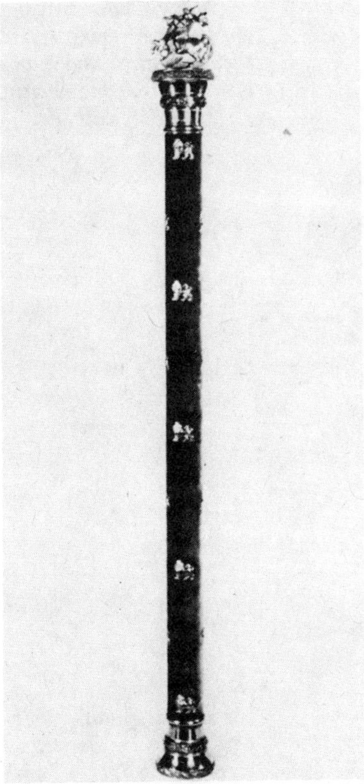

Field marshals' batons became one of the ritual objects of the military cults of modern times.

Walter Williams (1842-1959) the longest-living American Civil War veteran. Soldiers were thought to take up arms for their sides again after death.

Medallions, talismans and amulets were hung round the reins, girth and straps of horses, as in this Ancient Egyptian example.

Horses as man's companions on the battlefield became closely allied with the cult of militarism.

Armour and weapons of famous people were often invested with magical properties. This photograph shows King Henry VIII's armour in the Tower of London.

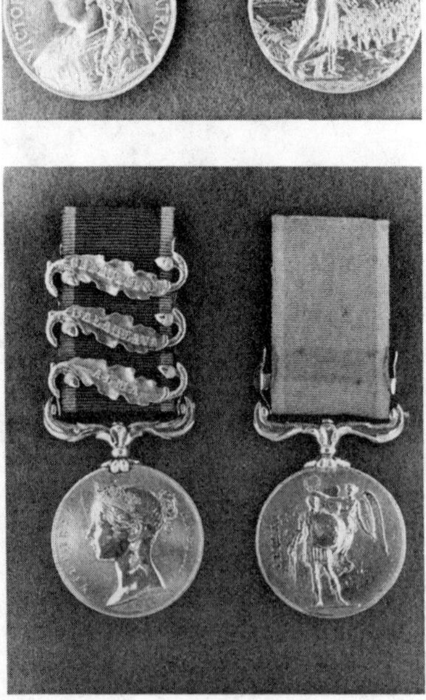

On the left are six of the medals awarded to British troops during the campaigns of Victoria's reign.

As occult objects medals rank with amulets and talismans, and it was only comparatively recently that they became marks of valour. It is known that prehistoric warriors decked themselves with slivers of wood and pieces of metal to ward off the evil spirits of death. Many inscribed their adornments with magic symbols for extra protection. Eventually these became uniformly square, round or diamond shaped and are older than coins. The art of specially engraving dies for medals is also very ancient, and was probably a by-product of the early Greek mints. Certainly the medals of Hellenestic Syracuse, Acragas and Athens are the oldest known examples. Under the Roman Empire medals reached a high skill and beauty. Because gods and imperial portraiture appeared on medals they soon became objects to be used in magic spell working and as votary offerings.

Today we know the medal principally as a decoration for war service, with those given during the two World Wars as the most common examples.

In the past, medals cast to commemorate certain victories often themselves became cult objects, worn to induce the spirits of luck to bless a present battle with a former's success. One researcher noted how old medals were the most popular 'mascots' of soldiers serving in the Crimean War. (Cf 'Flags and Badges'.)

Asian conflicts. They strongly believed in the intensification of occult powers during war-time and now their emperor was the focal point of this occultism. The following reply, made by Admiral Marquis Heihachiro Togo (1847-1934), Commander-in-Chief of the Japanese fleet during the Russo-Japanese War, to an imperial message of commendation received after the second attempt to blockade the entrance to Port Arthur, is characteristic of this belief in occultism: 'The warm message which Your Imperial Majesty condescended to grant us with regard to the second attempt to seal Port Arthur, has not only overwhelmed us with gratitude, but may also influence the patriotic (souls) of the departed heroes to hover long over the battlefield and give unseen protection to the Imperial forces . . .' (*Japan Times*, 31.3.1904).

Incidentally, Admiral Togo himself became a cult figure in Japanese occult thought, as did many of Japan's war heroes. After Togo's death multitudes visited his tomb at Tama cemetery, 35 miles from Tokyo, to petition his spirit, and to pray that his occult influence might act as a mediator with the gods.

So *bushido* and its occultism, its moral values and standards of behaviour remained and, for better or worse, became the most powerful foundations for the Japanese as they progressed in the 20th century. The cult of *bushido,* however, fell into disrepute in the eyes of the world during World War II. In reporting the rape of Hong Kong (December 25 1941), the then British Foreign Secretary Anthony Eden (now Lord Avon) described *bushido* as 'nauseating hypocrisy'. This became the general opinion of the West towards *bushido* ethic which permitted such barbarity to prisoners of war, although the selfless *bushido* spirit of the *kamikaze* suicide pilots showed another side, the ultimate bravery. By the 1930s the occultism of *bushido* had taken on a more intensely fanatical approach with greater overtones of nationalism. To many the uncivilised treatment towards prisoners and conquered peoples was the logical interpretation of *bushido.* It was considered cowardly to surrender, or to show one's back to the enemy, as by so doing one would bring dishonour to the family name. Anyone who surrendered had lost not only honour, but also all communion with the *kami* (gods) and deserved the most painful and ignominious treatment.

Japan, of course, has had many secret societies whose rationale has been based on military occultism. One such society was the *Shinpati,* known as the Soldiers of God. Incidentally, it should be remembered that contrary to Inazo's thesis, *bushido* was particularistic and concerted, never abstract or universal; the *Hagokura,* the so-called bible of *bushido,* a handwritten manuscript by Tsunetomo Yamamoto (1659-1719), makes this clear.

Superstition and the soldier

A community is never so superstitious as in those times when calamity, whether natural or man-made, threatens its existence. Consequently in time of war superstition is rampant. The trauma of war itself produces a mass urge towards any and every form of reassurance and produces, furthermore, a wide assortment of delusion. Certainly nothing else really explains the fantastic boom in astrology and allied forms of pseudo-scientific prediction and occult divination which was prevalent in Britain at the outbreak of World War II. So great did the boom in occult delusion become that a vociferous lobby arose in the British House of Commons to bring about legislation to muzzle the astrologers and diviners. Even though the latter invariably predicted a rapid victory for the Allies, at least one Member of Parliament feared for the country's war effort.

More localised delusions were fostered in Britain and America by the tensions of total war. Soldiers' wives came to believe that it was tempting fate (ie, a relic of primitive taboo) to refer in conversation to their husband's leave. Families with loved ones in the forces went to great, and sometimes ridiculous lengths, to prevent the occurrence of the best-known omens of death (ie, letting the sun shine through coloured glass in a window onto a bowl of apples, or allowing dogs to howl near a house at night). Some even set extra places at table, on special occasions, for relatives fighting abroad, following the old 'good luck by transference' superstitions.

Others tried the ancient idea of transference in death curses: many working in munitions factories scrawled the names of Nazi and Japanese leaders on bombs and shells, with the mystic prayer-hope that these particular bombs would kill the persons named. Names and images have always figured in magical charms, and in World War II it was common belief that one would not be killed in battle until one's 'number came up'. Similarly an insulation against anxiety came from the widespread superstition that an enemy bullet or shell had a 'soldier's number on it'. Sometimes these ideas prevented soldiers from becoming panicky about every bullet. While British and American propaganda agencies warned the people against 'careless talk' in public concerning the regiments and manoeuvres of their loved ones serving in the forces, the superstitious made such topics taboo anyway, lest they somehow jeopardised the lives of the soldiers with unconscious naming spells.

For a time, however, in London the universally 'unlucky' number 13 (see: *A Book of Superstitions*) had a period of glory. Bus drivers and conductors along route number 13—'The Bell' in Hendon and London Bridge Station, via Golders Green, Child's Hill, Swiss Cottage, St John's Wood, Baker Street, Oxford Street, Regent Street, Piccadilly Circus, Trafalgar Square, Strand, Fleet Street, St Pauls, Cannon Street and London Bridge—maintained a non-stop service through the terrible German bombing raids of 1940, and came through virtually without a scratch; so many felt that the mystic number had kept them safe.

Some time after US Air Force bombers made their first attack on Germany on January 27 1943, superstitious belief began to build up in America; so much so that the US War Production Board became worried. The Board declared that superstition was 'unpatriotic' and that it was costing the country many thousands of dollars in wasted products. To back up their allegations they quoted the 'three light' superstition and actually supported a campaign by match manufacturers to make it clear that the refusal to light three cigarettes on one match was a waste of valuable paper, wood and glue! The latter superstition is perhaps the best-known of all soldier superstitions. It is probable that no one will ever discover the real origin of this superstition, that the third soldier lighting his cigarette from the one match was doomed to die. But we know that the number three has been a mystic number for thousands of years. It is still commonly said that luck, good and bad, has a threefold aspect. If two accidents or deaths occur, another may be expected soon after; letters, gifts and visitors are similarly defined. Also some incantations/prayers were chanted three times before their devotees really believed that they would work or be answered. Although I have not been able to trace this superstition beyond the South African War (1899-1902), it is possible that the basic racial memory for the superstition may have originated in Imperial Russia. In the Russian Orthodox Church, during the service for the dead, three candles are lit with the same taper.

In war-time the real fountain-head of superstition is to be found in the armed forces themselves. Indeed, protective magic really came into its own during World War II. One group of American social psychologists in a detailed study of American servicemen, noted the most prominent magic practices. The most common amulets to be carried in battle were crosses, Bibles, rabbit's foot charms, four-leafed clovers, billikens, dice and kewpie dolls. Indian troops on the other hand favoured animal tusks, or human teeth set in gold mounts, while Italian troops carried miniature sucking pig amulets, and Japanese soldiers engraved black carp on their sword-guards. War amulets and charms were a flourishing industry in Japan during 1941-45.

One Dutch psychologist, J. A. M. Meerloo, shed some light on North European and Scandinavian superstitions during World War II and noted: 'We all went into war with amulets and mascots, convinced that while we possessed them we could not be harmed. We also made use of magical formulae which took away fear'. Meerloo went on to note that he had a personalised incantation which kept him sane while a prisoner of war. He would repeat over and over again: 'It is philosophically absurd to end my life at this very moment'.

American novelist John Steinbeck (1902-68), a war correspondent for the *New York Herald Tribune,* compiled a list of charms he noticed were the favourites among American troops. They included smooth stones, coins, rings, miscellaneous jewellery belonging to wives and sweethearts, metal in odd shapes, photographs, pieces of the garments of near relatives, and carved animals like pigs, goats, sheep and monkeys. In the Allied Forces General Dwight D. Eisenhower himself admitted carrying a particular gold coin for good luck, while Lt-Gen George C. Kenney of the US Fifth Air Force carried a pair of dice acquired in Paris (he also used the dice for good luck in gambling!).

To protect themselves against serious wounding, or to guard their wounds from profuse bleeding, soldiers of all ages have carried various fetish objects. Polish troops favoured packets of orris root, Russian infantrymen of the early 1900s carried pictures of the Tsar, ikons and bags of alum, Austrian soldiers preferred pieces of ivy wood, but Finns swore by small phials of spring water collected by a *tietäjä* (wizard). Strangely enough, in World War I, novels by British author Sir Henry Rider Haggard (1856-1925) were found by gunners at Ypres to be unlucky. Gunners of a particular battery found that unpleasant things happened to them when copies of Haggard's novels were included in boxes of books sent to them. So from that time on they burned every book by that author which arrived.

Psychologists found that a soldier's 'fear ratio' tended to increase when certain omens of disaster were apparent. It spelt bad luck, for instance, if a soldier stumbled as he went into battle. Several birds too provided fearful omens: the Romans feared the appearance of vultures as they marched into battle, and British troops once feared the mystic 'Seven Whistlers' (Plovers, curlews, whimbrels, widgeon, herring gulls, cuckoos and swallows). Eagles, however, were good luck signs because of their size, strength and aristocratic bearing, and because they could outsoar all other birds. The eagle became a recurring emblem of divinity and kingship, and Romans, French, Persians and Americans, among others, have used the eagle as a war emblem. The worst possible omen of course, was to lose one's emblem, flag, banner or regimental colours in battle: this was related to the old totem superstitions.

Folklorists might perhaps hold that the clearest indication of the influence that magic had over the armed services lies in the prevalence of mascots (ie, living animals), owned by particular units. Once again the totemistic inference is clear. Certainly it must be realised that mascots also have duties to perform, as with dogs trained for rescue work, but many animals kept as pets (ie, the unusual varieties) are clearly instances of the beasts being thought of as the repository of the unit's or regiment's good luck. Examples extant today are the goats belonging to the Royal Welch Fusiliers and the wolf-hounds of the Irish Guards. So it is shown in terms of military occultism that, while superstition multiplies rapidly when people are under some kind of stress, it does not entirely disappear to a corresponding degree in settled times.

The prophecy of war

War casts such deep shadows in history that many psychic people have claimed that they 'saw' clear indications of its coming. No less the superstitious claim to 'recognise' omens of war. Because of their swift and unexpected passage through the sky, and their 'mystic disruption of the orderly regularity of the heavens', comets have been deemed omens of war. Similarly the Aurora Borealis has been regarded as a war-omen by the superstitious. Just before the declaration of World War II, September 3 1939, the Aurora Borealis was reported as being seen as far south as London. Also in America, just before the Japanese attack on Pearl Harbour, December 6 1941, startling displays of 'lights' were seen for three successive nights from Anchorage, Alaska, clear across to Cleveland, Ohio.

Americans say that war is heralded by the appearance of a great number of harvest flies (*cicadas,* also known by the general term 'locust'), especially the ones with the curious markings on their wings resembling a 'w'. Again to the sheep farmers of the American plains, an over-large yield of lambs forecasts war, while to the cattlemen of Kansas an increasing number of rats means the same. Ants in New Mexico spell out a similar omen and some folk in Pennsylvania still forecast that a war is due to break out if the bees are idle, or are unsuccessful in their honey production.

The appearance over Britain of a large number of wax-wings was considered a war omen, while in Sweden the hoopoe indicates a coming conflict. Elsewhere in Europe war-omens are indicated when ravens are seen flying towards each other, or if the eagles swoop low in the valleys. Numerous folklorists in Europe have collected data from Madrid to Amsterdam, concerning the war omens said to be represented in the sudden change in the level of the water in dams, rivers, wells, polders and lakes. Britain's own examples of this latter superstition are represented in the water levels observed at Assenden Spring, Oxfordshire, St Helen's Well, Staffordshire and the 'dry pool' in Devon, which is said to fill before a war breaks out (this land depression is said to have filled shortly before the death of King George VI in 1952).

To match the forecast of war said to occur when Drake's Drum mysteriously rolls by itself at Buckland Abbey, near Plymouth (see: *Phantoms, Legends, Customs and Superstitions of the Sea*), Americans believe that during impending civil disturbances red, white and blue stripes manifest themselves in the sky over the scene of major conflicts; this is said to have happened just before the battles of Bull Run, Fair Oaks and Gaines Mill during the American Civil War.

A wider-spread omen states that the Black Prince haunts Hall Place, near Bexley, where he once stayed on his way to the wars in France. His appearance is thought to be an omen of danger to England, in general, and in particular to the occupants of the house. During World War I, the prince was seen on three occasions before Britsh reverses in Europe, and during the 1920s and 1930s Lady Limerick saw him four times before family misfortunes.

Modern seers like the Irish born Cheiro (the pseudonym of Count Louis Hamon, 1866-1936) correctly forecast the South African War, and World War I, some considerable time before the politicians actually made them happen. Edgar Cayce, who was born March 18 1877 on a farm near Hopkinsville, Kentucky, similarly had a 'vision of [*World War II*] in which millions of men and women would die' in June 1931. He lived to see his terrible prophecy acted out, but died at the end of the war.

Again in the archives of the Society for Psychical Research is a number of papers on the 'automatic writing' of Dame Edith Lyttelton (1865-1948), who forecast World War I, the coming of Adolf Hitler and the 'Six Day War', which broke out between Israel and the Arab States on June 5 1967.

What really causes people to experience these 'visions of the future' is not known. The late Dr Alexis Carrel, the great physiologist, biologist and Nobel prize winner, wrote: 'The facts of prediction of the future lead us to the threshold of an unseen world. They seem to point to the existence of a psychic principle capable of evolving outside the limits of our bodies'. Professor J. B. Rhine, the American pioneer parapsychologist expanded the theme: 'The scientific tests that were initiated by prophetic dreams have already led to the discovery of a new fact about the human mind, a discovery so radical as to call for an eventual revolution in basic human thought. Perhaps the most significant finding that has emerged is that there is known to be present in the personality an aspect that is unbounded by the space and time of matter—hence a non-physical or spiritual aspect. Its boundaries and its capacity for growth may well be beyond the limits of our present power to conceive . . . Is it not then provocative, to say the least, to discover certain capacities of mind that appear to operate beyond the boundaries of space and time within which our sensorial, bodily system has to live and move? Here, surely, if ever, "hope sees a star", and the urge toward an inquiry into the question of survival receives valuable impetus and encouragement'.

They used dark forces

In this cynical age when war and its preparations are an accepted way of life, it seems hardly credible that only some three centuries ago such evils were thought to be the direct result of sin inherited from Adam and Eve: the sin of disobedience, brought about by Satan's intrigues in the Garden of Eden. So, to expiate the sin and stop it ever occurring again, man's emissaries of good (priests), fought a continual battle with the forces of evil (personified by demons). This 'battle', which dates from the Middle Ages, was a popular theme in religion and social literary works, and coincided with the rise of the 'delusion of witchcraft' (see: *A Book of Witchcraft*).

Eventually a superstition grew up that, by following a certain ritual, or set of incantations, these demons and devils could be petitioned to fight man's individual earthly battles for him. Crusaders and local barons alike were not against petitioning dark forces to strengthen their arm. Among the superstitions of the Church, however, was one which ran conversely to the above. Following upon the expulsion of Satan from Heaven, as recorded in the Scriptures, his place was taken by Gabriel, 'a safe angel', who controlled an enormous army of 1,064,340,000,000 subordinate angels (Satan, according to Fromenteau, could only muster 7,405,926 minions). By careful prayer, therefore, the 'good Christian' could summon Gabriel and his host to fight his mortal battles.

Towards the end of the Middle Ages several of the more learned and moneyed occultists began to indulge in what is known as ceremonial or ritual magic. This, of course, was an extremely involved process of attempting to conjure up certain spirits, but when the demons had appeared they might be asked certain favours, including success in war. The ritual involved consecrations and incantations, and needed a great deal of preparation. It seemed very rarely to have worked, but devotees spent much time and money on the rites, and a definite bibliography was evolved. The textbook of the magician is called a *grimoire,* and from one such text *Le Lemegation*

(Bibliotheque Nationale, Paris) can be assessed the demons of most use in time of war:

Agares Demon from the East which rides a crocodile. On his wrist perches a hawk. He can bestow the gifts of diplomacy.

Aini A three-headed demon. A destructive demon useful when cunning is required in battle, he rides upon a viper and carries a blazing torch.

Amon A fire-breathing wolf with the head of a snake. One who can see into the past and the future, he can cause enemies to make love not war.

Andras He sports a raven's head on an angel's body and he carries a mighty sword to cut enemies asunder. Beware! This demon may kill the magician himself.

Asmoday Three-headed like Aini, this demon can answer all questions concerning military tactics. When evoked with the demon Furcas, both can help with all the sciences apertaining to war.

Cimeries The soldier demon on a black horse. He is especially knowledgeable in African campaigning.

Flauros A leopard demon, capable of assuming human shape. He is able to destroy the magician's enemies and keep him free from any temptation.

Gamygyn He arrives in the shape of a horse or donkey and can bring back the great soldiers from the dead for questioning. The demon Murmur also has this power.

Orias Takes the form of a lion riding a horse, and can transform enemies into allies.

Saleos A soldier riding a crocodile, he has great influence in conflicts requiring deception.

Vepar Mermaid demon of disaster in sea battles.

Vine Another lion demon which rides a horse. He can wreck castles and build defences.

Zepar He appears as a soldier in red armour and can make the women folk of the enemy hate their husbands, and love their enemies.

The tools and costume necessary to conjure up these demons included, the texts said, sanctified robes or red velvet, silken cloth, magic rod, trumpet, bell, sword, wax, salt, fire, trident and a circle to 'raise the power'. The magician must also have meditated and fasted for nine days before attempting a conjuration, and must have refrained from sexual activity.

A centre of East European witch power in military affairs was thought by many to be at *Cetatea Babei* ('The Witch's Castle') at the head of the Prahova valley in Roumania. Here emissaries might be sent to acquire potions, charms and ritual of use in battle.

For many centuries witchcraft has allied itself with war and revolution in Africa. In the East Congo, for instance, in the territory once held by rebels against the government of the late Moise Tshombe, posses of Babembi warriors wore clothing prescribed by their witch-doctors as making them invincible to the bullets of the government troops. Among the charms used for good luck in war by the Babembi were the following all blessed by the witch-doctor: leopard fur hats, wreaths of palm frond, spirals of creeper, sprigs of Bougainvillaea, plastic tulips (pillage from houses), button photos of Patrice Lumumba (the assassinated left-wing leader), osprey and bantam feathers, and in one particular case, the stuffed head of a crested crane.

Congo rebel leader Gaston Soumialot put 'protective' palm leaves across the radiators of his lorries and was a devotee of *dhawa* war ritual. Basically this witchcraft was a cult of avoiding all contact with Caucasian women, refusing to touch white people, swearing oaths and drinking certain potions brewed by the witch-doctors. Such potions were made principally from a drug known to the Belgians as *chanvre* (blue lotus). The juice of this plant creates a wild exhilaration and immunity to fear and pain followed by severe depression. This drug was widely used by the African *gendarmeries* in 1960 and 1961; in particular by Baluba tribesmen in Katanga. After a battle against these tribesmen, white mercenary Col Huguet said: 'The onrush of men having eaten *chanvre* was not affected by bullets striking them in the body. I have seen one savage still advance after four heavy-calibre revolver bullets had struck him and he fell a few feet from me'.

At Congolese Army Headquarters at Bukavu, the Area Commander Col Leonard Mulumba filed a report about witchcraft in modern African military tactics, of which this is an extract: 'The rebels, after taking the [*drugs*] advance several hundred strong, making no effort to lay ambushes, to take cover or avoid rifle fire. They are so close together that a dead man is often carried along by the pressure of bodies around him. They chant and wave their weapons but do not quicken their pace. If they suffer a defeat, it is said to be because the witch-doctor was not strong enough, and that they will rise again on the third day'.

Music, dance and the spoken word

There are few religions and cults in which music has played no part at all, for beneath the structural differences of all types of music, whether it be Peter Ilich Tchaikovsky's *Eugene Onegin*, or the resonant sounds of Australian aboriginal tempos, it is used to help express and heighten the content of ritual action of some kind. Without music mystic ritual is impoverished. Probably the earliest military, or war occultism was expressed in terms of simple dance routines in which participants used imitative magic; that is they acted out the routine of killing their enemies. Armed with weapons and dressed to kill (the origin of the modern phrase, meaning that a person is well groomed to make a conquest), the Watutsi warriors of the former Ruanda province, for instance, right up to modern times danced themselves into a frenzied pitch of exultation before going to war.

The next stage in the development of music in military occultism was probably reached when the voice was brought into play. The participant initially strained his vocal chords to imitate the fear, or death cries of his enemies. Dance and rhythmical music together developed as highly emotive routines, which were also thought to form a link with the spirit world when at their climax. This music and dance therefore evolved as a mystic petition to the various gods and spirits of war for assistance in battle, and for advice in war strategy. Certainly North American Indians like the Rocky Mountain tribes of Utes, Bannocks and Shoshone, and the Plains Indians like the Sioux, Cheyenne and Arapaho, for instance, used this type of spirit communication. Hence from the mystic chanting of the early cave man to the military music of such as American bandmaster John Philip Sousa, there is a close link with military occultism.

The importance of musical expression in military occultism may be explained by the fact that music is an intangible medium. It can have a direct, emotional effect that could, perhaps, encourage a spiritual awareness. Also the impermanence of musical sound may be considered as suggestive of the unseen and the supernatural. As far as scholars today are aware the Ancient Egyptians were the first to deliberately use music for occult reasons in battle. This idea of petitioning the gods with music for good luck, during and before battle, persisted right up to modern times. The Hungarian Army, for instance, were much taken with the idea of catching the good luck and inspiration of music in wartime: for centuries the melodic Hungarian musicians known as *verbunkás* helped recruit soldiers with ballads, and Hungarian gypsy violinists led troops into battle. This use of music in military occultism was by no means dead in the late 18th century; for example, the *Marseillaise,* the national anthem of France, evolved from this half-forgotten primeval memory of music and the occult powers.

In early 1792 King Frederick William II of Prussia and the Emperor Francis II of Austria concluded a pact with the designed purpose of opposing the dangerous new revolutionary ideology taking shape in France. The two rulers pledged at Pilnitz, near Dresden, to combat the 'insidious power' that had made Louis XVI, the nominal king of France, no more than a tool in the hands of the French Legislative Assembly. In retaliation to this pact the French declared war on Prussia and Austria in Louis XVI's name and a *levée en masse* took place immediately. As usual on such occasions, French patriotic fervour ran high and the populace in general sent the troops off to their war stations with great enthusiasm. The preparatory events of war at Strasbourg, one of the key fortresses on the Franco-German frontier, were to have particular importance in the field of occult-inspired patriotic music. And in this the Mayor of Strasbourg, Philippe-Frédéric, the 54-year-old Baron de Dietrich was to play a significant part.

Baron de Dietrich was a fervent patriot and a competent musician. His musical evening at his house in the Marché-aux-Chevaux (now the Place Broglie) were legendary, and the mayor passionately believed that music was a spiritualistic medium and the oil in the patriotic and military war machinery. A regular visitor to de Dietrich's musical evenings was one Rouget de Lisle, a captain in the Corps of Engineers. A talented officer, musician and poet, de Lisle was a worthy guest at any musical soirée. Although de Dietrich numbered the famous composer Ignace Pleyel and many other talented musicians amongst his friends, he chose de Lisle to compose a patriotic song (with implied inspirational and occult overtones) for the military 'raising of Strasbourg'.

De Lisle, a keen though discreet revolutionary, set about the song, which he no doubt based on other works of similar idiom. His theme was to have a later switch of emphasis, for the 'tyrants' he wrote about in the original script were the German princes and not the French aristocrats; and the 'hordes of slaves' not the French peasantry, but the German troops about to invade. The song was completed in a very short time and was first publicly played on April 25 1792. It was an immediate success and the words were printed on July 7 1792 in *Les Affiches de Strasbourg* and soon after the music was published by Th. J. Dannbach with a dedication to Marshal Luckner.

In June 1792, however, the song found its way through the salons and hostelries of southern France to Marseilles. There it was sung at a banquet by a certain Mireur to celebrate the departure of local volunteers for Paris. Again its success was immediate and with the song on their lips the volunteers marched across France. They arrived in Paris in late July and, on the morning of August 10 1792, headed for the Tuileries. By this time de Lisle's song had made a great impression on the people of Paris and as the march had come from Marseilles, it was thenceforth known as *La Marseillaise.*

Soon the whole French army was singing de Lisle's song (for which he received little credit) and, indeed, so were the entire nation. While the enemies of France and the anti-revolutionaries branded the Marseillaise as 'satanic', as Paul Martin wrote: '[*The song was*] copied by hand, sung in public, distributed throughout the musical circles, it soon penetrated into the repertoire of the military bands attached to various units of the National Guard'.

On September 20 1792 the Marseillaise achieved its first national anthem status at Valmy. The occasion was the victory of the French troops over the Germans. When victory was assured General Kellermann rode out in front of his troops and, raising his hat on high on the tip of his sword, he shouted '*Vive la Nation*'—his troops replied with the *Marseillaise.*

Fame and fortune being what it is Rouget de Lisle received no practical recognition for his achievement. For a long time he suffered partial obscurity in the army and eventually retired to his native village of Montaigu, near Lons-le-Saulnier, in the Franche-Comté. Although Louis-Philippe later granted de Lisle a small income, his life was lived in poverty and he died in very straitened circumstances on June 26 1836 at Choisy-le-Roi, near Paris. His patron Philippe de Dietrich fared even worse: he was executed in Paris in 1793 during *le règne de la terreur*.

The popularity of the Marseillaise, however, became universal, and on July 14 1795 it became a national song. Sung by friend and foe alike the song was translated into many languages including *Schlachtlied der Deutschen*, the most popular of the five German versions. Eventually of course, de Lisle's original authorship was forgotten, and its present form owes much to the pens of Gossec and Grétry, among others. Even the words are not an absolutely literal transcript of Rouget de Lisle's original score. In time a seventh verse was added called the 'Children's Verse'.

Introduced by Gossec in his *Offrande à la Liberté*, the *Marseillaise* was orchestrated by Berlioz, although the present official version (approved in 1887) is due to Ambroise Thomas. On February 14 1879 the *Marseillaise* became the *hymne national* of France, and a piece of pure military occultism went on to embody the spirit of a nation.

From time to time when no military bands or musical instruments were available, those charged with troop morale and the petitioning of the war-gods resorted to the use of the written word, or literary passages learnt by heart. Quite often tales of courage and bravery were spoken aloud to gatherings of troops before battle. In this way their minds would be filled with 'brave deeds', which might later be subconsciously imitated. From the back of a wagon, or high on a rock, such texts as *The Battle of Maldon* (c 991), one of the finest poems in Old English, telling of the magnificent ealdorman Bryhtnoth, or Beowulf (c 700), or even *The History of the Wars* (c 490-575) of Procopious of Caesarea, were recited to mystically inspire the troops. It is probable that the 'pep' talks given to American and British troops before battles in the two world wars were a forgotten but direct relic of these mystic recitations.

The realm of military phantoms

It is clear that even in modern times occultism is not dead in the field of military history. Many soldiers still have strange tales to tell; stories like that of a British veteran of World War II, Robert Loveday. A resident of Redhill, Surrey, Loveday was an NCO serving in Burma. His best friend served with him but apparently went out on a patrol one night and was reported missing. Some two weeks later Sgt Loveday was out on patrol himself when he heard his friend's voice shout: 'Watch out! They're right behind you.' This voice saved Loveday from a Japanese bullet which whizzed past his ear when he turned round. A day or two later the friend's body was found, and the medic's said he had been dead for several weeks!

Military history is full of such odd yarns which in many cases have become legendary. Again some stories are repeated so many times they rank as 'facts': some still say that Rudolph Hess, Adolf Hitler's deputy (1933), who flew alone to Scotland in May 1941, was a spiritualistic medium, and that he had been instructed by spirits to make the trip with proposals for a compromise peace with Britain. For his failure, the gossips say, he was assailed by evil Nazi ghosts and poltergeists during his captivity which gave rise to his being thought mad.

Have you ever been working late alone in a deserted office, or digging the garden, or tinkering with the car, when you thought you heard a voice call you, and having looked round you saw no one? It must have happened thousands of times to as many people, and not only to those who believe the dead are always with us. The realm of the modern military phantom is a very modern world for soldier phantoms appear all the time. Only recently the psychic newspaper *Psychic News* reported that in July 1972 Fusilier Kenneth Canham, who had been killed in Belfast, appeared to psychics in his home town of Newcastle-upon-Tyne. Hit by an IRA sniper while on patrol, Canham's mortal body died instantly but his spirit remained earthbound long enough to contact friends to assure them that he was not 'dead'.

Today there is an increasing interest being taken in ghosts. More and more people are including the occult sciences, and ghost-hunting in particular amongst their hobbies. This is a good thing, for only by constant research can we begin to understand ghosts.

Ghosts are very much a 'tomorrow subject', an essential part of the study of futuristics. As yet we are not fully prepared to understand ghosts and their world, for we have not to date developed equipment by which we can have a two-way link with the spirits of the dead. But this is possible, it will come, I am convinced. People who see ghosts today are still too emotionally affected to assess the situation properly, and professional 'mediums' are only vessels often controlled by amateur or unskilled spirits. The fact that we cannot control the time and circumstances of a ghostly visitation leads to scepticism. This is our most frustrating disadvantage at present. One positive step has been taken; people today do not automatically scoff at ghosts—they stop, and listen and ponder—such is the dividend brought by the mass media in projecting to the public such data as that on extra-terrestial science.

By the year 2074, however, when we have conquered such items as suspended animation, space-time distortion and artificial molecular adjustment, we shall be in a positive position to assess ghosts properly. In the meantime we need to be scientific. An unbelief in ghosts is neither sophisticated nor relevant. Ghosts exist, of that there can be no doubt; and perhaps this book goes some of the way to establish the probability of ghostly phenomena. In the meantime a scientific researcher's open mind is required, and a sympathetic approach. For who knows what benefits to mankind communications with ghosts might bring? It is a prospect as exciting as the first meeting between a man from earth and a being from the depths of space.

INDEX

Index